MW00461531

BY:- - - - - - - - - - - - - - - - - - -

Collisions with History

This series of publications on Africa, Latin America, Southeast Asia, and Global and Comparative Studies is designed to present significant research, translation, and opinion to area specialists and to a wide community of persons interested in world affairs. The editor seeks manuscripts of quality on any subject and can generally make a decision regarding publication within three months of receipt of the original work. Production methods generally permit a work to appear within one year of acceptance. The editor works closely with authors to produce a high quality book. The series appears in a paperback format and is distributed worldwide. For more information, contact the executive editor at Ohio University Press, Scott Quadrangle, University Terrace, Athens, Ohio 45701.

Executive editor: Gillian Berchowitz
AREA CONSULTANTS
Africa: Diane Ciekawy
Latin America: Thomas Walker
Southeast Asia: William H. Frederick

The Ohio University Research in International Studies series is published for the Center for International Studies by the Ohio University Press. The views expressed in individual volumes are those of the authors and should not be considered to represent the policies or beliefs of the Center for International Studies, the Ohio University Press, or Ohio University.

Collisions with History

Latin American Fiction and Social Science

from El Boom *to the New World Order*

Frederick M. Nunn

Ohio University Center for International Studies
Research in International Studies
Latin America Series No. 36
Athens

The books in the Ohio University Research in International Studies series
are printed on acid-free paper ⊗™

10 09 08 07 06 05 04 03 02 01   5 4 3 2 1

Library of Congress Cataloging-in-Publication

Nunn, Frederick M., 1937–
    Collisions with history : Latin American fiction and social science from "el
boom" to the new world order / Frederick M. Nunn.
        p.   cm. — (Research in international studies. Latin America series ;
no. 36)
    Includes bibliographical references and index.
    ISBN 0-89680-219-1 (pbk. : alk. paper)
    1. Latin American fiction—20th century—History and criticism.
2. Literature and history—Latin America.   3. Latin America—In literature.
I. Title.   II. Series.

PQ7082.N7 N86 2001
863'.6409358—dc21   2001036003

For Susan Catherine Karant-Nunn

A civilization acquires its character not from a display of prosperity or material supremacy, but from the grandeur of thought and feeling possible within it.

—José Enrique Rodó, *Ariel* (1900)

A modern literary, not sociological, theory divides the literature of a country into three periods: colonial, cosmopolitan, and national. In the first period, the country, in a literary sense, is a colony dependent on its metropolis. In the second period, it simultaneously assimilates elements of various foreign literatures. In the third period, it shapes and expresses its own personality and feelings. Although this theory of literature does not go any farther, it is broad enough for our purpose.

—José Carlos Mariátegui, "Literature on Trial" (1927)

riverrun, past Eve and Adam's, from swerve of shore to bend of bay, brings us by a commodius vicus of recirculation back to Howth Castle and Environs . . . .
A way a lone a last a loved a long the

—James Joyce, *Finnegans Wake* (1939)

Contents

Acknowledgments

There is never sufficient space to properly acknowledge all those who helped in some way to make a book possible. I want those whose names do not follow, however, to know that I do not forget them. You know who you are.

My daughters, Jessica Catherine Leslie Nunn and Tey Marianna Nunn, once again let me try out ideas with them, the former before, during, and since her undergraduate years at Carleton College; the latter all the way through her doctoral studies at the University of New Mexico—back at the place where this book really began. Susan Catherine Karant-Nunn, my wife and most esteemed colleague, to whom it is dedicated, was, as always, an inspiration.

Colleagues contribute in so many ways to an author's work, and mine has been no exception. Over the years I have discussed this work with Fernando Alegría, Kimberley A. Brown, Thomas M. Davies Jr., Iván Jaksić, Brian Loveman, Michael C. Meyer, Friedrich E. Schuler, Shawn C. Smallman, Howard J. Wiarda, and Craig E. Wollner. Michael F. Reardon, provost, Portland State University, was most supportive of this effort while I served as director of the Office of International Affairs, and later as vice provost for international affairs from 1992 to 1999. My former executive assistant, Mary Krug, never failed to come to my aid when the complexities of word processing proved daunting. She and her successors Annette Baumann and Debra Z. Clemans, and student assistants Arlene Brockel, Sophie Newton, and Jill Stoffers, were invaluable aides.

Decades ago, Perry J. Powers and Ned J. Davison introduced me to the wonders of Spanish and Spanish American literature. Then Marshall R. Nason and Sabine R. Ulibarrí took up where they left off.

Edwin Lieuwen's and France V. Scholes's history courses gave me a structure to which my thoughts on literature could be applied. Miguel Jorrín showed me ways in which literature and politics complemented each other. Albert R. Lopes taught me Portuguese, the literature of both Portugal and Brazil, and the history of Portugal, making the relationships between literature, history, and politics more significant still. The intellectual debt evinced by this book, especially to Al, can never be paid in full. My hope is that the efforts of these teachers were not in vain.

The pages that follow simply could not exist without a Fulbright Faculty Research Abroad Fellowship awarded me by the Center for International Education, U.S. Department of Education, and sabbatical leave from teaching and administrative duties at Portland State University during the 1993–94 academic year. To those who supported my fellowship candidacy I am most grateful.

Most of the research was done in the Biblioteca FLACSO-Chile, Santiago; the Ibero-Amerikanisches Institut, Berlin; and the British Library Reading Room, London. I thank the center, the institute, and the library and their directors and staffs profusely. In some cases translated passages have been slightly modified in accordance with my own reading and interpretation based on context. Therefore I also thank novelists and social scientists of Latin America for their figurative forbearance.

Finally, I wish to express my gratitude to Gillian Berchowitz, Nancy Basmajian, Beth Pratt, Sharon Arnold, Thomas Walker, and Bob Furnish, who guided this book through editing and production at Ohio University Press.

Introduction

In the face of what the conquistadors, the Creoles, and the imperialists
and their flunkies have attempted, our culture . . . has been in a constant process of formation.
—Roberto Fernández Retamar,
"Calibán: Notes toward a Discussion of Culture in Our America" (1971)

ONCE UPON A TIME the writing of history was more an art than the
fascinating mix of art and science that it is today. Over the course of the
last two centuries writers who purported to be historians, then historians with the academic credentials to assert their identity as such,
have come to see history as much more than mere chronicle, more
than great men, dynasties, battles, and such. As readers became both
more numerous and less detached from their past, history became more
the subject of protracted debate. The past ceased to be free from the
conflicts of the present, whether cultural, economic, political, or social. This is a book about how such conflicts encouraged Latin American novelists and social scientists to collide with their history.

In historical debates that take place where consensus on the meaning of history or on the past is utterly lacking, attempts to offer alternate versions of a canonical or officially sanctioned past to a wider
audience are often effectively made artistically. Style counts. Drama
and fiction can serve serious historical purposes, just as they did before history became a field of academic enterprise. Extradisciplinary
theories of history, cognition, and textual analysis influence the ways
in which historians think.

Somewhere between history and fiction there exist alternate views
of the past that go beyond the bounds of traditional differences of
opinion—Whig and Tory, liberal and conservative, canonical and

1

revisionist, Marxist and non-Marxist. One "somewhere" (not entirely unlike that discussed admirably by Lionel Gossman)[1] is in the minds of Latin American intellectuals, especially the foremost novelists of the late twentieth century. There and then history became the subject of collisions discussed in this book.

My interest in Latin American history is the result of an appreciation of Latin American literature. Having studied literature first, I would come to see it as a reflection of history, as one of Latin American history's other sides. Decades ago historians' versions of Latin America's past went far beyond chronicling. Access to archival materials assured that. Great men, dynasties, battles, and such yielded to more sophisticated examinations of just what made for history and who really had made it. But most scholarly history is meant for consumption within a refined, limited ambience. In societies that are less modern than those of North America and Europe the gap separating the majority from the historiographically knowledgeable is indeed wide. In much of Latin America the history profession has had limited impact on the historical mindset of the population at large until very recently.

Fictional versions of the past, like those described in the first three chapters, do not depend on archival sources so critical to historical scholarship, so fiction should not be viewed as chronicle. Rather, fictional histories are interpretations, vehicles for reflection and revision. This is especially valuable in places where the historian's profession is not well developed and where consensus on the past is shaky. Historians can learn a lot from novelists; novelists already have learned a lot from historians.

Reliance on fiction as document for the study of history is most justifiable if it provides evidence of ways in which an intellect deals with a historical theme or topic from another time. Reliance on fiction as document for the study of contemporary affairs is justifiable if novelist's license is taken into account. Fiction provokes thought in ways even the most exciting scholarly historical or political analysis may not. Fiction is more artifact than document when used by the historian. When they wrote their fictional histories, twentieth-century Latin Americans employed a lot of author's license. Because of this our knowledge of the facts of Latin American history may be no better or more accurate due to the collisions discussed here. Our perception of what history has meant to contemporary Latin Americans may be. And Latin Americans' perception of their history certainly is.

In the later decades of the twentieth century some well-known Latin American novelists turned their attention to distant and recent pasts for the express purpose of colliding with standard versions, revising misperceptions, and criticizing contemporary economic, political, and social injustices. Novelists and essayists had done this sort of thing before. But never with such an audience, and never more purposefully and successfully.

Authors of the Boom had additional motives that urged them to go further than their predecessors had gone. A new wave of authoritarianism—some have used terms like bureaucratic authoritarianism or national security regimes to distinguish it; elsewhere I have called it professional militarism—swept across the region from the 1960s on. In the next two decades national economic crises plagued both military-backed and civilian governments. Across most of the region there was a direct link between these crises and increasing transnationalization of capitalism and denationalization of economies. By the late 1980s it was apparent that the Cold War was headed either for a new phase or for conclusion. The times were interesting, to say the least, and it is in interesting times that history is up for grabs. What had it led to in Latin America? Was it worth remembering? Who was to blame for its injustices? What did history mean anyway?

CONCOMITANT TO THE wave of authoritarianism, which I have marked off historically as the "time of the generals," there occurred in Latin America what has been called by students of literature *El Boom*. Novelists of the Boom collided with history, asking and answering questions such as those just mentioned. Their collisions occurred in two principal ways: in "fictional histories" and political novels, and in their thought and self-perception expressed in the commentary contained in essays, articles, interviews, mutual criticism, and public presentations. In their fiction, novelists depicted what I call cataclysmic history. From between the lines of their commentary emerge thought and self-perception characteristic of a generation of intellectuals searching for the meaning of both past and present. When they offered commentary they sounded a lot like social scientists—and like historians who utilize the methodological approaches of social science. It is for this reason that I deemed it wise to investigate the possibility of social science's collisions with history.

Latin American novelists became world famous through their writing and their advocacy of political and social action, and because many of them had the good fortune to reach markets and audiences beyond Latin America through translation and travel—and sometimes through exile. Their views on contemporary matters became almost as well known to readers on all continents as did their fictional history.

In their fictional histories, novelists concentrated on three eras: the decades of discovery and conquest, the independence years, and the recent past, by which time history seemed to lead Latin America to repressive dictatorships of professional militarists and socioeconomic crises in the 1970s and 1980s. On the surface it might appear that their approaches differ little from traditional approaches to the colonial and early-national centuries.

But beneath the surface lies the truth. The novelists fictionalized discovery and conquest, and independence and early nationhood in order to attack and destroy historical icons. They wrote about the recent past in order to attack systems and institutions that were the legacy of history. The closer they got to the present the less interested they were in historical figures, the more interested in economic, political, and social results of half a millennium. From the very beginning they showed interest in defining Latin Americanness, *latino-*

americanidad, as a way of creating a common heritage and history. This is very close to what Latin American social science literature began to evince at about the same time.

In each of the first three chapters I discuss selected works that portray people, events, and institutions of those pasts: "great men, dynasties, battles, and such." Some are real, some are not. Real or not, the people and events portrayed represent a view of history that can only be called cataclysmic. The long stretches of time that connect the eras, referred to as spirals both in the text and by the authors discussed, received less attention than that accorded them in historical scholarship. The cataclysmic approach allowed novelists to bring out the most negative characteristics of historical heroes and expose them for what they most assuredly were not: still necessary to the identity of the region. It also allowed them to expose the recent past for what it was: the legacy of a failed history.

Novelists of the Boom saw the three cataclysms of their history connected to each other by time and place, each a cause, each an effect. The present in which the novelists lived urged them to see history this way, for it demanded explanations not forthcoming elsewhere. Each of the first three chapters is introduced and concluded in a way that shows how fictional histories provide links between times, people, and events, and that shows how novelists thought regionally more than nationally. Each chapter is accompanied by a list of suggested sources in translation, and is documented appropriately. I have based my choice of fictional histories on the directness of their relation to the three eras of cataclysmic history.

When they addressed history and history's legacy in places other than their fiction, Boom novelists evinced a common identity. They may have denied it or downplayed it, or even shifted positions over the years, but they did think a lot alike about what they were doing and why they were doing it. In chapters 4 and 5, I have let eight Boom novelists speak for themselves so that cultural, economic, political, and social views might emerge from between the lines of their thinking and conversation in printed form as sharply as do historical views from their fiction. Sources for these chapters come overwhelmingly from Latin America and are extensively used in this way for the first time. My choice of novelists is based on a combination of their literary stature, level of activism, and how well their commentary links fictional history to social science, which is the best way their collisions with history can be exposed for what they were. All were or are internationally known.

The ideas of fictional historians expressed beyond the pages of their imaginative works provide context in which fiction, commentary, and social science literature can be seen as ultimately resembling a consensus on something that might be called latinoamericanidad. Chapters 4 and 5 take the form of an interrogatory in which hypothetical questions are posed to the authors, questions cataclysmic history has begged. Both their thought on what that history has wrought and their self-perception make for illuminating commentary. Both these chapters are introduced, concluded, and documented appropriately. I mean by this that the corpus of critical and topical works on recent Latin American literature being as large as it is, I have limited citations to a quantity and quality appropriate to theme or author in the context of this book. Exclusion of a work by no means constitutes a judgment of its value to the study of Latin American fiction, or social science for that matter.

I PURPOSELY DEFINE the Boom more generously than others have done, for I see it more as the collective effort of an intellectual generation responsive to historical and contemporary stimuli than a purely literary movement of world proportion—as if that were not enough.

All sources agree that the Boom began sometime in the 1960s. Although there is difference of opinion on just which novels were its antecedents (Alejo Carpentier's early works are often cited), the Boom certainly can be associated with the publication of novels by Julio Cortázar, Carlos Fuentes, Gabriel García Márquez, Augusto

Roa Bastos, and Mario Vargas Llosa in the 1960s and 1970s. A reading of works on the Boom (all cited in these pages) reveals the following as characteristic of the movement: international focus or appeal, or both; stylistic innovation; urban settings as well as rural ones; historical and political focus; questioning of regional as well as, or more than, national identity; awareness of hemispheric as well as worldwide economic and ideological issues; polemicism; and timeliness. All associate the Boom with the Cuban Revolution with regard to cultural and literary independence from traditional norms and practices.

No argument that the Boom ended sometime in the 1960s or 1970s can claim definitively that these characteristics did not continue to grace the Latin American novel in the 1980s and 1990s, especially those works singled out as fictional history. Thus my protraction of the Boom—perhaps fictional history overcomes it as a movement, but I think not—until the early 1990s, well beyond the date of any specific work. Given this, the association of fictional history with Boom fiction seems proper.

Barely three years after Fidel Castro made the alarming pronouncement on revolution and intellectual freedom noted early in chapter 3, the Boom was underway, and the Cuban review *Casa de las Américas* devoted an entire issue to the novel in Latin America.[2] Now, the cause and effect relationship between the Cuban Revolution and literary and artistic activity on that island and the Boom is partially, but not wholly, responsible for collisions with history. Collisions of a sort had been taking place for over a decade. The "new historical novel"[3] predates and postdates a narrowly defined Boom. All authors considered in the first three chapters wrote new historical novels.

Characteristics of fictional history match those of the new historical novel. Fictional histories employ real characters (as well as imaginary ones). They rely on intertextuality (here meaning that they borrow characters from each other). They question the very nature of history (they do not simply rely on setting). They are cyclical, with unpredictable endings (they are not exclusively linear). They present conflicting worldviews (they are more than works of political and social protest). They utilize literary techniques to present (and represent) the past (they rely on stream of consciousness and intercalation). They are more than historical fiction. They are revisionist in form as well as content. In them the "official" past meets Vico, more about which below.

What is important, if one thinks in terms of cause and effect relationships, is the range of issues authors present. To the pages of that late 1964 issue of *Casa de las Américas* Alejo Carpentier, Julio Cortázar, Carlos Fuentes, and Mario Vargas Llosa, among others, contributed short pieces. In his incisive introduction, Angel Rama discussed every one of the discreet issues raised by fictional historians in chapters 4 and 5 of this book. Rama did not miss a one.

The isolation of Cuba by U.S. and OAS actions following Castro's triumph aided and abetted, as it were, something that was flourishing, gave it sociopolitical and worldwide dimensions it might have achieved anyway, owing to the impending quincentennial. In other words, Latin American intellectual and artistic responses to the Cuban Revolution helped solidify the Boom. Fictional history invigorated the Boom by colliding with standard versions of the past the way new novelists collided with standard versions of the genre.

Cuba's Carpentier, Mexico's Fuentes, Colombia's García Márquez, and Paraguay's Roa Bastos showed great concern for history when they commented on Latin America past and present. Argentina's Julio Cortázar, Chile's Isabel Allende, Peru's Vargas Llosa, and Brazil's Darcy Ribeiro were no less historically conscious. However, it is their commentary on the present that leads us in a more direct way to the scenes of collisions with history made by social scientists, whose sense of constricted history (based on commitment to apply as well as theorize) is the subject of the final chapter.

There I suggest that the literature of social science disciplines in Latin America by 1992 evinced a kind of historical mind-set in disguise. I also suggest that social scientists may be in the process of taking up the burden briefly borne by novelists: redefinition of the region's historical parameters through responses to, analyses of, and attempts to solve, contemporary problems. There I also raise the possibility of a constriction of history to the very recent past. If this should indeed prove to be the case, it may mean that Latin Americans will come to view history as the recent past alone, not so much a product of centuries of Iberian influence as solely that of the Cold War and its Western Hemispheric manifestations.

The dramatic events of 1989 to 1992 also resulted from processes begun in the 1970s—political democratization and transnationalization of capital, for example—but the rush of political events, following as it did the last decade of economic woes, served to encourage thought-provoking discussions of Latin America's past, present, and future. Latin American social scientists of the 1980s and 1990s were as worldly as their novelist colleagues for reasons that become apparent. The history that glares out from the works of economists, political scientists, and sociologists is indeed circumscribed, constricted history. The past that social scientists consider important for an understanding of the present is neither discovery and conquest, nor independence and early nationhood. For these Latin Americans, history—the collective of necessary cause and effect relationships leading to the present—began just about when World War II ended—with the onset of the Cold War. Dickens might have called it history-present.

Such a constricted history is nearly meaningless history. It is very close to a history that, having been collided with, is declared a total write-off in terms of the time and expense that should be devoted to its reconstructive study.

THE SAME RUSH of events that produced the New World Order (disorder?), as the post–Cold War years have been called, has allowed novelists to devote their creative and critical efforts to subjects other than history. Politics no longer drove them as it did in the early 1990s.

The Boom ended (at least it looks like it did), just like the era of professional militarism and the Cold War did. History will indicate, one day, if that was the case. Carpentier, Cortázar, and Ribeiro are all now historical figures in the truest sense. They have passed away. They and the others evince a consciousness of effort in both their total efforts that constitutes the "construction of self" alluded to recently by Jay Parini.[4]

Nowadays, and for the foreseeable future, collisions with history are more the result of social science circumscription and constriction of the relevant past than of literary attempts at revisionism. Novelists, it would appear, have turned away from activism—at least for the foreseeable present. Attempts to insure history (the idealized version of it, to be sure) against further damage may be by default the responsibility of the uniformed branch of social scientists, a possibility to which I allude near the end of the final chapter. It would be ironic indeed—and history is replete with irony—if the source of greatest veneration of the once-attacked past were to be found among those whose view of it has always been the most constricted in terms of thematic and topical content.

There is throughout these pages evidence of a Viconian (sometimes rendered Vichian) view of history. I refer to Giambattista Vico's theory of historical courses followed by resurgences—*corsi* and *ricorsi*, flux and reflux, flow and ebb—processes by means of which different geographical and cultural regions move through a continuum at different historical paces although guided by comparable causes, effects, and natures.[5] It would be helpful to apply Vico's meaning directly before continuing.

The titles of the books 4 and 5 of Vico's *The New Science* reveal the meaning of history's corsi and ricorsi. Fictional historians depict in form or content, or both, five hundred years of historical courses and resurgences introduced by dramatic endings and beginnings—what I refer to as cataclysms. The course of a given history may be replicated by different sets of characters in similar (but not identical) situations. History is never the same. Recourse may appear to be a coming back around to a very familiar starting point. It is never entirely cyclical. When Vico wrote, he saw history and all its attendant mores, practices, institutions, symbols, and intellectuality as having passed through three stages (and all corsi and ricorsi are divisible by three). History's causes and effects could be seen as the products of gods, heroes, and men. The mores, practices, institutions, and the like that dominated each stage (and stages within each) evinced divine, heroic, and human qualities.

Vico also theorized—and this is brought out tersely in book 5— that when nations (he used the term in its broad sense) needed solutions to their problems (I use this in its broad sense) they usually turned to strong leaders for solutions. Lacking these, foreign influences might prevail. Without either leadership or foreign influences, civil disorder was usually the result. Cataclysm ensued, and out of it a new course. In the fictional histories discussed in these pages the influence of Vico is manifest, and the vehicle for its penetration of the minds of novelists should be obvious.

The motivations and actions of humans in the making of their history can vary according to the makeup of culture, economy, politics, and society. Universal laws do not apply the same way everywhere; regional differences are not ahistorical at all. New institutions are created during a corso from the ruins of old ones based on historical experience. Vico's essential concept—corsi-ricorsi, I will be calling it—meshes dialectically with the synthesis of the Thomistic medieval and Machiavellian renaissance values once proposed as a theoretical framework for Latin American government.[6]

Vico certainly was known to nineteenth-century thinkers who struggled with problems of national identity and historical legitimacy. The Chilean José Victorino Lastarria's *Recuerdos literarios* (1885) showed Vico's influence, for example. Twentieth-century novelists avidly read European and North American fiction, and in James Joyce's *Finnegans Wake* they found more than enough inspiration for some of the specific works dealt with in these pages, as will be made clear.

Vico's influence on Joyce is as documentable as Joyce's on the likes of Fuentes, García Márquez, and Vargas Llosa, to name just three. Joyce adapted freely from Vico (he had read *Scienza nuova*); Latin American writers adapted Joycean techniques just as freely. I make reference to the divine, heroic, and human qualities of the history created by Latin American writers in the first three chapters. These ideas derive from Vico's; they permeate the fictional histories offered to Latin Americans and outsiders by Boom novelists.

In discussing both fiction, its creators, and social science and its practitioners, I make note of *la teoria dei corsi e ricorsi storici* because it is so obviously applicable, not because this book is about Vico and Latin America. Neither is it a work on literary criticism or theory, nor one on social science theory. Even less is it a critique per se of recent history writing. It is a book about what made late twentieth-century Latin American intellectuals from beyond the historian's academic discipline collide with their own history, and in so doing both contribute to its revision and communicate their ideas to an international audience.

History remains subject to human questioning because of its perpetually subjective content, as chapter epigraphs imply. Tediousness of standardized versions can be remedied by "hatching o'er again." There should be proportionately as few limits on what historians do as there are on what novelists do. History ought to praise and pillory. There can also be a Boom in literature and, as we now know in Latin America, the introduction of a new order is indeed a most difficult task.

Novelists and social scientists from Latin America have enjoyed the use of license in colliding with history. If in some way the words of the masters cited in the epigraphs were not intended to apply in precisely the way I have seen fit, well, that is historian's license.

Part One

Cataclysmic History

Chapter 1

The Epic of Discovery and Conquest

It was a pity he couldna be hatched o'er again, an' hatched different.
—George Eliot, *Adam Bede* (1859)

WE ARE FORTUNATE that the likes of Cristoforo Colombo, Pero Vaz de Caminha, Bernal Díaz del Castillo, and Alonso de Ercilla y Zúñiga wrote so passionately of the discovery and conquest of America. Their words confirm to us the awe, mystery, grandeur, and spirit of adventure that dominate fictional histories of the events that once brought Europeans face to face with a new world.

Chroniclers and Boom novelists may have more in common with each other than they do with historians who came in between them in the ways they render the forceful seizure of America, for they agree that the region's history begins around 1492. Thus, they both perpetuate traditional views of history as the product of great men, dynasties, battles, and such. Like scholarly interpretations of discovery and conquest written in the late twentieth century, however, fictional histories provide us with a better understanding of just what discovery and conquest were: aggressive expansion based on ambition, greed, exploitation, and religious convictions. Novelists were interpreting the past using their present as frame of reference, confirming the Black Legend fictionally for social and political purposes. Their fictional histories have didactic and revisionist ends.

Few events rival those of 1492 in terms of historical significance. The fall of Islamic Granada completed the reconquest of Iberia. Later that same year a Genoese mariner's trans-Atlantic voyage opened an age of discovery, exploration, and territorial aggrandizement that lasted the better part of four centuries in Africa, America, and Asia. For over three of those centuries the Iberian kingdoms held sway over what we call Latin America.

Every schoolchild of the Americas learns about the voyages of Colombo. We call him Columbus or Colón. Until recently he was a hero in the popular sense. In Brazil they learn about Pedro Alvares Cabral, who coasted along part of that country in early 1500 while leading the second Portuguese fleet sent out to India. What generations of ordinary Latin Americans have learned about discovery and conquest, of course, is pretty basic. Or at least it was until the late twentieth century, when Latin American novelists began to collide with history, and indigenes and their supporters protested the quincentennials in 1992 and 2000. European and North American revisionist works had very limited impact in Latin America until then.

Especially in the years preceding the five-hundredth anniversary of Columbus's great feat, and owing something to expressions of indignation from descendants of those he called *indios,* did writers of fiction take issue with the epic and heroic versions that participants and chroniclers, then historians, had concocted.[1] Unfettered by historians' need for documentary evidence to revise standard versions, but mindful of what actually had occurred to great numbers of innocent people, novelists invented their own versions of history, used their own devices to collide, and gave readers a darker view of heroism and epic, one that reveals the social injustices of the recent past as end results of half a millennium. Discontented with their present, these writers proved more

16

than competent in using history to register cultural, economic, political, and social concerns in ways that modern scholarship can. They would provide Latin Americans and others with alternative, not necessarily accurate, certainly thought-provoking versions of the region's bloody historical beginnings as what we call Latin America. Their fiction reached far more readers than historical scholarship has.

The novelists who collided with history most successfully—with impact in and beyond Latin America—came from throughout the region. Individually their works are impressive as fiction. Collectively they may be thought of as parts of an epic narrative based more on the values, ethics, and morals of the writers' times than those of their protagonists. Their novels found new markets at home, and others abroad through the medium of translation. Some are familiar to Europeans and North Americans, some are not; Mexican writer Homero Aridjis, Uruguayan critic Napoleón Baccino Ponce de León, Cuban writer and academic Antonio Benítez Rojo, Cuban writer and diplomat Alejo Carpentier, Mexico's great Carlos Fuentes, Argentine diplomat and novelist Abel Posse, Argentina's Juan José Saer, and Moacyr Scliar, the Brazilian physician and novelist are the principal fictional historians of discovery and conquest.

As a group they wrote between 1975 and 1992. They knew each other's work; some knew others personally. Above all, their works vigorously challenge long-held reverential views of Columbus and the Catholic monarchs, analyze the importance of America to Europe, relocate the place of indigenes and Jews ("others") in the history of Latin America, and question the very meaning of their history and the place of religion in it. They did all this more successfully than any Latin American literary school or generation has ever done. They wrote with a purpose at a time when a broad readership was receptive to their arguments. This renders them as historically significant collectively as they are in the field of literature.

By toppling the Admiral of the Ocean Sea from his lofty pedestal writers collided with traditional, at times fanatically Eurocentric,

"Hispanist" national views of a major historical hero and the past he created. By exposing godlike Ferdinand and Isabella as all too human they challenged authority itself. Their discussions of Euro-American relations helped frame late-twentieth-century arguments for latino-americanidad that would reverberate in social science literature. Overwhelmingly representative of the comfortable sectors of society though they were, their descriptions of native populations and European Jews indicated recognition of sociocultural prejudices against minorities or people of color still widespread in their own times. Their reflections on history and religion's role in it showed vividly how much they found makers of the past and the institutions they had created at fault for the troublous times in which they effected their collisions.

Epic heroes have flaws, human failings. If the gods do not exploit their flaws, they themselves find ways to do so. Achilles and Hector abound in history and literature as much as they did in myth. As flawed mortals, Columbus, Ferdinand, and Isabella made excellent symbols for fictional history to attack, just as the quincentennial appealed to the skepticism of a generation of intellectuals who perforce would question the results of five hundred years of history. Conscious of each other's efforts from the 1970s forward, some of Latin America's finest writers seized an opportunity to do what historians in the region could not or had not, owing to their continued concentration on colonial or national history and the limited clientele to which their work could be made available.

Latin American literature's Boom gave these novelists exposure. Markets and audiences waited for their next opus. The approach of 1992 gave them opportunities to explore something of truly epic proportions, and they were up to the challenge. Rejecting reliance on tried and true vehicles set in the past—historical fiction—they set out on their own voyages of discovery in *fictional history*. Their works are akin to what Milan Kundera once called "parallel history."[2]

Both their undisputed ability to write well and the prominence of the Boom made translation of novels dealing with discovery and conquest all the more probable from the 1970s to the 1990s. The market for Latin American letters expanded. The images presented of Columbus and his coevals, of Spain's relations with Americans and other Europeans, of Indians, Jews, and of the Church appealed to international audiences in the years preceding the celebrations of 1492 in countries where historians had long been focusing on cultural, economic, and social consequences, as well as to the growing readerships of Latin America. The accuracy of their fictional histories may not satisfy all historians—or ever serve to change all prevailing opinions—and their views on the nature of history may not be altogether scholarly. They succeeded as thoughtful revisionists nonetheless, in much the same way revisionist historians do. They reached new audiences.

Their attacks on traditional icons do not detract one bit from what they have to say about their history. Their collisions show us as much about the values of our own time as they do about what happened centuries ago. There is as much history in their fiction as there is fiction in the history with which they collided. Whatever else they may have achieved in their recreations of discovery and conquest, they have pretty much laid to rest the old Latin American canonical views of monarch, discoverers, and conquerors as generators of history there. To many, their fiction is indistinguishable from history.

A Hero and His Discoveries

How wondrous it must have been, that moment in October 1492 when Rodrigo de Triana knew it was land. And how wondrous it was each other moment a Spaniard or a Portuguese captain entered in his log that a new land had been found. Well into the sixteenth century wondrous moments fill the letters, chronicles, and epic poems set down by the first Europeans who came to America. Their wonder often got the better of their objectivity, and their chronicles grew in number.[3] Columbus, Cortés, and Vaz de Caminha in their letters;

Bernal Díaz in his history of the Mexican adventure, Alonso de Zárate in his of Peru; and Pedro de Oña and Ercilla y Zúñiga in their epic poetry of South American conquest all betray a sense of wonder and awe.

So do the novelists of our time—in terms equally human and epic that reflect the experiences through which the discoverers and conquerors went. It took a while for Iberians to know that they indeed were in a new world, not the Indies, not Asia.[4] The wonder of discovery as well as the need to make it sound worthwhile to backers is well known, but it prompted more vivid fictional reactions, like that of Carpentier's fictional Columbus: "This country is the most beautiful that human eyes have ever seen. . . . As for landscape, I didn't have to rack my brain: I say that the blue mountains I can see in the distance are like those of Sicily. I say that the grass is as tall as that of Andalusia in April and May, though there is nothing here that is anything like Andalusia. . . . I allude to the fields of Castile, here where not a single thing recalls the fields of Castile."[5] Spices, gold, pearls? No evidence of treasure yet existed to the Admiral, but treasure had to be in such a place, a place neither Europe nor anywhere known to Europeans. From the moment of contact Columbus's was another world—defined from without, by virtue of contact, not by its own existence.

Years later, after his return to Iberia, Saer's shipwrecked cabin boy begins his chronicle of a fascinating enforced sojourn with South American Indians thus: "What I remember most about those empty shores is the vastness of the sky. Standing beneath that expanse of blue, I felt how small I was; on those yellow sands we were as insignificant as ants in the middle of a desert. Now that I am an old man, I prefer to live out my days in cities because city life is bounded by horizons and because cities conceal the sky."[6] By the time the cabin boy adventurer—whose story really should be read in conjunction with *Robinson Crusoe* and Cabeza de Vaca's narratives—was an old man, there were cities on the shores of America, as this magical place where he had survived would come to be called. Another world was being transformed; it had only existed, theretofore, and in only a limited way, in the minds of its inhabitants.

Across a twenty-page span of *Terra Nostra,* Carlos Fuentes has El Señor (Charles V and Philip II as one) ponder from afar what he has been told about this wondrous place: "There is a new world beyond the sea ... There's a new world on the other side of the sea ... A new world exists ... Beyond the ocean ... Exists ... A world ... New ... Beyond ... The ocean ... From the other side ... Of the sea."[7] It was almost too much for a sixteenth-century monarch to bear, this (unseen) newness, this new world beyond Spain, Iberia, and Europe, for in the Old World itself newness was becoming hard to bear. Columbus's legacy would be Spain's mixed blessing from the outset. It is a burdensome legacy for Latin Americans to this day.

The Admiral was not only imperfect, he was doomed, and this made everyone's wonder and awe all the more epic in proportion. Argentina's Abel Posse argues that this was because Columbus did not know how to explain what had happened. He was aware of the potential for glory out there to the west, for had not the wife of the governor of the Canaries told him of earlier voyages that way, and tales of exotic visitors from out there, while he reputedly dallied with her, all too humanly, just prior to setting off for Asia?[8] Columbus was doomed by his times, by those who surrounded him, by those he would meet, and by his own boundless ambition. He was doomed, at least in fictional history, by the fact that what he would do might already have been done, and did not do him much good while he lived. He was doomed by the known and the unknown, the mundane and the wondrous.

Unable to explain it satisfactorily, Columbus invented America.[9] He was an egotist, a pitchman, a businessman, and an enslaver of Indians. His discovery not only fueled his ambition, it urged him to defend his actions and embellish his stories. Carpentier's Admiral portrays himself as such a fellow in a rambling discourse on pre-1492 lobbying for support that covers one-eighth of a novel (in which his sainthood is being contemplated early in the nineteenth century).[10] He makes it clear, does Carpentier's Columbus, that what he did was to advance himself as much or more than to extend Christ's dominion over the nations. Even so, Triana's cry, *¡Tierra! ¡Tierra!* "was like the music of the Te Deum to the rest of us." It is still as impossible to separate Columbus's sense of awe from post-1492 history as it is to ignore his dark side.

Ever the opportunist, Columbus most probably did not romance the queen, as Carpentier claims, and possibly did dally with the wife of the governor of the Canaries. Abel Posse, while concurring with Carpentier that Columbus was an opportunist, takes issue with the Cuban writer. The Admiral, writes Posse, "was intimidated. . . . Colón and Isabel were a sculptured composition, motionless amidst the forest of motionless columns." Posse, in fact, casts some doubt on Columbus's manhood. Carpentier's putative error re the Admiral and the queen, Posse claims, was based on the Cuban's incredible proclivity for the democratic.[11] So fictional history's Columbus becomes even less a man than once we were led to think. His life from 1492 onward is diminished by this alone. Might not the history of that which he discovered be similarly sullied because of his self-absorption—and that of so many others?

Ever the prevaricator, Columbus is taken to task by Carpentier several times in *The Harp and the Shadow* for his "stretchers." Columbus soon knew there was no gold in the Caribbean, no spices to trade for with Oriental potentates and their merchants in these islands, certainly not in Cuba, the largest of all the Indies. But he continued to lie about what he found, to the point of trying to convince his critics that he had found the earthly paradise near the island of Trinidad, there at the mouth of the Orinoco.[12] Benítez Rojo elaborates on what historians have known for centuries, that Columbus lied (at best, he thought wishfully) when he claimed that Cuba was not an island (Cubanacán = Kublai Khan) and that Cibao (the interior of Española) was Cipango—Japan.[13]

Ever the dreamer, Columbus would die disappointed, unfulfilled. He had not been to the East Indies and back four times, even if he passed away thinking so. Although he had achieved heroic status, only to die in semidisgrace, he did not die like "Tiphys, on a foreign shore, far from his natural land . . . [so that] now within a common tomb, midst unknown ghosts, he lies at rest."[14] No one really knows today where the Admiral rests.

Ever the schemer, Columbus was not trusted by Spanish authorities. All fictional histories remark on his suspect credentials, his behavior, his non-Iberian antecedents, certainly Genoese, possibly even Jewish.[15] Fictional history, for all this, has been kinder to him than has revisionist scholarship. Like all heroes at the end of their epic, too much attention diminished him.

Historical scholarship has made him vulnerable to harsh criticism of his conduct and his motives, and to his share of the blame for what he and others set in motion. To English-language readers, the difference between *Admiral of the Ocean Sea* and the Admiral portrayed in novels of the Boom is equivalent to the difference between the worldviews of 1942, when Samuel Eliot Morison wrote his classic biography, and 1992, when the quincentennial provoked so much protest. To Spanish Americans the five centuries preceding the quincentennial once constituted both a glorious and a tragic history generated by the actions of individuals holding power or contesting for it. Such a view no longer has much of a following, for power and the contest for it, we know, led to the tragedy of the recent past.

Godlike Monarchs

Autocrats are troubled and complex, every bit as troubled and complex as gods who toy with heroes. The Spanish monarchs of the sixteenth century, Isabel and Ferdinand, Charles and Philip, lived in momentous and troublous times. Luther and Erasmus, Loyola and

Machiavelli, Henry VIII and Sir Thomas More, Suleiman the Magnificent and Babur the Moghul Emperor, Bartolomé de las Casas and Torquemada, Elizabeth I and Catherine de Medici—they all lived while Iberians began the opening up of Africa, America, and Asia to them and theirs. The age of discovery and conquest was also an age of autocracy, intolerance, and violence for all involved. So has been much of the rest of Latin American history, hence this history's susceptibility to collisions.

It was the decision of the Catholic monarchs both to expel Muslims and Jews from Iberia and to encourage the Admiral to find a western sea route to Asia. The same Spanish monarch and Holy Roman emperor who confronted municipal revolt in Spain and Protestant heresy in Europe would reap the benefits of Mexico's splendor. He would struggle with the fate of the subjugated Indians of America, with conquerors, colonists, and clergy—and with his own subjects. Cultural, economic, and social forces not dependent on individual actions were as dynamic as the individuals who struggled for power. This is why those times—and the other two cataclysmic times in Latin American history—have been so exciting.

Above all, the Spanish crown was absolute in its conviction that order—political, religious, and social—had to be established at home, and this is one reason why Ferdinand and Isabella were so disappointed with the Admiral when he tried to administer Spain's first American settlements on the island of Española. They realized they could not replicate in the Indies what they were still trying to establish at home. Homero Aridjis claims that it was the Catholic monarchs themselves who had commanded unbaptized Jews to wear a symbol on their clothing, so that they could be more easily recognized, to live in specific parts of towns, and to be off certain streets after nightfall. Those who wielded power in fictional history's Spain believed it necessary to restrict the rights of others (this means non-Christians especially) in order to maintain control over all.[16] They did this to all they suspected and to many they did not. They did this at home and they would do it on the other side of the ocean. Scholars may find fault with fictional historians' claims such as these, but they may be less inclined to object if they see them as metaphoric in purpose.

Any criticism of the Spanish monarchy in the pages of fictional history is as much a metaphoric indictment of twentieth-century abusers of power as it is a clever, fictional depiction of history. Aridjis also asserts the prohibition of Jews from practicing medicine among Christians and from observing their faith in public. The conquest of Granada and the availability of the Inquisition did not temper the crown's commitment to orthodoxy in Spain: America would transmogrify it. Seizure of power would not temper, one day, the commitment of authoritarians to national security; the holding of power would facilitate it.

The crown's disappointment with the Admiral (perhaps a Jew himself, it has been mooted) was a blow. Prestige gained upon the fall of Granada was not enhanced by Columbus's feat: "your prestige if in fact you earn any, will be in the long term. Up to this point nothing has happened in these countries which we can't even imagine, no battles have been won, no memorable triumphs have been achieved."[17] No treasure, no gold, no pearls, precious stones, or spices; those who, godlike in their own demeanor, sent the hero on his quest were not satisfied with his efforts. Posse writes that after the death of Isabella, Ferdinand (as regent for Castile) "passed from grief to resentment, as if he had been cheated or deceived. Devastated by sorrow, he spent hours meditating on the curse of America. The figure of the Admiral was never far from the horizon of his wrath."[18] Gods never have let heroes (or each other) off easy, nor have contemporary novelists possessed of metaphoric license.

The Habsburg monarchs of the sixteenth century, Charles and Philip, were extraordinary men, worldly and spiritual, driven and disappointed. In the magisterial *Terra Nostra* they are one godlike El Señor, for history is not big enough for father *and* son. So one they become in Fuentes's fictional history, in order to regally grapple with the meaning both of Spain and the world "on the other side of the sea." Together they contemplate no worthy heir, no man who could be great enough to equal their achievements: "I must be the last *Señor*, and then nothing, nothing, nothing."[19] And next to nothing there was when we throw in the seventeenth-century Habsburg kings. The point here is that late-twentieth-century writers—Fuentes, certainly— consciously pointed their fiction toward negation of the legacy of pre-1975 Spain, or at least the diminution of its historical value based on discovery and conquest. And they did this by attacking the human symbols of pre-1975 Spain, not Spain or Spaniards per se.

Our own contemporaries' fictional treatments of authority, intolerance, abuse, and tormented lives are epic in form and content, clearly allegorical in meaning. Modern Spain, owing to its leaders, not its people, equates with an authoritarian and violent past cut short only with the death of Francisco Franco, El Caudillo (El Señor?), who left no heir of his own either, it should be remembered. Juxtaposition of negation of the past and affirmation of the present, which Octavio Paz associated with independence, finds its own way into fictional recreations of sixteenth-century history.[20] Spain did not deserve America then, nor would America deserve Spain ever after. If there has been any possible affirmation of a Spanish past, it is an idealized one more associated with the democratizing Spain of the post-1975 period than with historical Spain. In other words, the Spanish past must itself be constricted and depersonalized in fictional history in order to be part of Spanish America's. Perhaps this is where constriction of history, argued in chapter 6, really has its intellectual foundations.

"Neither the passivity of pleasure nor the weakness of illness will be able to govern these kingdoms," Fuentes tells us.[21] But from the end of the sixteenth century until the end of the eighteenth, neither passivity nor illness was enough to shake loose Spain's empire. The great kings and their heroes became history; new heroes would have to take their places. Philip (El Señor II) did not have an heir comparable to himself to whom he could pass a scepter the way his father had given his to him.[22] Iberian monarchies during most of the remainder of the colonial era were bereft of able monarchs. The inference for recent times is pretty clear.

Decadent Iberia, Living America

Fictional histories do not deal with very much of the three centuries of the colonial era per se. Reflections on relations between the *Madre Patria* and her colonies beyond the sea do give us a revised view of the colonial past, however. Observations on the role of the Church, faith, Euro-Indian relations, and Spain's relations with Europe, both beyond the Pyrenees and across the Mediterranean, provide us only with impressions of those centuries of imperial dominion when America first fell into the grasp of "tinhorn dictators and autocratic *corregidores.*"[23] Autocrats and tinhorns, as we shall see, figure prominently in the second two eras with whose history novelists collided.

Now, it needs saying that novelists are by no means the only Latin Americans who have pondered the region's relations with Europe and the world. All readers familiar with the history and literature of the region area are aware of the works of Andrés Bello, Lastarria, and Domingo Faustino Sarmiento; Euclides da Cunha, José Martí, and José Enrique Rodó; and more recently those of Germán Arciniegas, Edmundo O'Gorman, and Roberto Fernández Retamar, words that have found audiences beyond the sea. And, Europeans, Tzvetan Todorov and Hugh Thomas, say, have found readers on our side of the same sea.[24] Latin America's essayists initiated the debate in the nineteenth century, perhaps, but novelists have defined the recent discourse with a greater popular impact. The death of Franco, following closely the regime change in Portugal, helped make it possible to reopen discussions of the Ibero-American relationship in a new context, for historians to see Iberia as something other than either the source of all things evil, or good. Only from 1975 forward has it been possible to be Spanish American or Brazilian without having to *not* be Spanish or Portuguese. It has been possible to affirm without having to negate simultaneously.

The Mediterranean democratization experiments that began in the mid-1970s—Greece, Portugal, Spain—were followed by similar American experiments, most notably those in Peru (1980), Argentina (1982), Brazil (1985), and Chile (1990). Too, Mexico's official party began stumbling its way to *apertura* and expeditious coexistence with opposition forces, a process that culminated in an opposition victory in the presidential election of 2000. Through the initial stages of democratization, and until the collapse of the post–World War II paradigm, political issues were still life-threatening, and writers still believed themselves to be participants in struggles of a cultural, political, and social nature. They were determined to be more than "sheer entertainers," as Ilan Stavan put it.[25] This lends even more to the historical quality of their work.

In at least one sense, America was to Spain and Portugal hundreds of years ago pretty much what it is to them and others today—a collection of variations on Iberia, imagined and real. Fictional history portrays America as a most favorable—if not favored—variation. Fuentes's treatment of "our land" gives the world on the other side of the sea—not so new after five centuries—an air of mystery and fantastical qualities that it only partially retains nowadays. Carpentier's Columbus boasts of its beauty and the opportunities it presented to Spaniards. To Benítez Rojo's explorers of the *Sea of Lentils* (from *Antillas*, once translated into French as *Lentilles*), America had coasts "so broad and bitten out with coves to hide in, where the islands made you almost silly," and "where Negroes could be bought and sold for bags of pearls or silver bullion."[26] It really was a place for the taking. And may still be, sadly, if trends discussed in chapter 6 continue unabated.

America was a place where a fellow could find gold to buy favors at court, build a house with the labor of others, pay for the building of a church, dress in silk, buy indulgences, endow a daughter, make a son a rich man. America became the destination of choice for fortune hunters and freebooters, scoundrels and saints.[27] To the likes of sixteenth-century freebooter Lope de Aguirre, he who truly would go rogue, America was where gold secured all: not just favors from, but a place at, the court; one's own regiment; wine, women, and entertainment; El Dorado and "gloom and doom" as well.[28]

It was also the place where *bandeirantes* raged inland "from slaughter to slaughter, seizing for Portugal lands already usurped by Spain and assigned by papal authority." The redbeards ("mestizos of Jewish descent") fattened their dogs on the flesh of Indians,[29] and sacked Jesuit missions under the banner of the cross; America had something for everyone throughout the entire colonial era. It still offers much to outsiders.

The Admiral's earthly paradise was a place where dogs would run free regardless of whose usurped lands were seized by whom.[30] In *The Harp and the Shadow* Carpentier tells us that the Europeans with their firearms had the advantage of thirty centuries of development, "the gift of unknown desires . . . greed and lust . . . hunger for riches, the sword and the torch, the chain, the stocks, and the whip."[31] Paradise discovered became paradise fouled even before it was lost.

America was like a fantasy to Columbus, but no more than it was to those who followed him west. It remained so for centuries. El Dorado, the land of the Amazons, Cibola, Gran Quivira, the mountain of silver (Potosí)—it took the better part of a century for Spaniards to see the value of land that did not produce silver or gold. And when they and the Portuguese ceased to search for fantastic interior kingdoms, the Brazilians began their epic journeys into the South American heartland in quest of human treasure. There, and up on the northern frontier of New Spain, were the marches of the American empires, the frontiers both of faith and greed. Much of the region still awaits some kind of exploitation. Fictional history confirms this.

Fuentes, Benítez Rojo, and Posse each discuss early Latin America in terms of fantasy beyond the Edenic. Approaching Tenochtitlán, Spaniards "gazed in wonderment," asking if what they saw was not in a dream: snow-crowned volcanoes standing like guardians over this city . . . a gigantic sleeping man . . . a reclining, sleeping woman." Fuentes's speaker, echoing Bernal Díaz of course,[32] descends with his companions into the magnificent Valley of Mexico, and the conquest is on. Awe gave way to rapine in fact and in fiction. The natives confuse the Spaniards' presence with events surrounding the history of Quetzalcoatl (only briefly, scholars agree) and take their stand either for or against the light-skinned, bearded invaders. Welcomed, or opposed, and finally acknowledged as masters of cities and valleys, the Spaniards became the new rulers of Mexico. A cultural and social status quo crumbles, a new one takes its place. Fuentes's fictional description is no less epic than Bernal Díaz's, no less historical than any other version.

Spain (through royal government and the Church) had a mission; whether bent on prolongation of the peninsular reconquest or in quest of new opportunity, her monarchs and conquerors were collectively more than rapacious predators. Spaniards wanted to "carry to the New World the immaculate legacy of Christ our Lord."[33] They wanted to keep Jews out, those people who never had been "willing to work as laborers or herd cattle, or to teach those offices to their sons." They are portrayed as fanatics and bigots as much for political as fictional purposes.

Spaniards wanted, we know, to create a new Spain, and of course they would think they had. The monarchs wanted to establish an absolutism they did not fully enjoy at home, conquerors and colonists the kind they could enjoy. Once it came to be known as such, then accepted as something other than a hitherto undiscovered part of Asia, America would exist because Spaniards and Portuguese so needed it to exist.[34] Indigenes take note. This is to assert that Spain, at least, wanted to find something other than what she already was—but not threateningly different. Spaniards, too, had to affirm and negate in order to define themselves once they were in both fictional and historical America.

Here the beginnings of latinoamericanidad take form for readers of fictional history: something more easily to be found, but also to be altered, on this side of the ocean. Spain's mission was as much one to remake herself as it was to make the New World over in her image. Such a mythos of mission would become part of Latin America's history in the nineteenth century, when Latin Americans themselves sought to make countries over in a European image (but not in Spain's). Their continued addiction to both affirmation and negation, this is to suggest, is a legacy of the past, one brought to our attention through fiction as much as through scholarship.

The same order the Catholic monarchs, their Portuguese counterparts, and descendants of each sought for Iberia found its way to America, the same theoretically rigid, vertical hierarchies, the same theoretically absolutist government: "for the powerful, all the rights and no obligations; for the weak, no rights and all obligations."[35] Spain had her way. And would get her just deserts. Benítez Rojo's Antillian *Adelantado* reports to readers thus: "Here everyone works for himself and no one helps his neighbor. They rob His Majesty of his one-fifth, they defame the honorable, and they disobey all laws and contracts that might not favor them."[36] Until royal rule could be imposed everywhere, the disorder that drove Ferdinand and Isabella forward toward inquisition, reconquest, and expulsion in the fifteenth century would reign supreme in the ultramarine kingdoms-to-be.

"Great disorder breeds great order," El Señor's aide, Guzmán, tells him.[37] Royal rule in the form of governors, viceroys, archbishops, inquisitors, alcaldes, adelantados, corregidores, and intendants imposed order. And this order would prevail until there were no more Señores (no more authoritarians?). But while it did America was never free of disorder and rebellion, "the eternal rebellion of America." Posse's Aguirre would have those who heard such words believe that no one could conquer America. "Her soul pulses in the swamps, hides in the peaks, flees into forests unfathomably deep."[38] America the eternal, Lope de Aguirre claimed, transformed men, changed their ways; it could never be subdued by mere mortals.

Posse's telluric allusions recall Count Keyserling's.[39] America had the ability to transform both men and nations. America had identity without having to have a name. America had become a principal character in the epic of discovery and conquest. All novels dealing with this era personify the land, the water, and nature in the ways they are portrayed in mythic literature. "Where it's hot, it's *poor,*" the Admiral was warned once.[40] But neither he nor those who followed in his wake would be deterred by the heat or the poverty. Latinoamericanidad begins by being of the land as well as of the people.

None of the fictional histories considered here contains an argument for it being rich where it's cold. In truth Spain is portrayed in *Terra Nostra, The Dogs of Paradise,* and *1492* as either disorderly, monstrously orderly, or poor—or, at times, all of these.[41] It was not only poor where it was hot; it was violent. "Man destroys what he says he loves most," says Posse's Columbus near the end of *The Dogs of Paradise.*[42] He proceeds, saying that the men who first came to America found as much pleasure in sorrow as they did in happiness. "Like most readers of Dante," Posse writes, "they preferred Hell to heaven."[43] Like most epic heroes, they made the descent, they fell, or they were pushed from paradise to somewhere quite a bit less orderly—and often hotter too.

Posse's telluric Aguirre was every bit as much the man of action the Admiral was. Rogue and rebel, he is punished for his singular misdeeds by living an "Eternal Return" after death—an epic punishment of corsi-ricorsi dimensions. Aguirre cannot escape his crimes, his rebellion, his love of disorder. He finds America "a land of such living power that she routed vigorous men the way a hearty organism repels germs."[44] America could be militarily conquered, all right, but America could not be dominated, even by this latter-day Wrath of God. Posse's Aguirre represents Spain in America every bit as much as does Carpentier's Admiral. Both, and their kind, must take blame for historical injustices.

That Spain's stamp on her portion of America is still ever so discernible, is a point made again and again by fictional historians. That the Spanish and the Portuguese parts of America we know today were discernible as something quite *other* than Europe half a millennium ago, should be the inference drawn. Not all Europeans—not all Iberians clearly—appreciated then, nor do all regard now, the achievements of America's original inhabitants, the variety of cultures and climate zones. Not all indigenes, according to Saer's Witness could comprehend the meaning of the autonomous worlds that existed in close proximity to each other in America, "living in a dimension impenetrable to outsiders." It was not only the people who were different: "Space, time, water, plants, sun, moon, and stars were all different too."[45] I think this is a twentieth-century interpretation of a sixteenth-century recognition of distinct identity, of something quite other than Europe: out of disorder, order; out of order, disorder; out of affirmation, negation; out of negation, affirmation. It is a comment on contemporary Latin America as well as an assertion of history's Latin American variant.

Spanish America's stamp on Spain is less remarkable historically since the fall of the Spanish American Empire. Novelists who dealt with the period of discovery and conquest did so in order to show what history had led to as much as to collide with standard versions of regional historical origins. America becomes the principal character notwithstanding the Admirals, Señores, and Adelantados; the Aguirres and Witnesses of fictional history. Novelists revealed a sense of tragedy as well as one of epic grandeur in their works, adumbrating what prevails in novels of the independence and recent eras.

History's Others

The Spain of Columbus's, Charles's, and Cortés's times stood at a historical crossing place. The era of the Mediterranean was closing; the Strait of Gibraltar had ceased to mark the limit of long-term, open-sea navigation. It was the end of the Old World, the beginning of the New. Portuguese navigators had reached India by the end of the fifteenth century, America by 1500; Cortés conquered Mexico in 1521, the year before the Magellan expedition returned to Spain.[46]

Fictional history of this era portrays a set of interdependent relationships that may be best understood as metaphoric. I do not think anyone knows for certain if these metaphoric associations are of conscious or subconscious derivation, although authors' commentaries would lead one to believe them both. I believe them to be worthy of note as part of the Boom's revisionist thrust.

In the works of Aridjis, Benítez Rojo, Carpentier, Fuentes, Posse, Saer, and Scliar, Spain and Portugal emerge as products of historical processes initiated from without Iberia as well as from within: economic and political change in the Mediterranean, religious schism in northern Europe, the rise of the Ottoman empire in the Levant. Jews and Protestants played roles in this change as significant as the one played by Muslims. Englishmen caused problems for Iberians for national as well as religious reasons.

In portraying outsiders as causal agents, fictional historians place fifteenth- and sixteenth-century Spain in the same position they place Latin America in the postindependence centuries. Spain and Portugal are metaphorically Latin America; Latin America is to become, with independence, what Spain and Portugal once were. Iberia and America in the early modern era are in a relationship similar to that of Mediterranean and northern Europe with Spain at the same time. As portrayed in fictional history, Latin America is the ultimate victim of this linkage of unfavorable relationships, and remains so in its relations with the United States. So there is from the beginning an outside force, an other, both controversial and influential in the framing of the region's history, however this is to be defined. To Iberians, as depicted in the epic of discovery and conquest, it is first the Jew, then the Indian.

In fiction and fact Europe was an aggressor in America. The English had no scruples and were heretics to boot. "Whites," whether Anglo-Saxon (later North American) or not, always had evil designs on Latin America.[47] Europeans wanted "space! Precious woods! Markets! Spices and ivory from the Orient! Enough of things Turkish in Mare Nostrum!"[48] Indians, on the contrary were "naifs"[49] who had no understanding of what was happening to them upon the arrival of the whites from across the water. Is this all that far from portrayals of the fifteenth and sixteenth centuries by revisionist historians of recent times, especially the outsiders? Everywhere enemies: Italians and Levantines; Erasmus, Luther, and Calvin; foreigners who "deride our nation, for they treat us worse than Indians."[50] Benítez Rojo follows up this comment on Europeans' derision by opining that Spain, confronted by so many enemies, did her best to isolate herself from the rest of the West in order to achieve order at home and recreate it across the sea.[51] This, as we have been seeing, was to be no easy task.

Fictional history flails Spaniards for their treatment of Jews and Indians, indicating vividly just how difficult the conquests really were, metaphorically how complex the relations between dominant and subordinate cultures remain centuries later. In Jewish fictional history both Jews and Indians had reason to fear and obey the Christians of Castile and Aragon, and they had little reason to love them, making it ever so obvious that submission to authority need not be based on acceptance of it. "I felt fear of man,"[52] Aridjis's Juan Cabezón says when he witnesses an auto-da-fé. Fear of other men is no basis for productive relations between cultures and civilizations, but it was all Aridjis's Spain could extend, thus the best Jews and Indians could hope for.

Both would be apart from the influential social order of the era. Aridjis vividly portrays the ghetto status of Jews by noting the already mentioned requirement that they wear badges of identification.[53] Scliar emphasizes their commercial role in the Mediterranean, thus their association with Spain's other enemies.[54] Jews were reputed to have committed all sorts of social transgressions in Spain in addition to the crime their ancestors had committed against Christ. These sins marked them and *conversos* as others. The best term for what fiction portrays is institutionalized terrorism. "Castile and Aragon," Aridjis writes, "had ignited the fires, and Spain was ablaze." Soon America would be ablaze as well.[55]

The historical presence of the Jews in the Mediterranean, in old Islamic Iberia, and in Christian Aragon, Castile, and Portugal, marked them with the brand of suspicion. Their rumored associations with Genoese merchants and Columbus, financial dealings in Iberia, and skills in science, medicine, learning, and navigation, so vividly chronicled by Aridjis and Scliar, made Jews significant agents of change.[56] This agency occurred precisely when too much change of the wrong sort was unacceptable to most Spaniards on either side of the sea.

That is, 1492 would not be not a very good year for everyone, and the first few ensuing decades did not ease minds much about others. America, first contacts with Indians, the Protestant Reformation, Mexico—the growing list of unpleasant events and annoying people grew longer with each passing year. Novelists accuse Christian Iberians of associating Jews with all the wrong kinds of change; Spaniards suspicious or doubtful of the American enterprise might have seen it as a Jewish plot, we are told. I think there is a simple reason why Aridjis and Scliar saw fit to make this so clear: Change could be viewed as the work of the devil. Novelists used this same device to attack and deride the fanatical anticommunism (and much else in its name) of authoritarian administrations of the late twentieth century.

Seen in strictly colonial terms, what Sephardic Jews were to Iberian Christians, American Indians would soon be: other. Seen in a modern perspective, outsiders (the new others) had (have) more faults than Latin Americans, for the former deal with the latter from a power position. Spaniards thought Jews, Muslims, and their nefarious Mediterranean allies dealt with them in the same unjust way. Hypernationalism, the single most pervasive impediment to latinoamericanidad is a primary target of collisions with history.

Indians thus can be seen—and this may call for a leap of faith—as having become the new Jews. But they were not heretical. They were not tainted by the blasphemous Qur'an; nor had they clung to the Torah, rejecting, thus, the Gospels. Christians, therefore, would not have to treat them as they did Muslims and Jews, Levantines or Africans. Rather, there was something pagan (not heretical, though) about Indians; their otherness worked in favor of their survival, not in the attempts to eradicate them. They became subjects of the realm. The struggle for justice in the sixteenth-century conquests is our evidence for this conclusion.

Aside from population decline, which began with contact and began to reverse itself only in the first half of the seventeenth century, and labor conditions, Indians' status in America was portrayed as a lot better than that of Jews in Iberia. Fictional historians would have us believe this, not for historical but for political reasons. Indians cease to be a central component of fictional history early on in order that political agendas be better promoted at a regional level.

A previously cited passage from *Terra Nostra* also describes the Valley of Mexico and Tenochtitlán by calling it "a white city of tall towers and golden mists traversed by wide canals."[57] In short, these were places blessed with sophisticated cultures and peoples. They reminded invaders of home even as they were confronting the unknown. And Scliar allows an aged Indian to show a Portuguese Jew evidence that his people "no longer speak Hebrew; but in each generation, there is always one person in charge of taking care of the Torah, which our ancestors brought with them from Jerusalem."[58] Citation of these passages is not to mock fictional or real Iberians for their wishful thinking (nor to chide fictional historians for their selective idealization of the past), but to show that Indians ("Jews of the Lost Tribes") ultimately were regarded and treated with a respect not accorded Jews in the Old World.

When Indians became more numerous again, as their population began to increase in the seventeenth century, they were untainted still. They worked hard. Their acceptance (or simple apery) of Christian ways was a symbol of their acceptability into the Christian faith. They were part of a present as future-to-be, not of the present as past-that-was. They were honest, cautious, close to nature; they had a sense of history; they were not sneaky or corrupted by city life and the market place; and their sense of history did not get in the way of Christianity. In fictional history they were the lucky ones in the long run. But they were—as Americans—exploitable to the fullest.

Spain (America's own other) obliged herself to cleanse, reform, and purify her new citizen-clients, not to eradicate or expel them.[59] God demanded no less for *others*. This was Spain's self-assigned mandate. This "comparatively" benign exploitation stands in contrast to treatments of outsiders' behavior in Latin America in fictional histories of modern times, wherein outsiders (from North America in particular) are even more consistently attacked.

The fictional histories of discovery and conquest constitute a collective epic in which Columbian and Cortesian heroes and Aguirresque villains struggle against godlike monarchs like Ferdinand and Isabella, and El Señor. They reveal collective historical mindsets, these heroes and villains do, that are consistent with those revealed in fiction dealing with the independence era and in novels dealing with the recent past (wherein heroes gone bad become all too human tyrants). This mindset is associated, of course, with an ongoing struggle to assert latinoamericanidad in world context, in terms other than those used by traditional, nationally focused historians.

Identity clearly means both assertion and rejection, affirmation and negation. Spain had to reject northern Europe, Islam, Judaism,

38

Protestantism, and the Islamic Mediterranean in order to assert herself. Spain rejected in order to assure a destiny by absorbing much of America and by converting her Indians, unpolluted as yet, but still the *other*. America, in the mindset of Boom novelists themselves, is identifiable and independent through condemnation of discoverers, rejection of pre-1975 Spain's legacy, and wariness of some of Europe's and most of North America's continued influence. This all becomes even clearer upon examination of portions of these novels that address history per se.

History's Uses and Abuses

In *1492* Aridjis describes cases of heresy predating the establishment of the Inquisition being dealt with ex post facto: property confiscated from heirs of posthumously discovered heretics and disinterment of remains—in short, historical terrorism.[60] Redefinition of the past in such a way exceeds the boundaries of revisionism, surely. If the history of discovery and conquest can be revised in a commonsense way, as it is in fictional history, cannot others redefine portions of the Latin American past for baser purposes?

Benítez Rojo's "unfolding" history of the Caribbean provides readers with a maplike view of that geographic area.[61] In the novels of Carpentier, too, the Caribbean becomes an ur-Latin America where Spaniards had moved isle-by-beautiful-isle, instead of conquest-by-institutionalized-conquest, forward (as would be the case later). It was where what we now call "Latin America" was first identified through invention.[62] It was Columbus (ever a culprit, it seems) who shattered the "spatiohistorical horizon,"[63] he and his immediate successors who proved the extent of that horizon, both spatially and historically. Shattering of the horizon resulted in confrontation between European linear history based on an institutionalized chronology, and the cyclical history of America based on repetitive seasonal or

Whoa!
cyclical
history

astronomical phenomena. The result was a kind of spiral history[64] in which similar events occurred—and recurred—over centuries for many of the same reasons with many of the same results.[65] Beginnings and endings, the meaning of time to gods, heroes, and humans, and the nature of the future—all these changed once a name was given to America, especially once its own value exceeded that of a western all-water route to Asia.

"One needs multiple existences in order to unify a personality," Fuentes tells us.[66] He might just as well as have said Latin America needs multiple identities in order to achieve latinoamericanidad. The past, claimed the Mexican master, is characterized by illusion (canonical history?), the present by solidarity (out of exasperation with history?), and the future by hope (based on wishful thinking?). So it is quite possible for time itself to be relative, is it not?

In fiction it is. Intercalated history is a hallmark of recent Latin American prose. It surely is in the fictional histories of the authors discussed in this chapter. Daimon (Lope de Aguirre), Posse's Flying Dutchman of South America, engages in corsi-ricorsi with both a vengeance and tragic results. This hero gone bad is condemned to an eternity of suffering, an eternity of history, in the future as well as in the past.[67] He personifies Posse's "eternal rebellion of America." And of course he and the region are destined to see just what this means again and again. Fictional histories of independence and the recent past affirm this—again and again.

Change, or history as agent of change, also figures in the more linear fictional histories of Spain's and Portugal's American adventurers. The Brazilian Scliar's view is that the New World provided new opportunities for the Sephardim.[68] They were indeed history's principal human agent, he insists, in an age of change. They were the link between the Levant and the Indies, between Western Europe and America, and between faith, reason, and science. Their "racial memory" preserved the past for posterity.[69] Does this indicate anything more than the author's interest in providing a counterhistory of his coreligionists in Brazil? Probably yes; in the context of fictional history it further indicates acknowledgment of definition by outsiders, Christian and Jew, Iberian or Northerner.

In this context Daimon represents an important aspect of Spanish racial memory too: that of the eternal rebellion. Moreover the Marañones (Aguirre's sixteenth-century followers who rebelled against imperial rule) testify to the early and widespread descent of heroes to human—perhaps even subhuman—status or, conversely, to the ultimate triumph of humans over heroes and gods, a necessary part of the historical spirals under discussion here and in the next two chapters.

America gave them all their opportunity. "The Knaves of the Spanish Empire had trounced the Horse and even the King. Lowly, groveling servile knaves. They had triumphed in this elaborate artificial game known as real life." Their triumph was completed in the independence saga, as history reveals.[70] Heroic effort endured in human terms. Humans would also thrive on cataclysm. Their frailties would be as historically remarkable as the flaws of heroes.

Saer reveals a sense of history when he describes the routine of the Indians among whom the eponymous Witness spends time as an *other*. Resting meant "losing ground to the viscous dark that enveloped them." Autonomous action meant existence and identity of the collectivity. Once the Spaniards arrived the collectivity would, of course, cease to exist as before, and the Indians would be left "without a world."[71] Their losses were Spain's and Portugal's gain, but only for three centuries of history, at the end of which Spain's and Portugal's loss would be America's gain. Autonomy would be restored, but to what end.

Collisions with standard Latin American versions of the history of discovery and conquest helped destroy nationalistic myths propounded for centuries by chroniclers, then historians. Like revisionist scholarship, fictional history is not kind to the individuals most regularly portrayed; great men become villains, discovery and conquest become acts of aggression committed against sovereign peoples.

Novelists used canonical history's own icons to destroy a rejected past every bit as much as historians use archives to reconstruct better versions of a controversial one.

Fictional history of discovery and conquest, especially that which became available to foreigners and larger segments of Latin America's population, does more to perpetuate in our minds the deeds and events of infamy by attacking their perpetrators than it does to advance the cause of historiography in the ways scholars have advanced it. Boom novelists had the former in mind—for political, not scholarly purposes. They knew who they wanted to blame for injustices and what they wanted their readers to remember about the cataclysm of discovery and conquest.

Five centuries after the epic of discovery and conquest of their region began, Latin American novelists recreated it in order to denounce its perpetrators and much of its legacy. Viewing discovery and conquest in terms of an epic created by modern writers is tantamount to a rehatching à la Eliot, of the region's history. It is evidence of regional thinking in a time when Latin America cried out for definition as such.

Is it possible that fictional history may have abetted what Fuentes calls the "transportation of the historic past into a future that will have no history"?[72] Fuentes's turn of phrase will be central to arguments to come on the relationships between the social sciences and the past and present. Collisions with history, it will be shown, accelerated through the medium of Boom fiction, to be continued in social science literature devoted to aspects of the New World Order.

The Fictional Histories of Discovery and Conquest

The following list includes major sources for documentation of the cataclysmic history of the discovery and conquest of Spanish and Portuguese America. A similar list follows each of the next two chapters. Citations from these texts come from English editions listed here unless otherwise noted. English-language titles and publication data are followed by Spanish or Portuguese titles and publication dates.

Aguilar, Rosario. *The Lost Chronicles of Terra Firma.* Trans. Edward Waters Hood. Fredonia, N.Y.: White Pine Press, 1997. *La niña blanca y los pájaros sin pies* (1992). Not cited in text.

Aridjis, Homero. *1492: The Life and Times of Juan Cabezón of Castile.* Trans. Betty Ferber. New York: Summit Books, 1991. *1492: Vida y tiempo de Juan Cabezón de Castilla* (1985). Cited as *1492.*

Benítez Rojo, Antonio. *Sea of Lentils.* Trans. James Maraniss. Amherst: University of Massachusetts Press, 1990. *El mar de las lentejas* (1985). Cited as *Lentils.*

Carpentier, Alejo. *The Harp and the Shadow.* Trans. Thomas Christensen and Carol Christensen. San Francisco: Mercury House, 1990. *El arpa y la sombra* (1979). Cited as *Harp.*

Fuentes, Carlos. *Terra Nostra.* Trans. Margaret Sayers Peden. New York: Farrar, Straus and Giroux, 1976. *Terra Nostra* (1975). Cited as *Terra Nostra.*

Posse, Abel. *Daimon.* Trans. Sarah Arvio. New York: Atheneum, 1992. *Daimón* (1978). Cited as *Daimon.*

———. *The Dogs of Paradise.* Trans. Margaret Sayers Peden. New York: Atheneum, 1989. *Los perros del paraíso* (1987). Cited as *Dogs.*

Saer, Juan José. *The Witness.* Trans. Margaret Jull Costa. London: Serpent's Tail, 1990. *El entenado* (1983). Cited as *Witness.*

Scliar, Moacyr. *The Strange Nation of Rafael Mendes.* Trans. Eloah F. Giacomelli. New York: Ballantine Books, 1987. *A estranha nação de Rafael Mendes* (1986). Cited as *Nation.*

Chapter 2

The Saga of Independence and Early Nationhood

> All the history books which contain no lies are extremely tedious.
> —Anatole France, *The Crime of Sylvestre Bonnard* (1881)

IN "THE POET'S Answer to the Most Illustrious Sister Filotea de la Cruz," Sor Juana, citing 2 Corinthians 12:11, asserts "my writing has never proceeded from any dictate of my own, but a force beyond me; I can in truth say, You have compelled me."[1] In colliding with the history of independence and its immediate product, early nationhood, novelists may have felt compelled but they certainly saw no need to justify their compulsion by quoting scripture. Man's work, not God's, compelled them to write. Novelists attacked the traditional heroes of history when they wrote about independence and the early national era just as they did in works on discovery and conquest. They did something else as well: they took further steps toward answering those questions raised in the introduction by stressing the intellectual content of a developing latinoamericanidad.

No one's history ended with the independence movements, certainly not that of Spanish Americans who followed the likes of Bolívar and Sucre, Hidalgo and Morelos, O'Higgins and San Martín. It flowed anew from another perceived cataclysm: the rupture of political ties with Spain. Brazilians' history flowed more steadily still, for a branch of the Portuguese royal dynasty ruled in Rio de Janeiro until 1889. But as much as traditional interpretations of independence made mere mortals into seeming heroes everywhere, fictional history would assert that history's heroes were not godlike at all, merely men of the moment. It proved that mythic or spiritual influences could no longer be blamed for heroes becoming mere mortals as much as might be inferred from fictional histories of discovery and conquest.

Latin American treatments of independence until the last few decades were as subjective as North American works on the Revolution of the Thirteen Colonies. Octavio Paz's assertion of Mexico's independence as a rejection and assertion of identity bears remembering here,[2] for by extension this can be said for all Spanish America. The major failing of standard, national treatments of independence in Spanish American countries is that they asserted national identity before the concept of nation became consensual. Until recently, that is, independence was depicted canonically more as a *national phenomenon* in a region where nation-states were yet to be, than as a *regional phenomenon* with national cultural and social variations. The fact that for the vast majority things cultural, economic, and social changed very little has been accepted wisdom for decades, thanks principally to the work of scholars.

Nationalism made it all the more difficult for past historians to explain why independence heroes were such failures when it came to leading new governments. Throughout Latin America historians struggled against biographical and event-clogged standard views with increased vigor as the twentieth century wore on. But they often ran the risk of being labeled *hispanistas* or reactionaries, then "internationalists," if they did not confer national identities upon the early-nineteenth-century remains of regional independence struggles.

Both discovery and conquest, and independence and early nation-hood, as depicted historically, are somewhat analogous to origin myths. They assume their own spiritual dimension. They have been popularly to Latin America, say, what Genesis and Exodus are to the Pentateuch. Until recently literal interpretations (of mythic proportion) constituted canon, and it was bad form, if not downright folly—nearly treason in some cases—for Latin Americans to attack what heroes of independence and patriarchs of new nations had said they stood for and supposedly accomplished. To attack the genesis of the national past was to deny the validity of its present. When the present became unbearable, however, it became fashionable—and profitable—and wholly justifiable to say so in fiction as well as in revisionist scholarship. Novelists knew what scholars had proven for the region: Independence meant significant change for only a minority, and had not at all led to a very attractive present.

A story of independence anywhere has to be a validation of national existence and identity if it is to apply positively to human beings of the present. This is why revisionism in Latin America might lead to the branding of dissenters as extremists, antinationalists, and internationalists. Until recently the historical profession in Latin America did not successfully challenge standard views of the regional independence saga with which North American and European scholars had become familiar—and had challenged—decades ago. The most convincing challenges to traditional views of regional origins, existence, and identity have been made by scholars from without the region,[3] or by novelists from within it.

Over the decades of the nineteenth century, politics enabled those who chronicled the past to create the terms for late-twentieth-century collisions, for revisionism through fiction. Minor independence figures who involved themselves in politics—following passage into history of the frontline leaders—proved unable to implement the proposals and the dreams of their dead or exiled heroes. In Mexico and Peru, Chile and Haiti, caudillos wreaked havoc with nationhood. Each caudillo had a following; all had detractors. Liberals and conserva-tives, federalists and centralists, civilians and military, secular and re-ligious all had their own versions of independence and what it should mean.

Gradually, "received" versions emerged that served the purposes of national leadership more than they represented cultural, economic, and social reality. Fictional historians in the late twentieth century not only recognized these philosophical struggles of the epiphenomenal past, they freed them from the nationalistic and ideological con-straints that had bound "factual" historians. Here the lines between history and fiction both blur and stand out, encouraging all to con-tinue the search for both accuracy and consensus. By exposing the leaders of independence and early nationhood as all too human, fic-tional history ultimately serves the interests of modern scholarship.

Latin America's patriarchs may one day again be revered as are biblical ones: Abraham and Isaac, Jacob and Joseph, Moses and Joshua, Peter and Paul. But for the foreseeable future they will be view d as no more than humans—with all encumbrances pertaining to such figures. Because of their patriarchal roles, however, they provide a continuity with the colonial past, traditional historical icons with which fiction can easily collide. They are the figures to whom identity and nationhood have been attached in the ways discovery and con-quest were linked to actions of fifteenth- and sixteenth-century heroes. They are the warriors and leaders whose efforts resulted in both de-struction and creation, however fraught with complexity this last has proven to be. It was easier, in short, for novelists to use them for their own purposes than it was for Latin American scholars to reveal the truth about independence and early nationhood.

They and their deeds, moreover, lend support to a second surge in the spiraling of fictional history. Destruction of an empire and creation of weak nation-states, some with little legitimacy, maintain a regionwide historical paradigm of creation arising from destruc-tion, validation through negation. This is like saying that regionally, historical change comes not gradually but violently, through up-heaval: cataclysm. It is like saying that latinoamericanidad depends on cataclysm. If this is not sound disciplinary scholarship, it is intel-lectually provocative.

This chapter treats traditional heroes, the meaning of indepen-dence, the identity of America shorn of Iberia's ties, and other specific themes developed fictionally by Cubans Reinaldo Arenas and Alejo Carpentier, Carlos Fuentes, Colombian journalist and nov-elist par excellence Gabriel García Márquez, Paraguayan master Au-gusto Roa Bastos, and Brazil's Ana Miranda in novels—prose cantos of the independence and early nationhood saga—that deal with the late colonial and independence years. Miranda's *Bay of All Saints and Every Conceivable Sin* and Carpentier's *Concierto barroco*, ad-mittedly devoted to the middle and later colonial era, speak enough to pertinent issues of Latin American historical identity around the time of independence to merit inclusion in the list of fictional histo-ries of the saga of independence appearing at the end of the chapter.

From Heroes to Humans

In their fictional portrayals Simón Bolívar and José de San Martín were certainly as heroic as Cortés and Pizarro—as Ulysses and Aeneas, for that matter. They were equally human, too. García Márquez's and Fuentes's superb independence novels show this, the former's slightly more than the latter's, I think.

Bolívar is perhaps the best example of a modern mythic hero in all of Latin America. He was not known (condescendingly) as the George Washington of South America for nothing. But in *The General in His Labyrinth* he is portrayed all too evidently as flesh and blood. He is, after all, a hero caught in a labyrinth of tragedy. His plight at the hands of García Márquez represents a purposeful collision designed to banish heroes from history once and for all. It pretty well succeeds.

48

At the end of his career Bolívar had to leave the capital of his Gran Colombia for the Caribbean coast. He was on his way to exile, we know. He had failed to implement his geopolitical dream (the union of Venezuela, Colombia, and Ecuador was already doomed), he had alienated too many erstwhile supporters, fallen prey to his own egocentrism, become paranoid, and was living as a recluse. He was ill, nearly destitute, and he no longer counted for much politically. It was 1830, he was in his forty-eighth year, and he was an anachronism.

"It was the end," writes García Márquez. "General Simón José Antonio de la Santísima Trinidad Bolívar y Palacios was leaving forever. He had wrested from Spanish domination an empire five times more vast than all of Europe, he had led twenty years of wars to keep it free and united, and he had governed it with a firm hand until the week before, but when it was time to leave he did not even take away with him the consolation that anyone believed in his departure. The only man with enough lucidity to know he really was going, and where he was going to, was the English diplomat, who wrote in an official report to his government: 'The time he has left will hardly be enough for him to reach his grave.'"[4] This Bolívar was no longer a man on horseback; he was unable to ride. He was a constipated insomniac, decrepit, feverish, and crapulent. This Bolívar was convinced that "every Colombian is an enemy country."[5] This fictionally historic Bolívar was a tragic hero, all too human at the end.

Bolívar's fictional passing symbolizes at once three things historically. It is both coda to the saga of independence and prelude to implementation of its consequences. It also is the symbolic death rattle of the Spanish empire in America—the first of the great European overseas empires to take form and the first to pass into history. Only Cuba and Puerto Rico remained Spanish in America, and only until the end of the century.

Early on in *The General in His Labyrinth* the tragic hero finds that he is losing height as well as weight. He is in the "autumn of his patriarchy," as it were. "Even his nakedness was distinctive, for his body was pale and his face and hands seemed scorched by exposure to the weather. He had turned forty-six this past July, but his rough Caribbean curls were already ashen, his bones were twisted by premature old age, and he had deteriorated so much he did not seem capable of lasting until the following July [i.e., July 1830; he died December 17, 1830]."[6] Bolívar's pallor and scorch marks, his white hair and his twisted bones metaphorically represent the novelist's appraisal of what imperial decline and fall had bequeathed Colombia and her neighbor states: the independence saga and the impending tragedy of *an identity without a region*. What a shock this must have been to good Colombian patriots.

Bolívar and his kind were entering a transition period: Latin America's labyrinthine Middle Ages. "'Damn it,' he sighed. 'How will I ever get out of this labyrinth!'"[7] By dying he did. "Damn it, please let us have our Middle Ages in peace!"[8] he said. Independence ushered them in. The old empire crumbled, that which the heroic Bolívar proposed in its place fell apart, and the human himself wasted away. Lesser leaders would force themselves on society for both patriotic and self-serving motives. This was the stuff of which nation-states would be made and historicized.

Not all heroes of fictional history are real-life ones, to be sure. In Carlos Fuentes's *The Campaign* the fictional Baltasar Bustos serves to portray a composite hero of the entire Spanish American independence saga. Bustos is a wealthy young Argentine, a revolutionary whose love for a woman against whom he has committed a crime drives him to pursue her across two continents. Bustos's obsessions take him to Venezuela (whence Bolívar and Sucre), Chile (whence O'Higgins), Peru (where San Martín failed), and on to Mexico, the land of Hidalgo and Morelos. Bustos is more regional than national, Bolívar writ both large and small.

He journeys, he suffers, he fights alongside "the fearsome guerrillas of Miguel Lanza in the mud of the Inquisivi, with the legendary Father Ildefonso de las Muñecas at the head of the Indian hordes of the Ayopaya, with José de San Martín himself in the heroic crossing of the Andes."[9] His is the saga of a man seeking redemption—of a region seeking identity.

The love he seeks—the redemption and absolution he seeks, this elusive Ofelia Salamanca, Marquise de Cabra—is sighted in Guayaquil, then heading for Buenaventura, and in Panama crossing the isthmus, again in Cartagena de Indias on her way to Maracaibo.[10] She is nowhere. Bustos's America pursues its independence and identity; America's Bustos pursues his fantasy. It is everywhere. Independence is everywhere more fantastic than real when it finally comes to pass. It is the political equivalent of magic realism, beguiling, frustrating, filled with black as well as white magic, replete with identity that is suppressed by inept political leadership.

The San Martín portrayed by Fuentes is a heroic figure, a man who "dreamed he had stilts and could cross the mountains in one stride."[11] And cross the Andes he did, in 1817 with his *Ejército de los Andes*. They suffered from cold and from *soroche,* the altitude sickness, but they won in Chile, and those who went on to Peru would ultimately see their efforts succeed in the liberation of a continent.

Fuentes's San Martín is as mindful of the future as García Márquez's Bolívar, for that matter as the real Bolívar, whose "Jamaica Letter" of 1815 has been long lauded as evidence of his vision of America. Both fictional patriarchs are ably portrayed in this respect. Bolívar knows what he has done will be undone. His own campaigns descend into a "fandango for lunatics who can't get along even after they've made their revolution."[12] San Martín, in the same vein, tells the hero of *The Campaign,* "We joined together to beat the Spaniards. We saw that if we were divided they would beat us. All I ask . . . is that you realize this and that you be aware of the danger of a lack of unity. That lack of unity may well be our undoing; we have to create institutions where there are none. That takes time, clear thinking and clean hands. We may think that laws, because they are separate from reality, make reality unreal. It isn't so."[13] San Martín goes on to forecast the breakup of federations and the fragility of newly created governments. He is predicting, in so many words, the history of Spanish America, both national and regional. Fuentes was lamenting it.

What San Martín meant, held in his soul, according to the novelist, was "the vision of a world without heroes, in which men like himself and . . . his friends would no longer be possible."[14] This hero would be a dying god. Dying gods and demigods litter the landscape of Spanish American independence as surely as they do the pages of *The General in His Labyrinth* and *The Campaign*. The San Martíns and the Bolívars, historical, fictional, and would-be, proved all too mortal, for they were caught in the trap of conviction. They believed they would be able to build something better than what they knew, the old Spanish American empire. In this they differed from Columbus, Cortés, Pizarro, and their ilk, who were guided by far simpler and baser motives. Once again cataclysm would produce disastrous history. Once again collisions reveal it.

Independence leaders had faith that what they destroyed was unworthy, all right, for it was not theirs, it was now the *other*. History indicates that faith alone rarely induces reality, but that is nearly what did occur in the sixteenth century. History also indicates the rarity of sheer will resulting in reality, and that is precisely what would not occur three centuries later. Independence heroes and their political and military spawn lived in an age dominated by Napoleonic egos. Beginning with the end of the independence struggles and the death of Bolívar (ca. 1826–30) the second-rank caudillos took over.

Most of them had been involved in the wars against Spain and France, and the break with Portugal (*caudilhos* may not have the same historical significance as caudillos, but such there were). Few, though, boasted the credentials of the great liberators—Bolívar, San Martín, O'Higgins, Sucre, Páez, and the like, as flawed as those heroes clearly were. With few examples, leaders of the early national decades had primarily local constituencies, limited experience, great ambition, and only a modicum of talent. Their egos equaled those of the heroes. Their talents, alas, rarely did. They were more interested in provincial and national power than regional identity. By the early 1830s they dominated national affairs in most of Spanish America. Of them all, only one was historically remarkable in both positive and negative ways, in fiction as well as fact.

A Godlike Human

Not all had played military roles. José Gaspar Rodríguez de Francia, a civilian, ruled Paraguay with a firm hand as Supreme Dictator for Life from 1814 until his death in 1840. In his wake lesser leaders would nearly destroy the country. Dr. Francia is the subject of one of the most highly regarded works of fictional history to ever come out of South America, *I, the Supreme.* The significance to the discussion at hand of Augusto Roa Bastos's classic is not so much its literary merit (which is substantial), but rather its portrayal of its human hero, the archetypal civil caudillo known as El Supremo.

Even paranoids have nemeses. Francia rendered fictional is like Bolívar and Columbus, a tragic figure beset on all sides by enemies and temptations and incompetents. He is the only person capable, he is convinced, of fulfilling a quest—not in this case the discovery of a new world, or even the independence of new countries, much less a region, but the maintenance of an independent Paraguay, landlocked and isolated in a hostile world. This fictional history is national, but regional in a grand metaphoric sense too, for it relates to nearly all the significant strata of history that great men, dynasties, battles, and such do not.

Paraguay's, we know, is a tortured history. As with most of Spanish America in the past century, Paraguayan independence created as many problems as it solved. Unlike most of Spanish America, but like Brazil, Paraguay enjoyed relative stability immediately following the break with the mother country (in Paraguay's case, with Buenos Aires as well). Roa Bastos's Francia, therefore, is a supreme egotist. He is convinced that he is the sole Paraguayan capable of preserving his country's integrity. He may have been right in fact as well as fiction.

Similarities with, and distinctions from, contemporaries notwithstanding, Francia's guarantee of independence and identity marks him as a prototype caudillo—human, in other words. No other independence figure, save possibly Bolívar, is treated the same way. Roa Bastos's fictional history reveals some of the historical consensus that marks the works of novelists in the later twentieth century. *I, the Supreme* is a transitional historical work that moves us from the independence saga on toward early nationhood: an age of caudillism and authoritarian rule regionwide. It can be asserted that the early national decades constitute a continuation of the struggle to establish sovereignty, identity, and legitimacy (the three are not synonymous). Without legitimacy, independence and sovereignty meant nothing; without identity, independence meant nothing.

Along with Carpentier, Fuentes, and García Márquez, Roa Bastos is one of the major fictional historians discussed in the portion of this work that treats the social science–like commentary of Boom novelists. Along with that of the Cuban, the Mexican, and the Colombian, the fiction of the Paraguayan collides with history head on and by intent. *I, the Supreme* reveals the dictator Francia as neither savior nor demon, rather as a human being, subject, just like his contemporaries, to all the limitations of our species. Can the message for twentieth-century dictators have been made more clearly? Can the fact that all fictional history speaks to the present?

The first law in the code of the postindependence caudillos might well have been stated thus: "He who trusts people builds on sand."[15] But El Supremo monologically tells his listeners/readers that he is "fighting not with a people of sand or of phantoms, but with a people of men with a thousand miseries and more."[16] Human resources available to early-nineteenth-century Spanish American leaders (and to Brazilians, for that matter) were not impressive by European standards of that time. Colonial policy had not allowed for much involvement on the part of the majority in high-level affairs of state, after all. Impressive enough to fight and bleed and die, but not impressive enough to live *politicamente* (as Spaniards of Columbus's time had hoped Indians would one day do), *el pueblo* needed guidance, leadership. The people needed literacy and economic security too. El Supremo's statement rendered by Roa Bastos is as much historical judgment as it is replication of a dictator's hauteur.

In fictional (and real) early national Paraguay "functionaries and servants of the state have not learned, and give few signs of being about to learn, to judge from the way you [functionaries and servants] make my head swim with your dispatches full of questions, request[s] for advice, [and] dull-witted pondering of the least trifle."[17] Independence had toppled whatever infrastructures Spaniards had erected for governance; the inheritors of responsibility reconstructed little of this commodity themselves. They served *el pueblo* poorly.

"And when at long last you finally do something, I must also find a way to undo all the harm you've done."[18] Soldiers, intellectuals, lawyers, historians who produced "History Books, novels, accounts of imaginary facts seasoned to suit the taste of the moment or their interests,"[19] oligarchs, Jesuits—these all did more damage than good. That is to say they did not automatically seek to fulfill the wishes of El Supremo.

Surely an indictment of twentieth-century politics, both of those in power and of their lackeys, *I, the Supreme* provides us with a sole example of worthiness among the children of independence. "Nowadays," the supreme autocrat tells us, "the Indians are the best servants of the State; it is from such cloth that I have cut the most upright judges, the most capable and loyal functionaries, my most valiant soldiers."[20] These were the same folk who for centuries had provided Hispano-Paraguayans with the manpower to build and sustain a New World culture and civilization in the wilderness. But their lot would not improve much because of independence. Among the fictional historians of independence and early nationhood, Roa Bastos did the best job of giving indigenes their due.

Francia was an exceptional man, all right, but he was a ruthless dictator nonetheless. He knew the bureaucrats, the soldiers, the intellectuals, the lawyers, and the oligarchs for what they were. He distrusted them, and they him. In this sense he was no different from other would-be great men of his time, or from those who had come before. In the early nineteenth century he alone approaches positively the independence and the discovery and conquest heroes in historic stature. He rivaled the all too human dictators of this century, too, and in all the negative ways.

Among those discussed herein only he (El Supremo)—in fiction as well as fact—ever dwelled much on the similarity between deities and men. "The Dictator of a Nation," he allows, "if he is Supreme, does not need the help of a Supreme Being. He himself is that."[21] As Supreme Being it is only fitting that he render judgment both on mortal novelists and historians. What really interests such people as these, in his words, "is not recounting the facts, but recounting that they are recounting them."[22] Roa Bastos's Francia minces no words— ever. All the dilemmas of early nationhood are his. His country was independent, but still bound uncomfortably to a greater whole.

Latin America(s) and Europe

If independence of this greater whole did not mean much beyond separation from Europe, what did it mean? What was Europe to America now? Carlos Fuentes's *Distant Relations* is an imaginative novel in which American identity, asserted over the centuries since discovery and conquest, is tied to the great age of change that began with the French Revolution and ended (for Latin America) with the independence movements. Many Spanish Americans considered themselves ultramarine Spaniards until de facto separation was established in the 1820s. "Napoleon was unable to subjugate Spain," Fuentes tells us, "because the Spain of the Napoleonic era was not to be found on the mainland but in her colonies—which was where the French Revolution was to continue once it had been interred in Europe."[23] Far across the Atlantic, so epic a voyage for Columbus centuries before, the struggle begun in 1789 lived on in the minds of liberator-heroes and a few of their lieutenants, in the "petrified disorder" of the Spanish American republics.[24]

Not by happenstance did Fuentes set much of this fictional history in the Caribbean. Carpentier did the same in *Explosion in a Cathedral, The Kingdom of This World,* and *Concierto barroco.* The Caribbean, where cataclysmic history began, is where Bolívar spent much time formulating plans, and where he would die; it had been the laboratory for social and institutional experimentation by imperial Spain. It is where Haitian slaves revolted, igniting fears of slave and Indian revolts throughout Latin America. The Caribbean is the connection between Europe and America, discovery, conquest, and independence, freedom, revolution, and authoritarianism. It is the New World's Mediterranean.

Independence would mean violent protraction, to different ends, in parts of Spanish America, of a struggle begun in Europe. It was indeed both affirmation and negation. Cuban Reinaldo Arenas supports such a thesis in *The Ill-Fated Peregrinations of Fray Servando Teresa de Mier,* a picaresque tale of the Mexican revolutionary thinker's Caribbean and European adventures. While in France, Fray Servando meets Lucas Alamán and Simón Bolívar, as well as Humboldt and Madame de Staël, who tells the good cleric that "a revolution is not accomplished in ten years, or in a century. It is a long accumulation of eras, of men."[25] Independence, that is to say, was just the beginning. Beginnings can take a long time.

Beginnings are built on endings. As Bolívar tells Agustín de Iturbide in one fictional conversation, "The damn problem is that we stopped being Spaniards and then went here and there and everywhere in countries that change their names and governments so much from one day to the next we don't know where the hell we come from."[26] When Spanish Americans stopped being overseas Spaniards they had nowhere to go but to the places they were in the process of creating. These were places that needed changing, hence a historical process had to begin. Attempts to resume history by salvaging it from the wreckage of independence were ill-fated in Spanish America. It would prove hard enough to create nation-states much less to endow them with a past.

Beginnings are a central part of fiction as well as of history.[27] What fictional historians have done is to provide us with vivid representations of "characters and societies more or less freely in development." These characters "mirror a process of engenderment or beginning and growth possible and permissible for the mind to imagine."[28] They are more than individuals; they are the raw material of latinoamericanidad. If what begins (again and again?) in Spanish America is based on endings, the question arises for historians: when did the endings take place in the minds and imaginations of both those involved and the novelists?

Not just with revolt against Iberia, but with the beginnings of either "national" or American awareness, with a sense of being the *other*. Most standard versions of Latin American history acknowledge emerging creole identity, especially in the eighteenth century, as a significant ending and beginning point. A history of wealth, limited participation in decision-making processes, increased taxation, discriminatory acts by *peninsulares*—these all served to complicate and destabilize the endings of imperialism and the beginnings of American identity. Independence was an unfinished ending, so it was a poor beginning to nationhood for at least a half century.

As an example, the expulsion of the Jesuits, from Brazil in 1759 and from Spanish America in 1767, had jolted creole elites as much as it pleased them some years before they took up sword and gun to preserve their status and declare their independence. The Society of

Jesus was the main provider of high-quality education (for men) in the colonies. Baltasar Bustos, hero of *The Campaign*, "had had a Jesuit education." The expulsion of the Jesuits had "left an immense void behind them. People protested the expulsion [and many applauded it], demonstrated in the streets, wept . . . And the Jesuits of America had their revenge."[29] Some returned without their "priestly vestments, the better to fool the colonial authorities," but damage had been done nonetheless. Voids had to be filled because of it.

"They taught, tutored, mentored: national history, national geography, the flora and fauna (and the form and fame [*la forma y la fama*]) of the nascent nations from New Spain to Chile, from the Río de la Plata to New Granada."[30] Jesuits, according to Fuentes, had their young men read books banned by the Church: *The Spirit of the Laws, The Social Contract*, Diderot's *The Nun, Candide*. Young girls read breviaries, Catholic pamphlets, and sermons, not much more unless they were fortunate, rebellious, or both.

Such reading was inflammatory stuff to eighteenth-century young creole males. Where such study actually did occur it made intellectuals (or would-be intellectuals) pretty nearly rebels with or without causes—sometimes before causes were manifest. A sector of the Church would assist, all this implies, Spanish Americans in developing an identity other than that of American Spaniards—at the end of one era and the beginning of another. Partial filling of a void can be dangerous, for the void still begs attention; however powerful its spiritual content may be, identity needs material form. Latinoamericanidad needed more than symbol; it still does.

Now, the young men so affected, among whom were more than a few liberators, were members of the social elite—or aspirants to elite status. So their rebelliousness was hardly very radical.[31] Only a handful ever sought significant change in the social order, despite what we read about their Jacobinism, liberalism, or revolutionary convictions. And these would not be frontline leaders of the independence movement(s) anyway.

Fuentes tells us bluntly that the elitist liberators ran the war, ordered the mestizos about, relied on the Indians for food, labor, and women.[32] Independence was a thing of the mind, but the mind was that of members of an elitist caste who represented at once the end of an era and the beginning of another. And elitists were not about to let any ideas alter their status, unless it was to improve it. Independence was a thing of violence as well, and the violence consumed quantities of human and natural resources. This is another reason why what was left at the confluence of ending and beginning was poor material with which to build, and why there were few leaders left capable of designing anything, much less building it.

The term *balkanization* has been applied anachronistically to what happened in Latin America nearly two centuries ago. The term Spanish Americanization is one more cumbersome but less anachronistic for describing what went on after independence there, and even in the Balkan peninsula after the collapse of the Habsburg empire early in the last century. Fuentes wrote forcefully on the disintegration of the viceroyalties during the campaign(s) for independence: "Lima can't beat Buenos Aires," he writes, "and Buenos Aires can't beat Lima. The two powers cancel each other out. We're right between them."[33] García Márquez agreed, all the while seeing the United States as another cause of this negative process.[34] Consolidation of independence was going to be but the dream of some laic elitists imbued with ideas transmitted by clerical elitists, based on a desire for revenge against an elitist mother country, revolution and rights of men notwithstanding. The saga of independence rendered in fictional history is more tragic than epic, and elites must share in the blame for this.

Having resorted to organized violence to achieve their ends, all too human historical heroes fell prey to geography, distance, and isolation. Their campaign(s), both fictionally and in truth, took place in the vastest of labyrinths. The strongest influence on Spanish Americans, as they assessed the wreckage of their recent efforts, was their newfound sense of *other*ness. This was, perforce, out of resignation in some cases, in others it was genuine. Where it was the former, consolidation would prove forthcoming much later; where it was the latter, consolidation was more peacefully achieved. All endings and beginnings are not the same in Latin America.

"British colonies enrich British subjects," a character in *Distant Relations* tells us, "but Spanish colonies enrich only the Spanish crown. Spain isn't growing rich, only the coffers of her rulers. You will see, it will be the same story with the rulers of these new republics."[35] Spanish Americans were not Spaniards anymore, but they were in charge. And they would mask their perpetuation of sociocultural exclusionism with facades of French respectability, fictional history emphasizes. This made them different, French rationalism being antidotal, as it were, to "Latin American Delirium."[36]

Spanish America was not, of course, "in the same latitude as the Champ de Mars,"[37] so even Francophilia had its limits. Carpentier's *Explosion in a Cathedral* (i.e., reverberations in the Caribbean of the French Revolution) provides as realistic a portrait of the coming of the West's first great social upheaval as his *Kingdom of This World* does an impressionistic one. Recurrent references to goings-on in the Old World, especially France, and the presence of the main character, Victor Hugues, in the lives of two young Cubans avails readers of a grand canvas of the Caribbean on the verge of forsaking Spain for independence, casting off Iberian culture for French, all the while experiencing little change in the social order. France had become "the final homeland of every Latin American,"[38] writes Fuentes, but the great revolution that broke out there would not penetrate all that deeply the minds of those Spanish Americans and Brazilians who were forsaking Spain and Portugal. Haute culture, yes, social and economic radicalism, no. The latter gave life to the likes of Victor Hugues, but not to all Spanish American elitists. Violence gave independence to mainland territories, but not to all Caribbean islands.

The Fantastical Qualities of Independence

As portrayed in fictional history, independence reinforced in Spanish Americans an (updated) sense of the fantastic. It reinforced images first created in the sixteenth century. García Márquez's Bolívar recounts how a delay in Vera Cruz (during his first journey to Europe in 1799), gave him an opportunity to visit the capital of the viceroyalty of New Spain, "climbing almost three thousand meters between snowcapped volcanoes and hallucinatory deserts, which were nothing like the pastoral dawns of the Aragua Valley, where he had lived until then. 'I thought it was how the moon must look.'"[39] Fuentes also has Bolívar describe Mexico's capital in terms reminiscent of Bernal Díaz's, as we have seen.

All Latin America was fantastic and exotic to its new Creole leaders—both because they knew so little of it as a continent and a region, and because they had Europe to compare and contrast it with. These neoconquistadores and those they would leave in charge of independent countries were as awed by what they were doing as were the Spaniards of three centuries before.

Early on in *Explosion in a Cathedral*, Carpentier's Hugues tells his young Cuban acquaintances of "coral forts of the Bermudas"; "spirits made from mint and watercress in Veracruz"; of Guiana, "that iridescent colony where the banquets were served by negresses decked in bracelets and necklaces and wearing skirts of Indian silk, with delicate, almost transparent blouses stretched tight over their hard quivering breasts"; of the Antilles, "where one came across ... enormous anchors abandoned on lonely beaches, houses fixed to the rocks with iron chains, so that [hurricanes] could not sweep them into the sea; a huge Sephardic cemetery in Curaçao ... sunken galleons, petrified trees, unimaginable fish; and in Barbados, the tomb of a nephew of Constantine XI, the last emperor of Byzantium [1449–53], whose ghost appeared to solitary wayfarers on stormy nights."[40] And this is not to mention the wondrous sites of central

Mexico or those of the Andean highlands, many of which still had not been found. The wonder of what they confronted, one can infer, overwhelmed Latin Americans from the moment they identified themselves as such. The rapid descent from the realm of the exotic and fantastical into the world of squabbling, would-be nation-states must have been traumatic, accompanied as it was by the tragedies of caudillism, resulting as it would in the bitter struggles between advocates of democracy and authoritarianism.

From the very beginning, we know, this New World was considered to be *other,* and sixteenth-century descriptions and colonial adventures still fascinated Europeans in the eighteenth and nineteenth centuries. A variety of Orientalism existed especially among northern Europeans, who longed for exotic lands where rare commodities might be found.[41] Explorers and scientists, travelers and diplomats all kept a sense of the fantastic alive in Europe by bringing back tales of Latin America. Independence and the ensuing chaos compounded all senses of traumatic, fantastical, racial, and national *otherness.* For something to begin in toto, something had to end in toto.

Latin Americans took a long time in the nineteenth century to come to grips with the human dimension of the fantastic. Indians did not count for much besides labor and conversion in Mexico and Peru. There were few left in Brazilian territory fully occupied during the Empire. Chileans and Argentines pushed their native populations beyond frontiers, then defeated and confined them. Not until this century would *indigenismo* become a sociocultural force associated with political and economic reform, and more importantly, with latinoamericanidad. Collisions with independence history destroyed images; they did not forcefully substitute new ones.

America's historical identity clearly had an indigenous base, and it was conceived of as fantastically by Europeans as it was accepted reluctantly by Latin Americans. The weaker the sense of the fantastical and the quicker the recognition of some kind of indigenous contribution to "national culture," the easier the achievement of identity, sovereignty, and legitimacy. This holds for the entirety of the post-colonial centuries.

In *Concierto barroco,* one of Carpentier's lesser-known but more inventive works, the main character, a Mexican of means traveling in Europe, asks Antonio Vivaldi (no less) if he does not consider "the history of America glorious or important?" He has already questioned Vivaldi's portrayal of the Aztec chieftain Moctezuma in the eponymous opera (premier: Venice, 1733). His question to the Italian, it needs saying, has been prompted by Vivaldi's own assertion that "poetic illusion" was more important to the theater than "that history crap." But it is Vivaldi's answer to the Mexican traveler's interposed query that conveys both an eighteenth- and nineteenth-century European and Latin American identity-linked sense of the fantastical: "In America," says the great composer, "everything is fantastical: tales of *El Dorado* and Potosí, fabulous cities, talking sponges, sheep with red fleece, amazons with only one breast, big-eared Indians who eat Jesuits."[42] *Fantastical* quite simply was not the same as *glorious* or *important.* Nor was postindependence reality.

Once the fantastical, the glorious, and the important gave way to the quotidian, the gruesome, and the inglorious of the early nineteenth century, Latin America ceased to have a history—by European standards, the ones applied from without and embraced by many Latin American elitists themselves. Americans had to work so hard to avoid national disintegration in the nineteenth century, it was hard for them to maintain even a mythical past to claim proudly. So they had to make one (or make one up), and later, as we are seeing, some would resort to doing it in the pages of fictional history.

The French Revolution had enlightened literate and learned Spanish Americans and excited many others. At least they had abandoned monarchy in order to confront their history. They and Brazilians had broken with Iberia. French culture and a superficial understanding of foreign philosophy and political theory of the eighteenth century—an olio of European and North American ideas and practices—served moderately well at best to inspire those who strove to keep fledgling Spanish American nations from descending further into the depths of anarchy—or simply from changing too rapidly.

In some places race played a preeminent part in all this. Fictional portrayals are most vivid when set in the Caribbean, and there are no comparable treatments of Mexican, Peruvian, or Brazilian blacks or indigenes during independence or postindependence times in the Boom's fictional history canon. Both Carpentier's *Explosion in a Cathedral* and *The Kingdom of This World* deal with race, indicating as they do the gulf between privileged, Europeanized Creoles and de-graded Afro-Americans, a gulf that would widen with nationhood.

Blacks fared poorly indeed when the French Revolution arrived in Carpentier's Caribbean and independence took the place of empire: "Victor Hugues [as revolutionary symbol] showed more sympathy towards the Caribs than the negroes."[43] In another part of *The Kingdom of This World* Carpentier notes the prejudice toward darker skin tone that has prevailed: "The Surveyors who came down to the Plaine from distant Port-au-Prince beyond the cloudy hills were silent, light-skinned men." These surveyors, of course, were out to do dark-skinned men no good.[44] Sympathy for people of color was not widespread among Creoles following Spanish American independence; lighter skin won out everywhere, even among the mixed sectors of society, even in the Caribbean. Fictional histories are no less convincing of this than are the traditional accounts.

History versus Past, Present, and Future

Like the fictional histories of discovery and conquest, those of the in-dependence and early nationhood evince a historical consciousness abuilding—all the more so as the emphasis moved closer to the present—among contemporary writers. The works of Arenas, Carpentier, Fuentes, García Márquez, and Roa Bastos all have a keen appreciation of history. They address institutional and social problems that stem from the colonial past, for their authors had centuries of documentable history from which to glean perspectives on independence and its aftermath. History tumbles off their pages as if the printed words had an energy of their own. This is true as well of Ana Miranda's exquisitely titled *Bay of All Saints and Every Conceivable Sin*.

Arenas saw scholarly history as largely boring stuff: dates of battles, body counts, stark facts about the fleeting, ephemeral, and fugitive. Because of this, he said, he "always distrusted the 'historical,' those 'minutiae,' the 'precise date' or 'fact.' Because what, finally, is history? A file full of more or less chronologically ordered manila folders?"[45] In the prologue to his fictional history of Fray Servando he goes on to refute the validity of chronological, linear time. It cannot be quantified, he insisted, raising at once questions about both cause and effect, and their relationships to each other that historians study so assiduously. Arenas's fictional history challenges such relationships as much or more than do others examined herein, and reveal his appreciation of what had passed for history in his native Cuba before 1959.

In *Concierto barroco* Vivaldi's outburst about the fantastical qualities of America embraces the defense of his historically incorrect operatic account of the Aztec leader whose legions fell to those of Cortés. The basis for argument: equally spurious sources Vivaldi chose to read that gave him the right to make Montezuma over.[46] History, to Carpentier, was something to make over because it had been made over tediously so many times already—certainly in Cuba both before and after 1959.

Then in *Explosion in a Cathedral* the fantastic battles with the mundane in an almost Manichean way while Sofía and Esteban, the two young Cuban companions of Hugues, reach adulthood. They in fact symbolize the Caribbean—Spanish America drawn through the open door of history toward a perilous future: "The play time of adolescence had come to an end. . . . Words were beginning to take on new meaning. What had happened—what had not happened—was acquiring a vast significance."[47] Carpentier's legitimate history is also something that must be accompanied by change lest it remain a plaything of privileged processors of minutiae writing about elite strata of Latin American countries. Change becomes necessary to history, and not just political change. One would expect this from a Cuban who had experienced history prior to the Cuban Revolution.

And in *The Kingdom of This World,* Ti Noël realizes that man is so minute as not to count for much historically: "He suffers and hopes and toils for people he will never know, and who, in turn, will suffer and hope and toil for others. . . . But man's greatness consists in the very fact of wanting to be better than he is. In laying duties upon himself."[48]

Received history, in short, is not worth remembering unless it has resulted in betterment of all mankind. Fictional historians knew full well that what had passed for standard versions had not done this didactically. Is this why a corsi-ricorsi construct embellishes the thought of fictional historians so? I think it is their disappointment in what followed the independence saga, not just the impending quincentennial, that made them see their entire history as cataclysmic rather than linear and superficially progressive. It was the failure of the fantastical that led to the unacceptability of the quotidian.

Perhaps because of his own country's controversial past (and present), the Mexican Carlos Fuentes described independence as a process through which history is transformed into the "presence of an absence,"[49] a commentary, I believe, on affirmation of independence as negation of the Hispanic past that, nevertheless, will not go away. "Would the South American patriots," Fuentes asked in *The Campaign,* "ever understand that without [the] past they would never be what they so desired: paradigms of modernity? Novelty for its own sake is an anachronism: it races toward its inevitable old age and death. A past renewed is the only guarantee of modernity."[50] But a past allowed to repeat itself just once is a curse.

"The modern age," one of Fuentes's characters avers, "which for an Englishman . . . is a breeze, will be a hurricane for a Peruvian. We who speak Spanish were not born for it."[51] Stagnant economies, societies of privilege, and politics bereft of foundation: not much of a legacy by the end of the independence saga and the beginning of nationhood.

Fuentes's respect for the Hispanic past (with both its limitations and negative aspects) shows through as well in *Distant Relations.*[52] Of the authors whose works document the history dealt with here and in chapter 1, Carlos Fuentes has been the most mindful of the need to remember, as well as the need to look ahead with care, in order to avoid revisiting the past.[53] He is the most historically fluent novelist in the history of Latin America.

One of the most oft-recalled lines from García Márquez's fictional history of Bolívar is Marshal Sucre's, in a conversation with Bolívar: "It's destiny's joke. . . . It seems we planted the ideal of independence so deep that now these countries are trying to win their independence from each other."[54] The creation of independent states would be the result of destruction of both an empire and its old constituent parts, after all; a destruction that obviously left little with which to create anew, either regionally or nationally.

America was hopeless, "half a world gone mad."[55] This is the decidedly negative view of the history that led to the madness of a nineteenth century in which independence became a "fandango for lunatics who can't get along even after they've made their revolution."[56] Independence to García Márquez and others was discovery and conquest redux: cataclysmic, dynamic, as destructive as it was creative. It was an unstable conflation of beginnings with endings. Its human heroes were as tragic as the historical heroes of the fifteenth and sixteenth centuries had become. In fiction as well as fact they became so at a more accelerated pace, with a greater meaning for the present. For this they deserved to suffer the ill effects of collisions with history.

Brazilians have not done fictionally to the history of their independence what Spanish Americans have to theirs, for they have less reason to do so. Ana Miranda's impressive first novel, set back in seventeenth-century Salvador da Bahia, raises issues dealt with by the likes of Carpentier, Fuentes, and García Márquez in later contexts, as discussed herein. Luso-Brazilian relations, colonialism, Church-state relations, the role of Jews, and that of Jesuits—these all make Miranda's work a transitional fictional history of the time between the epic of discovery and conquest and the saga of independence and early nationhood. Miranda's is the foreword to the independence saga. Roa Bastos's is both its postscript and the foreword to early nationhood. They ought to be read jointly with this in mind.

"Ah, if only one could undo the past, turn the clock back and achieve the impossible, if only what has happened had never taken place," intones a fictional Father Antônio Vieira to a young listener.[57] Without that past, however regretful, Miranda makes it clear, there would be no Brazil: "Without African slaves there would be no Bahia. Without Angola there could be no Brazil."[58] Without an Old World, no New World. Without a confrontation with history, none with the present.

It follows that without a history, there can be no future either. The continuation of monarchy made Brazil's transition to nationhood easier for the elites, surely, but it did little or nothing to energize the economy, change society, or generate a modern polity. Dynastic institutions would continue to define Brazilian history until the last decade of the nineteenth century.

"There is always time to have more time," Roa Bastos's Dr. Francia would have all believe.[59] According to his own fictional historian, Francia also believed that Paraguay would be "the political destiny of the American continent."[60] Geographically, historically, and socially was this not already so? Paraguay's mediterranean location, its institutions, its social structure did not change much with independence. There would be time, all right, but how much change? History was the moment at hand, not much more. As with colonial Bahia, rendered by Miranda, the present was history still; but unlike her Father Vieira, Roa Bastos's Dr. Francia would never advocate turning back any clocks. Rather he would still their ticking lest awareness of time's passage create a sense of too much change, thus foment chaos. It almost had done that to the South American heartland state when it became an independent country and had done so to the rest of Spanish America. If the independence and early nationhood saga did not turn back any clocks, neither did it speed them up.

Arenas, Carpentier, Fuentes, García Márquez, Miranda, and Roa Bastos all found fault with history. For the most part history was boring to Arenas, useless sets of dates, places, and names—a reaction, probably, to the fitful history of his native Cuba. Before Castro what was Cuba's canonized history, after all, but that of seminationhood at best? Since 1959, Cuba's history has proved to be more national in character. This may make it more politically meaningful to that island's people, more worth remembering when Cubans confront the future without Castro.

Carpentier's musings on history inform us that while he recognized the powerful force history can exert, he thought it essentially meaningless unless it resulted in betterment of the human condition. History had to lead to something worthwhile whether its path was linear, spiral, or cataclysmic, or all of these. He clearly saw the Caribbean in terms of despair and hope in equal measure. He demeaned neither history nor the past but respected both, acknowledging all the while their intimate relationship.

Mexico's Fuentes reveres the past, for he sees history as a dynamic mix of form and motion, the construction of everything the Mexicans and their Latin American neighbors are and are not. Without their past they would have no way of confronting the present. With it they cannot forget who they want to be. Nobelist García Márquez viewed independence as destructive to those who championed its cause and to those who came after. His history is an aggressive force. It devours its makers in the same way gods punish heroes for their successes and failures. García Márquez's history is truly cataclysmic.

Ana Miranda's Bahia is a living historical monument to Iberia and Africa, to the Portuguese and their African slaves, culturally, economically, and socially unique. In her fictional historical preface, Brazil is portrayed as a living monument to the entire colonial experience as well. And Roa Bastos reminds us over and over in his postscript that change does not occur at the same pace everywhere, that sometimes humans who would be godlike and heroic in the classical sense, really do make the difference in the drama that we call history. In the next chapter we shall see just how few humans proved capable of making a difference by the time institutions had become entrenched and authoritarian regimes became vehicles for realization of individual and group ambitions. With the rise of institutional authoritarianism, history as portrayed fictionally becomes more a thing of the present than the past.

We can now see plainly that fictional histories were an indictment of the past and the way it has been recorded for posterity by Latin American scholars. Those of the independence and early nationhood eras contribute to the quest for latinoamericanidad by debunking myths, attacking heroes, and challenging nationalized and regionalized canonical versions even more harshly than do those of the epic of discovery and conquest. They lead us further toward an understanding of what made novelists see history as having been misused by both heroes and traditional chroniclers. If they are admittedly something quite other than factual depictions of a tumultuous age, they are certainly not tedious in the sense Francia saw so much history as being. In the following chapter we will see even more clearly that the distance between thought and self-perception of the fictional historians expressed in their commentary and that manifest in their creative works shrinks in direct proportion to their proximity to the tragedy of the recent past.

The Fictional Histories of Independence

This list includes the principal sources for documentation of the cataclysmic history of Latin American independence and the beginnings of authoritarian rule. As in the previous chapter, citations in the text come from English editions unless otherwise noted, and English-language publication data precede Spanish or Portuguese titles and publication dates.

Arenas, Reinaldo. *The Ill-Fated Peregrinations of Fray Servando Teresa de Mier.* Trans. Andrew Hurley. New York: Avon Books, 1987. *El mundo alucinante* (1966). Cited as *Peregrinations.*

Carpentier, Alejo. *Concierto barroco.* Trans. Asa Zatz. Tulsa: Council Oak Books, 1988. *Concierto barroco* (1974). Cited as *Concierto.*

———. *Explosion in a Cathedral.* Trans. John Sturrock. New York: The Noonday Press, 1989. *El siglo de las luces* (1962). Cited as *Explosion.*

———. *The Kingdom of This World.* Trans. Harriet de Onís. New York: Farrar, Straus and Giroux, 1989. *El reino de este mundo* (1949). Cited as *Kingdom.*

Fuentes, Carlos. *The Campaign.* Trans. Alfred Mac Adam. New York: Farrar, Straus and Giroux, 1991. *La campaña* (1990). Cited as *Campaign.*

———. *Distant Relations.* Trans. Margaret Sayers Peden. New York: Farrar, Straus and Giroux, 1982. *Una familia lejana* (1980). Cited as *Relations.*

García Márquez, Gabriel. *The General in His Labyrinth.* Trans. Edith Grossman. New York: Knopf, 1990. *El general en su laberinto* (1989). Cited as *General.*

Miranda, Ana. *Bay of All Saints and Every Conceivable Sin.* Trans. Giovanni Pontiero. New York: Viking, 1991. *Boca do inferno* (1989). Cited as *All Saints.*

Roa Bastos, Augusto. *I, the Supreme.* Trans. Helen Lane. New York: Aventura, 1987. *Yo, el Supremo* (1974). Cited as *Supreme.*

Chapter 3

The Tragedy of the Recent Past

> The advantage, the luxury, as well as the torment and responsibility of the novelist is that there is no limit to what he may attempt as an executant—no limit to his possible experiments, efforts, discoveries, successes.
>
> —Henry James, *The Art of Fiction* (1888)

WHEN GEORGE ORWELL's Winston Smith reluctantly repeats the party slogan, "Who controls the past controls the future; who controls the present controls the past," to his oppressor, O'Brien, he vocalizes a dilemma confronted by novelists of the Boom. Unless they could bring their creative efforts to bear on their own present(s) they could not effect definitive changes in interpretation of their past(s). This is why they chose the subjects they did for fictional histories discussed in the preceding two chapters. The subjects they chose to attack in works discussed in this chapter make their fictional history both more comparable and recognizable to that of modern scholars, especially social scientists, for the economic and social forces of the recent past were not only timely, they were historical.

If the historical roots of independence are fictionally traceable to discovery and conquest, and their legacy, it stands to reason that those of the recent past may also be traced to independence and early nationhood, and their legacy. Cause and effect relationships being what they are in the historical sense (i.e., often tenuous), they ought to be analogous in fiction, and they probably are.[1] Fictional historians spent a lot of time and effort on contemporary politics, authoritarianism, and military-civilian relations as institutionally entrenched, systemic. And for good reason. Because they did so we have a better opportunity to see the extent of their collisions with the full trajectory of Latin America's history. We are closer to answers to questions about the meaning of history, about what it had led to in Latin America, about who were the responsible parties for history's injustices. And we can more easily see the intellectual similarities between fictional history and social science.

The quarter century or so preceding the closing of the Cold War paradigm was a painful time for most of the region's inhabitants. The time of the generals[2] encouraged novelists to criticize harshly the conditions, historical and contemporary, national and international, that had brought about the authoritarian governments of the 1980s.

Social scientists from abroad responded with formulas for democracy and development. Latin America's social scientists followed suit when and where they could. Fictional histories of this third cataclysmic era differ from those of earlier times in their direct focus on institutions and themes rather than controversial historical figures who represent those themes allegorically or metaphorically. Even when the subject is an individual, the analysis offered is institution-based. In these works novelists not only collide, they offer new means of interpreting history to their fellow citizens and to the world.

Corruption, repression, torture, dirty war, dispossession of peasants, suppression of labor organizations, violation of human rights—these all found their way into works of both leading and lesser-known authors, some of whom resorted to metaphor by setting stories in the late nineteenth and early twentieth centuries—for political and historical as much as for artistic purposes. The three decades preceding World War I are an ideal metaphoric time, for all the characteristics of the recent Latin American past are present there and then in abundance. Reading some of this fictional history is like reading revised and carefully edited versions of social protest novels from the 1920s, 1930s, and 1940s.

A growing number of younger or (initially) newer writers were translated between the mid-sixties and late eighties, so that their work became imbedded in, and identified internationally with, the Boom and the alternative history canon that we have seen it engender. For every Carlos Fuentes, say, there was an Humberto Costantini bursting upon the international scene from Argentina; for every Mario Vargas Llosa, there was an Arturo von Vacano, a Bolivian novelist; for every Ariel Dorfman, one of Chile's finest novelists, an Osvaldo Soriano from Argentina; for every Chilean like José Donoso, a Brazilian like Ignácio de Loyola Brandão; and for every Isabel Allende, a Luisa Valenzuela, yet another Argentine star.

As some of these newer writers approached, then achieved, major status the Boom gave way to the New World Order, and the sheer number of authors being published and translated precluded Boom-identity maintenance. Then, when the Cold War ended, when domestic political reasons for fictional collisions with history diminished, authors turned elsewhere for inspiration. This does not mean that conditions propitious to collision were no longer extant, it means that new conditions encouraged collisions by other means and encouraged novelists to essay other subjects in their fiction. Perhaps their original mission had been accomplished.

The Failure of the Fantastical

The documented failure of her leaders to extricate Spanish America from the backwardness and stagnation of the early nineteenth century has cast a pall over politics and government until the present day. The wreckage of the colonial era became that of the postindependence decades. Practically speaking, negation of the past took precedence over assertion of the future. The present became a permanent condition in the minds of some authors because they saw the past in terms of spiral, not linear perspective.

It is some three and a half centuries from the beginnings of discovery and conquest—Columbus's zenith—to the endings of independence—Bolivar's death, say. It is much less than that, about a century and a third, from 1830 to the Boom and the tragedy of the recent past. The spirals of cataclysmic history have tightened and become more dynamic in socioeconomic and cultural terms, less dependent on the deeds and mistakes of individuals in political ones. This tightening indicates that the next significant set of historical events of cataclysmic importance may occur in a half century or less. This may sound like a more substantive assertion upon reading chapter 6, wherein collisions occur by other means. Whether or not fictional history ever again becomes the vehicle for collisions depends on the magnitude of events and personalities involved, but is not assured by any means.

As mentioned, fictional renditions of the late nineteenth century are in reality commentary on the recent past, for just like those of the contemporary era, they evince real disillusionment with what nationhood had wrought. Politics and government routinely appear in fictional history set a century ago as unnecessary sicknesses and necessary evils respectively. Authoritarianism comes across as an almost natural result of the mistakes and miscalculations of those who gave independence over to their followers. The military depicted in the pages of fictional history is a multinationally influenced, goose-stepping band of predatory and bloodthirsty hypocrites—sometimes armies are rendered even more negatively than that. All this makes for exciting reading. It complements as well as supplements historical and social science scholarship devoted to the recent past from the region and beyond.

history as arbitrary leads to oblivion

Disillusionment with the present and the recent past casts a nihilistic pall on one's historical mindset, makes of history a meaningless experience to be forgotten or arbitrarily rewritten. It almost does make one want to posit the disappearance of history as possible, and almost does lead to the conviction that, with few exceptions, a historical mind-set no longer need obtain among intellectual elites and leaders of government. Writers who focused on the recent past did not want for examples of disillusionment in it and in their present, and would proceed to reject both in ways that helped initiate the constriction of historical thinking discussed in chapter 6.

Preludes to the Recent Past

José Donoso's *A House in the Country* is a case in point. Set at the end of the nineteenth century, long after Roa Bastos's eponymous supreme one has gone to his reward, Donoso's extended Ventura family seems a collective metaphor for the decadent aristocracies that sprawled across the history of the early national decades. Opulence and misery have increased side by side. Lackeys of the landlords, *mayordomos*, and others, now serve their masters in order to keep the peasants and natives from destroying what the aristocracy has created, or appropriated, for its own benefit, and what little the lackeys have retained for theirs. The Venturas represent the upper crust, cannibals the lower sectors of society. The lackeys are in between, and their choice, like that of Latin American middle sectors and professional classes, is relatively simple.

Opportunity-based loyalty to the elites results in survival, just as it did for armies that propped up the haves and kept them on top of society well into the present century, all in the name of stability and order. "Your Grace's hands must be kept clean to set the example without which there can be no order," Donoso has a lackey tell a master. "That's what we servants are for, to dirty our hands."[3] Politics and government meant so little to so many in the last century, is the inference: order was the result of ignorance and force, not program or policy.

Donoso would be the first to remind us that metaphors are both necessary and shaky. "I make no appeal to my readers," he writes, "to 'believe' my characters: I would rather they were taken as emblems— as characters, I insist, not as persons—who as such live entirely in an atmosphere of words, offering the reader, at best, some useful insight."[4] But metaphors are what his book and others like it are based on, and insights abound. At the least this 1978 novel is an apocalyptic indictment of the sociopolitical past that produced the present in which it was written and published. At most it is an indictment of the present. I think this is clear in the context Donoso himself established.[5]

This may also be said for Vargas Llosa's *The War of the End of the World.* Set in the 1890s, during the Canudos revolt led by the messianic Antônio Maciel (Antônio Conselheiro), it chronicles in fiction what Euclides da Cunha did in his documentary *Rebellion in the Backlands:* republican Brazil's struggle for sovereignty and legitimacy—its very identity—against a millenarian revolt in the hinterland known as the *sertão.*[6] Read along with each other, Cunha's and Vargas Llosa's works provide readers with an ideal juxtaposition of fictional and early social science approaches to a cultural and political struggle of epic proportions. They complement and supplement each other in the same important ways other works mentioned in chapters 1 and 2 do.

Vargas Llosa's novel of Brazil is packed with allegoric and direct allusions to history as a mechanistic, linear passage of time—for modern, Atlantic Brazil, but not for the *sertanejos* of the vast, undeveloped interior. And, it illustrates the dilemma of those go-betweens who spend their lives in politics and government in lands where the seeds of democracy still have little to sustain growth, and where linear time still seems to lead nowhere, despite the insistence of those in power that it will.

The collapse of the Brazilian monarchy in 1889 left the majority of citizens there without two mainstays of their historical past: a comfortable (over the long run) relationship between the Church and the state, and the once socially atrophying institution of slavery. Change was in the wind. Galileo Gall, one of Vargas Llosa's witnesses to the Canudos rebellion, expresses his own view of history thus: "We know, comrades, that there is no such thing as chance in history, that however fortuitous its course may seem, there is always a rationality lying hidden behind even the most puzzling outward appearances."[7] Written in 1981 and translated just three years later, *The War of the End of the World* indicts a nineteenth-century history that produced conditions in the Brazilian hinterlands analogous to those in the Peruvian sierra a century later. "The explanation of Canudos [or of Sendero Luminoso or Movimiento Revolucionario Tupac Amaru, Peruvian popular revolutionary movements of the late twentieth century] does not lie in race but in ignorance," according to one of the army leaders sent to crush the Brazilian backlanders.[8] The present, in short, can be understood by looking back to its most appropriate origins. If this is so, what does change mean? Which origins are most appropriate? What are the stabilizing institutions of a future if intellectuals agree that rationality is still out there waiting to be found? These are the important questions that stem from works that deal with the prelude to the recent past.

Dictatorship is dictatorship, whether in the nineteenth century or the twentieth, and rebellion is rebellion. Authoritarianism and opposition to it are as much constants in post-independence Latin America as are politics and government per se—at least until the 1980s. Dictators and those who oppose them figure more prominently in fictional history than do senators and those who run against them. Individuals still count, but not as prominently as before; they are symptoms as much as causes.

Fictional history from the recent past per se deals with dictatorship from several principal vantage points and through a variety of themes. In a historical context they are connected to works on earlier times because of continual interest in authoritarianism as both cause and effect. In the last century, political theories imported by elites proved unadaptable to Spanish American reality; in that century's last decade they proved barely adaptable to Brazil. Lack of adaptability led to alternatives less theoretical, principal among which were institutionalized and personalized authoritarianism. The politics of democratic processes proved either meaningless or frivolous, a plaything for aristocrats and their lackeys throughout the region.

During this century most of Latin America has alternated between putatively democratic and blatantly authoritarian systems of government. This explains the interest of fictional historians in the present as perpetuation, not continuation, of the past, and their conviction that history is either without meaning, inevitable, tragic, or all of these.

Authors whose works went into translation in Europe and North America paved a way for newcomers. They, in turn, found their reputations and marketability enhanced through both timeliness of publication and rapidity of translation. The Boom was a political and social phenomenon as well as an economic and literary one (and a capitalist-publisher windfall to some) owing to its place in the historical flow. Dictators make good targets. Politics can be just as inseparable from literature as history is. Each must become controversial for collisions to occur and for large numbers of people to take notice.

The gravity of things political during the last decades of the twentieth century enlarged markets and emboldened the growing number of fictioneers to elaborate on aspects of authoritarianism already treated in the well-known works of Miguel Angel Asturias, Carpentier, García Márquez, and Roa Bastos. Realism spiraled into a kind of neonaturalism precisely when authoritarianism began to justify itself under the rubric of national security. Torture was no longer visited upon known opponents exclusively; anyone might be caught up in the formalized institutional violence commonly known as counterterrorism. Anyone might be branded procommunist, at any time for a multitude of reasons. Literature became, thus, even more a weapon in the war against authoritarianism—history's principal legacy.

By now professionalized and indoctrinated in ways to fight Marxist subversion and any perceived threat to institutionally defined historical, national values, armed forces became more than mainstays of authoritarian alternatives to putative democracy. Their leaders became the theoreticians of a new form of governance: professional militarism. Thus members of the military profession may be considered the modern version of discoverers, conquerors, and independence leaders—major role players, all too human ones. Officers became at best antiheroes and villains, forces of evil in the pages of fictional history. Politics, authoritarianism, military-civilian relations and history's meaning (or lack thereof) are the main features of the collisions discussed in this chapter, where they become more head-on in their depictions than metaphoric and allegorical. I think this indicates a tightening of history's spirals that enables the constriction of history.

now what sought to expose may be replicated

Collisions with Dictatorship

Like aristocrats, dictators must have lackeys. El Señor Presidente had his share. Asturias's central character (like those of Donoso and Vargas Llosa, and Carpentier's in *Reasons of State*) first came to fictional life in 1963. He spans the historical and institutional gulf between Roa Bastos's *I, the Supreme* and García Márquez's *Autumn of the Patriarch*—even if their publication dates do not encourage one to see it this way.[9]

As a group these novels of Caribbean, northern Andean, and southern South American dictatorship, and their main characters have become as familiar as El Supremo. The dictators' followers and lackeys have become models as well for other authors. Asturias's novel serves as chief model for most recent fictional renditions of the horrors of dictatorship and abuse of power. The most recent political manifestations of authoritarianism have not been portrayed any more vividly (I do not mean more accurately) than in these novels of prelude.

> Long live the President.
> Long live the President of the Republic.
> Long live the Constitutional President of the Republic.
> Let our applause go on echoing throughout the world forever: Long live the Constitutional President of the Republic, Benefactor of his Country, Head of the great Liberal Party, and Liberal-Minded Protector of Studious Youth.[10]

And on and on it goes throughout Asturias's great work, reminding readers of those things shouted about well-known circum-Caribbean dictators like Fulgencio Batista, the Somozas, Rafael Leonídas Trujillo, François Duvalier, Marcos Pérez Jiménez, Gustavo Rojas Pinilla, and so many other real-life presidentes of the middle decades of the twentieth century.

Fictional leaders in these novels, however, are not portrayed as tragic heroes à la Bolívar or San Martín. They are purely evil creatures of history spawned over time in the chaos following the disappearance of the leaders of the early nineteenth century. These tyrants prolonged postindependence caudillismo and set the stages for those of the late twentieth century; they are neither more nor less responsible for what happened in Latin America than the aristocrats and lackeys who set stages for civilian political collapses of the 1960s and 1970s.

One can easily place these novels in a historical setting—*I, the Supreme* in the early nineteenth century; *A House in the Country* and *The War of the End of the World* at century's end; *El señor presidente, Reasons of State,* and *The Autumn of the Patriarch* a little later. In each, time spends a lot of history standing still. It does not seem to matter "whether something back then was true or not, God damn it, it will be with time."[11] Throughout this limbo of time or history military men would fulfill roles of both leaders and lackeys: dictators and policemen. Bureaucrats would also fulfill theirs: upholders of the regime without which they, like the military rank and file, would have nothing. This would change, of course, during the time of the generals, when *uniformados* not only carried out policies but made them, so as to uphold their own historical creations.

In each of these classic works on authoritarianism, dictators, their civilian and uniformed allies, and foreign influences are censured for their perpetuation of timelessness and terror, for not moving the region ahead in a linear historical sense. In the works of Donoso and Vargas Llosa, especially, aristocrats and republican forms of government receive less than kind treatment. Works that these fictional historians devoted to the nineteenth and early twentieth centuries chronicle the long-term legacy of independence as pessimistically as novels dealing with the end of empire portray Spain's colonial legacy. Little wonder, then, that fictional history of a past remembered firsthand should be so negative in its portrayal of a present lived. For what was the present but a current version of an unpleasant history, what was the past but a series of unproductive corsi?

Competitive politics still has a bad name in Latin American literature, although not enough to give dictatorship a good one. Writers have been cynical in their treatments of the politics of what passes for democracy in the region, and for good reason. Politics in recent fiction comes across as prelude to dictatorship and imposition of military rule. In some countries Boom writers were reluctant to publish at home, for what they put on paper might easily have placed them in institutionalized harm's way. Indeed, they wrote a lot from exile or during long sojourns beyond the reach of authoritarians, who either discouraged or prohibited them from publishing in their native land.

The Remembered Past as History

As Chile's Ariel Dorfman tells his readers, "a lot of good it'd do us to have a literary renaissance if we ended up without a country; it was the same old vicious circle. We had believed the government was eternal, giving us time to work out the future peacefully, and now the fascists wanted to cut out our tongues; they were getting their public back, talking about the highest patriotic values, and for us, well, we would be screwed. What sense did it make to write at times like these?"[12]

But write they did, with the past and the future ever in mind, for the present was too awful to bear. For some writers, Luisa Valenzuela of Argentina, for example, the present was nothing more than a cruel continuation of the past: a sleight of hand played on the people by the Peróns and the López Regas of the Southern Cone.[13] The Eva Duarte and Juan Perón, and the Jose López Rega (insidious confidant of Argentina's first family—in real and fictional versions) of both Valenzuela's *The Lizard's Tail* and Tomás Eloy Martínez's *The Perón Novel* are portrayed as no more than contemporary patriarchal types who regarded Argentina as their fief. In fiction as well as fact their way of dealing with an opposition was not to negotiate within the bounds of a constitution but to do what threatened patriarchs always have done: eradicate the opposition, for "THE BEST ENEMY IS A DEAD ENEMY."[14] This is precisely what late-twentieth-century tyrants did across the region.

Violence and politics went (iron) hand in (velvet) glove much of the time in fact as well as in fiction. When politics in Argentina, Brazil, Chile, and Peru, say, became infected with too much populism (i.e., when popular causes became fundamental to the democratic process), politicians on the right succumbed to the great temptation of reliance on the military. Works of Dorfman, Valenzuela, and Vargas Llosa bear out this assertion. In the latter's words, for example, " '*El Comercio* [the major Lima daily] calls Odría the Savior of the Nation because it hates APRA [Alianza Popular Revolucionaria Americana, the radical reform party],' Colonel Espina said. 'They only want us to keep the Apristas in the clink.' "[15] Peru's most recent experiences with military rule, it needs saying, owed as much to the weakness of its civilian leadership as to the ambitions of its officers. Fictional history has made this just as clear as has historical scholarship.

There is a fatalism in Boom novels that deal with the tragedy of the recent past. Either politics is a meaningless historical exercise undergone to perpetuate elites and putative democracies by any means, or it is simply a façade for authoritarian control. "Somoza will govern Nicaragua," one of Antonio Skármeta's characters argues, "until the end of the Twentieth Century."[16] No matter that dictators, like seasons, come and go, and always have (the Somoza dynasty fell in 1979), their style of government remained the principal alternative to populism and what authoritarians thought of as democratic excess.

Fatalism can lead to alienation, or just plain hopelessness—especially when the military becomes institutionalized, more than a pack of lackeys, as was increasingly the case as the century wore on. Humberto Costantini's eponymous Francisco Sanctis felt as if he were standing on the sidelines of life, powerless, watching history: "He felt he was a sort of spectator . . . in a world that seemed to reject him and into which he had trouble fitting. . . . That world struck him as violent and obscene."[17] And he could do nothing to change it. Few Latin Americans could.

Alienation can lead to an activist, an antipolitical, or even an *a*political stand, in which cases the individual reflects the existing alternatives, as in the following exchange between two characters in Skármeta's *I Dreamt the Snow Was Burning:*

> I don't like politics [says Arturo]. Just want to live with no problems, making trouble for no one and no one making trouble for me.
> So nothing changes? [replies Fats] The same injustice?
> Is that my fault?[18]

It should amaze no reader, activist or alienated, antipolitical or apolitical, that Latin American political vacuums would be filled by uniformados. Nor should it amaze anyone that military-political action ("they've built a school and a barracks")[19] restores a stability still seen by some as preferable to the inherent instability of modernizing democratic regimes. We may not need fictional history to instruct us thus, but Boom novels serve a corroborative purpose. They remain another form of documentary evidence derived from an intellectual generation whose perceptions of their world were significant, given changes Latin America is still experiencing. Their supplementary and complementary value derive chiefly from their collisions with all facets of the recent past.

In this vein, Isabel Allende's *Of Love and Shadows* serves as a valuable study of women's changing roles in politics and resistance to professional military rule.[20] The transformation of the indulged heroine, Irene, into a valiant opponent of the military regime is an allegorical approach to the historical transformation of women into political activists to a point where their activism cannot be ignored. No longer content to emulate preceding generations, women like Allende's Irene—and, for that matter, Dorfman's Paula of *The Last Song of Manuel Sendero*—become a collective power to be reckoned with by authoritarians, then by political leaders who follow them on into democratization processes in the wake of military rule. Even if they stand by their man, as Paula claims to do, the experience of the time of the generals transforms them.[21] Nowadays they stand beside, not behind.

This is obviously the case in the Southern Cone. Dorfman's *Widows* and his 1991 play, *Death and the Maiden,* are prime examples, both clearly Chilean-based yet appropriate to the study of other countries. Such works are also valuable for their insights on divisions within the Church re the brutal stability of authoritarianism as contrasted with the instability of democracy and its respect of human rights. There is no fatalism about politics displayed in Allende's political works, neither in *Of Love and Shadows* nor in *The House of the Spirits.* It will be more than interesting to follow the fictional course of women in politics and government during the century ahead, more interesting still to follow the social science literature on this subject.

The end of dictatorship always brings political readjustment. Parties adjust to new circumstances. Leaders scramble to retain influence in newly shaped arenas of discussion and debate. Coalitions realign. Those who once resisted actively fault those who did not—or those whose opposition was lukewarm or inconsistent. Exiles come home to a different country. Those who suffered want justice. Who deserves the democratization dividend most? This is still a question, for women, labor leaders, and one time *others* who continue to think themselves treated less than equitably. Nothing yet approaches an answer, although social scientists are making strides in this direction, as we will see further on in these pages.

When civilian party politics, with all its advantages and shortcomings, returned to countries like Nicaragua, Peru, Argentina, Brazil, Uruguay, and Chile in the last decades of the twentieth century there were recriminations aplenty. It is hard for the formerly persecuted and exiled, for the tortured and maimed, to reconcile with those who had chosen the apolitical or fatalistic approach to survival. A conversation between David and Felipe in *The Last Song of Manuel Sendero* amplifies this for us. Christian Democrats, we know, condoned the military rising of 1973 in Chile, then opposed the Pinochet government when it became clear that the armed forces were going to make serious structural changes, especially in the polity and economy. But the Left suffered from the outset, both for past deeds and timely opposition. A chasm (i.e., more than just a gulf) of distrust opened between the Chilean Left and the Christian Democrats, and was bridged (perhaps only temporarily) only by some careful political engineering prior to and following the 1988 plebiscite. Dorfman's Felipe cannot trust the Christian Democrats; his David does, but reluctantly.[22] This kind of schism does not bode well for the future, neither fictionally nor politically. Healing still goes on in Latin America—in Argentina and Chile, for example—among larger numbers of affected citizens than ever before.

Politics had made for "make-believe nations,"[23] let alone strange bedfellows, well before the authoritarian experiences of the 1964 to 1990 epoch. If this is so, fiction encourages us to see it that way, and politics allows us leeway to consider it possible, then history may have brought little substantive change along with it after all. Social scientists would have us consider this, as chapter 6 will indicate, and I think they are justified in doing so. The pessimism of fictional historians evinced in their writing on earlier parts of Latin America's past compounds itself with what they remembered firsthand. This may not bode well for the security of history's place among intellectuals in the future; nor does it lend much intellectual support to democracy's sustainability in that same future. Chapter 6 (which may be read immediately following this one for contextual purposes alone) elaborates on this also.

"You think that in this day and age anyone knows anything about parties? There are no more political parties, buddy. This is the disgrace, that they can't agree on anything. . . . All of us have retired from the political scene, even though we keep telling ourselves that the people united will never be defeated [*el pueblo unido jamás será vencido*]."[24] This mindset bodes ill for the political future. If Latin American (re?)democratization processes begun in the 1980s should falter, what alternatives will there be? This is one of the questions being mooted by social scientists of the region.

Collisions with Institutionalized Authoritarianism

Based on what fictional historians have told us over and again (and what social scientists allude to), we cannot exclude new beginnings for authoritarianism and military involvement in affairs of state from history's onward flow(s). These beginnings may not take the forms they have in the past; they never fully do. In fact the armed forces may be able to exert more influence from behind present and future scenes than they ever did as principals, more like technicians (I do not imply stagehands) than actors. What began in 1980 with devolution of leadership upon civilians in Peru may be part of a democratic wave, but all waves create some undertow, some reflux—for each and every corso there must be ricorso, in other words. Expectations of an end to authoritarianism in Latin America, are, I fear, a little like those of an end to history. Bolivia's Arturo von Vacano likened such expectations to "waiting for the end of an agony that will never cease."[25]

Fictional history, then, portrays authoritarianism as the result of politics gone bad in the recent past—for historically systemic reasons. This is surely akin to novelists' views of discovery and conquest (good intentions gone bad) and independence (better intentions gone worse). But it goes a step further. Latin America's ills are no longer the work of individual failings, much less the result of battles. Latin America's ills are the results of systems both economic and social.

Authoritarianism is rarely as cold and calculating in its inception as are politics and government in their operations. This is because the former is only slightly less rational than the latter. Increasingly in this century military political actions have reflected professional refinements in staff planning and use of technology, not the crass ambitions of *exaltados* (although there is evidence that there is still time for such political creatures, witness the behavior of cliques of officers in Argentina, Paraguay, and Venezuela during the 1990s). This is because the action was directed against increasingly complex, if thinly based, political systems. Following seizure of power, the ability to conduct national affairs, for better or worse, by military leaders becomes easier proportionate to their ability to seize power.

"The coup," wrote Chile's Fernando Alegría, referring to 1973, "is an empty truck that comes from the South and comes from the North, halting, grinding, uphill until it almost stalls, and finally stops at dawn, douses its headlights and draws out its small shining muzzles."[26] Dawns like that one did break across the region. The nights were long and dark for years.

"Mili-techs" took over across the region.[27] Men steeped in national security doctrine, some trained in the United States, moved into government positions. Ministries, the diplomatic corps, policy-making offices, new agencies all felt the influence of men in uniform. In some cases—Peru in the 1960s and 1970s is the best example of this—both cabinet-level policy formulation and execution fell to professional officers. In other cases—Chile in the 1970s and 1980s, say—military men and civilian fellow travelers shared control. But everywhere mili-techs, technocrats, replaced professional politicians. Antipolitics prevailed,[28] confirming novelists' views that political processes were immediately and primarily to blame for recent examples of authoritarianism. This is tantamount to saying that tightening of the historical spiral has indeed occurred ever more rapidly.

Carlos Martínez Moreno's novel *El infierno* takes readers into the authoritarian hell of struggles between the Uruguayan military and the Tupamaros, in which the forces of order did much more than just wage war against those of populism. These River Plate authoritarians of the 1960s destroyed the fabric of a society in much the same way conquerors, and independence and postindependence caudillos damaged social structures and economies. In *El infierno* the enemies of the state are "always watching you," ready to "stab you in the back," they are "everywhere," and "always lurking," "laying a trap," "spying on you," "pursuing you," "waiting for you," "coming to get you," they "know your movements," and they may "leap on you" at any time.[29] The forces of order must suppress enemies of the state at all costs like the Holy Office once kept Islam, "Judaizing Heresy," and Protestantism at bay. To oppose this suppression is to give succor, to become one of them. Better "to scurry around, to take refuge in the first available hole" than to stand up to the authorities, thus incurring the wrath of the armed forces and their civilian allies.[30] Fatalism was not limited to politics.

Military-designed authoritarianism was not just an Argentine, Chilean, Bolivian, Brazilian, Peruvian, or Uruguayan phenomenon. It was a regionwide tragedy. In El Salvador, and Guatemala and

Nicaragua too, the majority would have to pay a high price for both democracy and authoritarianism. Ivan Ângelo's recounting of Brazilian statistics on income distribution (1 percent of the population with an income greater than that of the bottom 80 percent ca. 1970) is as germane to his fiction and history as are such statistics to any social science analysis of Brazil's or Central America's twentieth-century reality.[31] And vice versa. Societies everywhere were rent by professional military leaders who preached security, nationalism, and community, perpetuating damage done hundreds of years before and prolonging the suffering of millions.

Historically, authoritarians have been demagogues as well. The reclusive Francia was an exception. The "Somozas of today," said René Depestre, "and the Batistas, the Trujillos, and the Pérez Jiménezes of yesterday . . . played to the point of hysteria the roles of imperial saviors."[32] So did Peru's Velasco Alvarado; his successor did not. Nor did Brazil's Garrastazú Médici, Argentina's Galtieri, or Chile's Pinochet, for example. The tragedy of the recent past is one in which a return of historically minded, calculating dictators gave full dimension and ample definition to authoritarianism. Fiction portrays South Americans more often than not as the cool and calculating professional soldiers of Alegría's dawn, Central Americans and Caribbeans as flamboyant and demagogic patriarchs like García Márquez's eponymous patriarch. Fictional history portrays them about as accurately as do other sources. It also portrays the cultural, economic, and social forces within which they flourish.

Authoritarianism depends on hierarchical subordination and oppression. All novels dealing with the tragedy of the recent past have as a principal theme authority and subordination. In their most positive sense they are essential to discipline and hierarchy—fundamentals of traditional societies, the Church, and the armed forces. In their most pernicious manifestations they are essential to dictatorship and its accompanying suppression of opposition, which is a legitimate activity by authoritarian definition. Oppression once institutionalized may be

based on class, ideology, racial, or even clique rivalries. It has historical as well as contemporary dimensions, and should not be relegated
to an irretrievable past.

Novels of discovery and conquest, and of independence, showed us
this. One Brazilian novelist once went so far as to draw an analogy between sixteenth-century Iberian suppression of Judaism and twentieth-
century suppression of political dissidents: "It was destined for us to
inherit the stigma that followed the Hebrews for millennia. Persecu-
tion and segregation and oppression: transplanted. I realized that it was
our turn to be humbled, spit upon.... A cycle was ending in that green-
ish yellow moment, the Jew making way for the Latíndio-american."[33]
So a theme begun with conquest reappears in a new guise over the
course of centuries. The "terror of the state"—a historical phenomenon in Ângelo's opinion—is revisited in barbaric form: "Attila, the
Vandals or the terrible Avaros [Avars]";[34] officers, mili-techs, hysterical saviors, maintain a tradition at the expense of *others*, the weak and
the unconvinced—over a long span of history.

Collisions with History's Foreign Influences

However enduring its essence or hysterical its perpetrators, authoritarianism had its foreign inspirations and abettors. Brazilian, Uruguayan,
and Chilean fictional historians recognized the influence of the major
hemispheric power among all the forces that defined late-twentieth-
century descents into the inferno of dictatorship. Dorfman's Dragon
Pinchot (Pinochet) allegorically invades Tsil (Chile) from "up north,"
but allows as how he may have been asleep in the mountains until the
day "the people's arguing [political conflict] woke him up." "Up
north"[35] means only one thing: the United States. Ideology, national
security, and geoeconomics pervade the fictional history of the recent
past, and in so doing cast the United States in all historical roles once
restricted to Iberia.

Increasingly during the past century dictators themselves wore uniforms proudly and were highly educated career professional officers. As such they represented their profession's views more than their own and were at ideological odds with civilian career politicians as often as not. The links between politics, authoritarianism, and the military are depicted as clearly in fictional history as they are in scholarly monographs on the same subject.

The professional attributes of Latin American armed forces and their derivation from the United States have been systematically studied by North American and Latin American scholars for a half century. U.S.–Latin American military relations figure prominently in works of Allende, El Salvador's Manlio Argueta, Costantini, Skármeta, Brazil's Márcio Souza, and Vargas Llosa.

These writers portrayed foreign-trained military leaders as acting like men whose vocation forces them to stand *apart from* the very society they profess to be *a part of.* Cold War emphasis on national security and ideological warfare drove generals and admirals to think and act on behalf of a nation in order to defend it from the enemies of—the United States. Frequently misguided, usually overreactive to perceived threats, always reliant upon their professional thought and self-perception, and often poorly served by civilian allies (the new lackeys), these officers did some terrible things in the name of saving their countries from the clutches of what they believed was an insidious worldwide Marxist-Leninist grand scheme for domination.

Armies must have enemies if they are to maintain their professional identity, after all. Their education—both at home and in the United States—helped military leaders see their countries' problems as homegrown as well as induced from without. The enemies within might be rural or urban insurgents, and were often defined in military literature as Marxists whether or not they indeed were. This meant that in lieu of the Soviet Red Army and the domestic Communist Party as their foe, armies fought insurgent and downtrodden Indians, peasants, and workers. These domestic enemies were not easily defeated, officers were told by their North American instructors, and of this they also convinced themselves, because nefarious outside forces aided and abetted their every move. So the campaign to save countries and a region had both domestic and foreign fronts, both domestic and foreign allies and foes.

The perceived docility and stupidity of their own troops convinced fictional Nicaraguan officers, Skármeta claimed, that brute force was the only discipline they understood.[36] In other words, they gave their fellow citizens of less than modest means very little credit; they underestimated their real foes. El Salvadoran demographics convinced them, according to Argueta, that there were just too many peasants and workers, too many poor.[37] Argueta's fictional soldiers learned to tie their demographics to Marxism-Leninism from North Americans who came down to El Salvador to advise on how to roll back the Moscow-and-Havana-inspired insurrection of unwitting but nevertheless culpable nationals, Donoso's cannibals with an ideological theory base. These advisers, one of Argueta's characters counsels his readers, "come to our country in big airplanes. They tour the countryside in their helicopters. They wear dark glasses so they can't see our light. They drive bullet-proof Cherokees. They don't speak Spanish. How are they going to understand us like that?"[38] How indeed?

Argueta's two novels of El Salvador and Skármeta's Nicaraguan-inspired opus depict rapacious armed forces cut off totally from society owing to their contact with outside benefactors, entities unto themselves, convinced of their professional and institutional superiority over all human beings who did not wear a uniform. In reality these Central American militarists were no more professional than conquistadores or caudillos. In *One Day of Life* the Salvadoran army acts to defend property, money, and privilege against poverty, hunger, and misery; it draws the line between domestic allies and foes. Grim-faced, devoid of humor, as tropically cold as Alegría's Chilean trucks of dawn, the army can only save "endangered democracy" by vicious acts designed to intimidate the majority.[39] Argueta's two novels of the

94

struggle against brutal institutionalized authoritarianism are representative of Central American fictional histories of the recent past in more ways than can be described here.

Once, during a lecture at the Chilean War Academy, sometime in the 1980s it was, the author of these chapters told his uniformed audience that Isabel Allende's *Of Love and Shadows* showed unusual understanding of the military profession, its thought and self-perception. This statement did not meet with the listeners' approval, nor with that of the faculty.

Only after the question-and-answer period was over did a few officer-students want to pursue the matter. I cited a passage well into the novel where Allende discusses the vocation of one of her most interesting characters, Captain Gustavo Morante. It "was an absorbing vocation," she had written. "He had chosen it as a career because he was fascinated by the rigorousness of the life and the security of a stable future, and because he had a taste for command as well as a family tradition. His father and grandfather had been generals before him."[40] None of these reasons for choosing a military career is invalid. Indeed to a lot of Latin Americans all this makes a lot of sense. It finally did to Chilean officers who had heard it said but never had read anything by an author named Allende.

Later in the same book Allende discussed the dilemma of officers and noncoms who must dispatch a prisoner of the dictatorship. The lieutenant holding the revolver had been prepared "to fight against neighboring nations. . . . But no one had told him he would have to beat a bound man to a pulp to make him talk, they had not taught him anything about that."[41] Where had he learned it then, somewhere "up north"? Even the most historically professional of Latin America's armies found in the tragedy of the recent past their undoing.

Authors mentioned in this chapter addressed in firm tones the great gap separating theory from practice in military political action and resultant authoritarian rule. Souza elaborated on this throughout *Death Squeeze* by placing a Brazilian captain of his own, one Miguel

Gouveia, in the unenviable position of abandoning his career after the return of civilians to power. His disillusionment is symptomatic of the plight of numbers of young officers in Latin America during the second half of the past century. Had they become cadets only in order to make war against their fellow citizens at the behest of outsiders? Had history duped them somehow? Had they been forgotten by their former benefactor, the one, in Dorfman's words, "up north"? Already social scientists are addressing this theme.

Collisions with the Military Profession

Apart from its linkage to foreign influences the military profession receives pretty rough treatment in fictional histories of the recent past. Corruption, bribery, public works, palliatives to workers and employees, demagoguery—these all characterize the political action of the Pérez Jiménezes, the Rojas Pinillas, the Peróns, and the Odrías of Latin America, those mid-century tyrants who preceded the professional militarists of the latter part of the century. Manuel Odría's flirtation with APRA support in the 1960s (to get himself reelected in the 1962 and 1963 contests against Fernando Belaúnde Terry) figures in Vargas Llosa's *Conversation in the Cathedral.*[42] This fictional history stands as an example of the cupidity of military strong men before 1964 in South America, and of the entire twentieth century elsewhere in the region. Vargas Llosa's ridicule of Odría is matched in sharpness only by his send-up of the military in the person of poor Captain Pantaleón Pantoja in *Captain Pantoja and the Special Service.*

As true to life as any officer portrayed in *The Time of the Hero,* Pantoja expresses a fictional reality of the individual as part of uniformed bureaucracy. A "soldier-administrator" by his own career choice, Pantoja organizes (under orders, of course) a special service of prostitutes to serve the needs of men posted in Peru's Amazonian hinterland. This effort at nation building, modernization, and development, as part of the Peruvian army's self-proclaimed "civilizing mission," is a mockery of military procedure and policy. Pantoja, the ever-idealized soldier-administrator, is no Lyautey.[43] Indeed, when the word gets out about what is going on, it is he, not those who gave him his orders, who must pay the price of loyalty. The novel is a farce in part because Vargas Llosa and others of his generation saw the military as farcical and retrograde. This book is a natural supplement to his tragic and powerful *The Time of the Hero*. Together they expose the military to popular scrutiny and judgment very effectively. No other author has seen fit to deal with the military profession based on such inside knowledge (Vargas Llosa temporarily prepped at Colegio Militar Leoncio Prado, where his record was less than exemplary).

One other fictional historian has, though, elaborated extensively on the chilling, bureaucratically inhuman dimension of professional militarism gone bad. In *The Long Night of Francisco Sanctis* and *The Gods, the Little Guys, and the Police*, Argentina's Costantini leaves his readers with images of calculating, gangsterlike death squads preying upon civilians, the innocents and those involved in resistance alike. An episode from each of these two novels is worth pages of scholarship owing to the vividness of imagery provided and accuracy of setting.

"With a chilling squeak of rubber tires on pavement they'll come to a halt in front of this well-established residence, and then a trained group of untouchable murderous para-policemen, whom the morning newspapers will hypocritically refer to as 'a group of strongly armed individuals' will descend from the cars."[44] "Ford Falcons that cruise the city like phantoms . . . murderers armed with . . . submachine guns . . . torturers who at three in the morning climb into their cars, slipping the safety catches off their weapons. . . . My God, what have we come to?"[45] Argentines had their dirty war, Peruvians their overly ambitious military socialism, Brazilians and Chileans their technocratic professional militarism. In each case violence and terrorism accompanied them all along the way. Democracy collapsed and professional militarism took over their lives more than old-fashioned dictatorship ever had.

Did democracy's failure signify history's failure? Will democracy's revival mean history's end? Are the two necessarily related? Probably yes. If it is perceived by intellectuals as having lead to nothing, history can be considered as having failed to justify remembrance of the past. If it is worth remembering, the past must mean something. If it is a series of essentially bad memories, though, history must be either revised, selectively idealized, or constricted to allow only the most felicitous and expeditious cause-and-effect relationships to be its form and content. Blame must be assessed to someone for history's injustices.

Thematic Collisions

Some years ago, at about the same time I discussed with Chilean army staff aspirants the merits of Isabel Allende's work, it was my good fortune to give a paper at a conference on literature in translation. No critic or translator I, the paper urged the use of fiction in translation as collateral reading in history courses—no major novelty per se, except in its focus on thematic history.[46] These chapters go well beyond the scope of that paper, but here at the end of the portion dealing with cataclysmic history its central argument bears placing in context in order to lead us into the next three chapters.

From the earliest days Latin American literature and history have been inseparable. Only with their separation in the eighteenth century, then the rise of academic disciplines in the nineteenth, did they diverge as subjects of study and comment. Even so, I argued, in our times anthologies of literature retain a historical flavor and comparable historical compilations show the influence of literature. Works dealing with discovery and conquest and the early colonial period are interchangeable; historians and teachers of literature often use the same colonial-period readings. Not many works on independence find their way into more than one discipline, and only a few nineteenth century–based classics do: Sarmiento's *Facundo: Civilización y barbarie,* José Victorino Lastarria's *Recuerdos literarios,* and Cunha's *Os Sertões,* say.[47] In this century there was a severe dearth of belles lettres (excepting the essay) to bridge interdisciplinary gaps— until the Boom.

As noted, there is as much history in fiction as there is fiction in history, maybe more. I do not mean by this that *Terra Nostra* or *The General in His Labyrinth* or *Reasons of State* should be considered *good* history. They are, rather, good *history.* They are historical in more than one way. First, they add dimensions to our vision of the Latin American past. Second, they help us understand what about their history has puzzled intellectuals of the late twentieth century. Third, they evince the values and priorities that guided writers as they attempted to provide alternative visions of the past. Fourth, they demythologize traditional, nationalistic history and its godlike and heroic national icons, reducing all in the process to something nearer a human scale. Fifth, they provide us with stimuli to revise further.

Neither by linking history to literature nor literature to politics do I mean that Ivan Ângelo, or René Depestre, or Mario Vargas Llosa have written definitive works on politics, authoritarianism, and the military in Latin America. Their work is historical, nevertheless, for by colliding with recent history they describe situations analogous to real life in such a way as to enhance readers' knowledge of the past and the present, and to make them ponder the future.

Recent Latin American fiction gained more acceptance outside the region than the concurrent output of disciplinary scholars inside the region, with the possible exception of that of some social scientists, because fiction is easier to read, either in translation or in the original, and it is usually more entertaining. It will have a more lasting effect in Asia, Europe, and North America than most other published materials emanating from Latin America owing to the wider audience it reaches. Such was the gist of that paper; such is the purport of these chapters.

At the end of the paper appears a selected list of "archival" works of fiction deemed worth using in thematically structured history courses. The list is now dated, but is still worth consulting with regard to the present work; themes emphasized in the list—authority and subordination, gender relationships, military-civilian relations, the city and the countryside, contemporary politics, and history and possible futures—all figure prominently in works examined here that portray collisions with history. It is insufficient, obviously, to view history solely in chronological chunks of time, but it is appropriate to demonstrate how Latin American novelists saw fit to interpret their own history during one of its most important eras.

Narrative history still counts for a lot. History is also thematic, and its writing and teaching are the better for it. History is cataclysmic—when viewed through the lens of novelists with manifest interest in both themes and topics from the recent and distant past. Latin America's history is indeed spiral; violence, exploitation, subordination, and oppression recur in ever changing guises: corsi-ricorsi. Latin America's history is indeed influenced by exogenous forces: Spain, the Mediterranean world, Portugal, northern Europe, Africa, Asia, the United States, and now the transnational economy of the New World Order.

Latin American history is dramatic. It is a broken and incomplete history, an invertebrate, inchoate history, both spiraling and cataclysmic, still without enough meaning for far too many. This is why, I think, novelists felt so compelled to collide with it and did it so artfully in the form of fictional history that portrays it as cataclysmic and characterized by so much recurrence.

Authority and subordination encompass a lot. Some of the novels already mentioned, those by Asturias, Carpentier, García Márquez, and Roa Bastos, for example, deal with historical dictators of the independence and national periods in ways that give them life unattainable in other genres. Presidents, patriarchs, and dictators, as well as discoverers, conquerors, and independence leaders stride from the pages of their fiction into our present. And why not, given the way history has flowed and eddied? Carpentier, García Márquez, and Roa Bastos join Carlos Fuentes as subjects for further examination in chapter 4.

Gender relations constitute a metaphor-filled Latin American variation on authority and subordination. And it is for this reason I have selected Isabel Allende as one of the subjects for my discussion in chapter 5 of thought and self-perception. Vargas Llosa, Dorfman, Donoso, and others depict military-civilian relations, another variation on the authority-subordination theme, quite convincingly. Vargas Llosa joins Allende, Julio Cortázar, and Darcy Ribeiro (the last two for reasons to be made evident) as subjects of discussion in chapter 5.

omg- that's it?

Fictional Historians as Historical Figures

Some Boom novelists were exiles; others chose to live abroad, but, had not conditions been so unpleasant in their homeland, they might have avoided such notoriety. Experience abroad internationalized their reputations, as well as their outlook on native land, region, and world. It encouraged translation too. Internationalization of their fiction helped accelerate the internationalization of Latin American culture, and helped disseminate the new outlooks highlighted in this chapter. Multiple collisions between literature, politics, and history became frequent and more intense as the Boom played on. Latin American fiction became part of the mainstream. A few of the names cited in these pages may not be all that familiar to English-language readers, but they are well known in the literary, diplomatic, academic, and political circles of Latin America.

In a quantity never before imaginable, Latin American authors

exile helped popularize

latin american lit helps politics

became celebrities between 1964 and 1990. They won prizes, gave lectures, appeared at conferences, had symposia devoted to their work, taught in Europe and the United States, and lived and traveled abroad in numbers. Their celebrity gave them new fora, access to a worldwide, multilingual public. They were in demand; critics, scholars, teachers, learned societies, and publishers demanded their time and their words as well as their writing. Their accomplishments and their audiences made them influential. Their opinions expressed beyond the pages of fiction counted—especially in the media-rich countries where they resided when and if they were not living at home. Their talent made them novelists; their eagerness to collide and their propensity to insist on new themes made them figures of historical import. By the time Orwell's figurative 1984 had passed into history their literary collisions with history were having an influence on Latin America's future, for they had assumed the responsibility of ignoring the limits of fiction, as James would have had them do, to experiment with recent historical themes and topics.

In the two chapters immediately following this one I will discuss commentary of the novelists noted above on several timely subjects. This two-part discussion will show that those who collided with history were consciously members of a generation (defined by publication dates more than by birth and death) that achieved something of a group consensus on the ever-elusive latinoamericanidad, the Latin Americanness, that so many readers have found in Boom fiction. Some of these do not figure at all in the writing of cataclysmic history—well and good; their intellectuality and idiosyncratic ideations add even more luster to their recognized literary prominence to a degree that warrants their inclusion in any discussion of this type.

Even if they disagreed on specifics or did so ideologically, they understood what they were about as something more than production of marketable fiction. They had come to believe that past(s) portrayed in history books compelled them to challenge their veracity and utility of this history in order to understand present(s). They spoke for Latin America and for their own countries every bit as eloquently in essays, interviews, lectures, and panel discussions as they did through the voices of their fictional characters. The eight are, in order of discussion: Alejo Carpentier, Carlos Fuentes, Gabriel García Márquez, Augusto Roa Bastos, Julio Cortázar, Isabel Allende, Mario Vargas Llosa, and Darcy Ribeiro.

Where is Belli?

The Fictional Histories of the Recent Past

This list includes the principal sources for documentation of the cataclysmic history of the recent past and the struggle against authoritarian rule. As with those at the end of the preceding two chapters, citations in the text come from English editions unless otherwise noted, and English-language publication data precede Spanish, French, or Portuguese titles and dates. See also note 9, this chapter for additional documentation of the fictional struggle against authoritarianism.

Alegría, Fernando. *The Chilean Spring.* Trans. Stephen Fredman. Pittsburgh: Latin American Literary Review Press, 1980. *El paso de los gansos* (1975). Cited as *Spring.*

Allende, Isabel. *Of Love and Shadows.* Trans. Margaret Sayers Peden. New York: Bantam Books, 1988. *De amor y de sombra* (1984). Cited as *Love.*

Ângelo, Ivan. *The Celebration.* Trans. Thomas Colchie. New York: Avon Books, 1982. *A festa* (1976). Cited as *Celebration.*

———. *The Tower of Glass.* Trans. Ellen Watson. New York: Avon Books, 1986. *A casa de vidro: Cinco histórias de Brasil* (1979). Cited as *Tower.*

Argueta, Manlio. *Cuzcatlán: Where the Southern Sea Beats.* Trans. Clark Hansen. New York: Aventura, 1987. *Cuzcatlán: Donde bate la Mar del Sur* (1986). Cited as *Cuzcatlán.*

———. *One Day of Life.* Trans. Bill Brow. New York: Aventura, 1983. *Un día en la vida* (1980). Cited as *Life.*

Brandão, Ignácio de Loyola. *And Still the Earth*. Trans. Ellen Watson. New York: Avon Books, 1985. *Não verás país nenhum* (1982). Cited as *Earth*.

———. *Zero*. Trans. Ellen Watson. New York: Avon Books, 1983. *Zero* (1979). Cited as *Zero*.

Costantini, Humberto. *The Gods, the Little Guys, and the Police*. Trans. Toby Talbot. New York: Avon Books, 1985. *De dioses, hombrecitos y policías* (1984). Cited as *Gods*.

———. *The Long Night of Francisco Sanctis*. Trans. Norman Thomas di Giovanni. New York: New American Library, 1985. *La larga noche de Francisco Sanctis* (1984). Cited as *Night*.

Depestre, René. *The Festival of the Greasy Pole*. Trans. Carol F. Coates. Charlottesville: University Press of Virginia, 1990. *Le mât de Cocagne* (1979). Cited as *Festival*.

Donoso, José. *Curfew*. Trans. Alfred Mac Adam. New York: Weidenfeld and Nicolson, 1988. *La desesperanza* (1986). Cited as *Curfew*.

———. *A House in the Country*. Trans. David Pritchard and Suzanne Jill Levine. New York: Aventura, 1984. *Casa de campo* (1978). Cited as *House*.

Dorfman, Ariel. *Hard Rain*. Trans. George Shivers and Ariel Dorfman. London: Readers International, 1990. *Moros en la costa* (1973). Cited as *Rain*.

———. *The Last Song of Manuel Sendero*. Trans. George Shivers and Ariel Dorfman. New York: Viking Penguin, 1988. *La última canción de Manuel Sendero* (1987). Cited as *Song*.

Martínez, Tomás Eloy. *The Perón Novel*. Trans. Asa Zatz. New York: Pantheon Books, 1988. *La novela de Perón* (1985). Not cited in text.

Martínez Moreno, Carlos. *El infierno*. Trans. Ann Wright. London: Readers International, 1988. *El color que el infierno me escondiera* (1981). Cited as *Infierno*.

Skármeta, Antonio. *I Dreamt the Snow Was Burning*. Trans. Malcolm Coad. London: Readers International, 1985. *Soñé que la nieve ardía* (1975). Cited as *Snow*.

———. *The Insurrection*. Trans. Paula Sharp. Hanover, N.H.: Ediciones del Norte, 1983. *La insurrección* (1982). Cited as *Insurrection*.

Soriano, Osvaldo. *Winter Quarters*. Trans. Nick Caistor. London: Readers International, 1989. *Cuarteles de invierno* (1982). Cited as *Winter*.

Souza, Márcio. *Death Squeeze*. Trans. Ellen Watson. New York: Avon Books, 1992. *A condolência* (1984). Cited as *Death*.

Valenzuela, Luisa. *The Lizard's Tail*. Trans. Gregory Rabassa. London: Serpent's Tail, 1987. *El señor de Tacuru* (1983). Cited as *Lizard*.

Vargas Llosa, Mario. *Captain Pantoja and the Special Service*. Trans. Gregory Kolovakos and Ronald Christ. New York: Noonday Press, 1990. *Pantaleón y las visitadoras* (1973). Not cited in text.

———. *Conversation in the Cathedral*. Trans. Gregory Rabassa. New York: Harper and Row, 1975. *Conversación en La Catedral* (1973). Cited as *Conversation*.

———. *The War of the End of the World*. Trans. Helen Lane. New York: Farrar, Straus and Giroux, 1984. *La guerra del fin del mundo* (1981). Cited as *War*.

von Vacano, Arturo. *Biting Silence*. Trans. anonymous. New York: Avon, 1987. *Morder el silencio* (1980). Cited as *Silence*.

Part Two

History between the Lines

Chapter 4

The Commentary of Carpentier, Fuentes, García Márquez, and Roa Bastos

One must allow the best to be shown so that it reveals and prevails over the worst. Nations must have a pillory for whomever stirs up useless hates, and another for whomever fails to tell them the truth in time.

—José Martí, *Our America* (1891)

GIAMBATTISTA VICO COULD never have imagined how much influence he might have over writers of fiction from a far off part of the world that long after his death would be called Latin America. The author of *The New Science*, whose corsi-ricorsi schema clearly is at the core of "cataclysmic history" would have marveled at the fictional history of Alejo Carpentier, Carlos Fuentes, Gabriel García Márquez, and Augusto Roa Bastos, whose thought and self-perception this chapter examines. Each of them, in turn, owes the eighteenth-century Neapolitan rhetorician an intellectual debt; each wrote fictional history that evinces a historical consciousness akin to his that permeates their commentary.

Collisions with history that take place in essays, interviews, lectures, panel discussions, mutual criticism, and casual conversation are less cataclysmic than in fiction. They have far less to do with great men, dynasties, battles, and such. They deal far more with the themes and topics, and the institutions and systems discussed in chapter 3 than those of the first two. That is, the closer to the present fictional historians got in their thinking, the sharper their emphasis on subjects being dealt with by scholars.

This chapter and the next take the form of a virtual interrogatory: the position of four interrelated questions and responses to them using the authors' words gleaned from a variety of sources—always with historical and literary contexts in mind. Here the writers speak for themselves, not through fictional characters. I have purposely arranged the responses thematically to substantiate conclusions, and chronologically to both establish continuity and take into account shifts in political or ideological stance, given the contemporaneity of ideation.

The questions are: (1) Is there a collective Latin American consciousness that defines or sets apart writers of the recent past (i.e., the Boom era)? (2) Who constitutes the generation associated with such a consciousness? (3) Should writers and intellectuals play a political or social role? (4) What is the historical or political viewpoint that defines either their writing, or their role, or both? In chapter 5 the same interrelated questions will be asked of Julio Cortázar, Mario Vargas Llosa, Isabel Allende, and Darcy Ribeiro. In each case the response takes the form of a summary answer followed by elaboration that cumulatively comes to resemble a dialogue similar to that which characterizes both Boom fiction and recent social science scholarship.

Why these questions, why these authors? I think it is important to show that the outpouring of quality, translatable, marketable, and timely fiction was, more than a felicitous literary coincidence, an intellectual phenomenon of historic proportions. It is also important to know just who inspired writers and whom they likened themselves to. Who their models, their idols were. Reading their nonfiction or hearing them speak, one is struck by the mix of sophistication and candor manifest in discussions of roles they saw themselves fulfilling. Their historical viewpoints need to be seriously considered if the idea of a historical phenomenon is to be seriously considered, and I think it should be. The choice of writers dealt with in these two chapters represents both the regional quality and worldwide appeal of the Boom. Carpentier, Fuentes, García Márquez, and Roa Bastos, Cortázar, Allende, Vargas Llosa, and Ribeiro represent countries, subregions, and Latin America well. For one reason or another their international stature was established during their lives, not after, either within the Boom or by it, however the latter is defined.

If Darcy Ribeiro was not the stylist Carpentier was, he certainly straddles with ease an increasingly shrinking gap between late-twentieth-century Latin American fictional and social science approaches to history. If the words of Isabel Allende and Julio Cortázar do not display the historical sense found in those of Carlos Fuentes and Augusto Roa Bastos, so much the better for purposes of both synthesis and contrast, and definitions of latinoamericanidad. If Mario Vargas Llosa and Gabriel García Márquez have disagreed so much (most important, on Cuba, and in this respect Vargas Llosa has not stood alone), so much the better for the sake of argument. And so on.

All the writers dealt with in this chapter consciously collided with history or contemporary politics in their fiction. The next chapter's group was even more intensely political in their lives and their writing. Choice and placement, thus, are designed to advance the idea of collisions with history toward the final chapter, wherein social science is the vehicle for collision. Placement of Ribeiro at the end of the next chapter is specifically designed to complete this transitional process. Had such questions ever been asked in the form they are in these chapters, the responses would, over the long run, be essentially as constructed here, I am convinced. Allowing for creative individuality, their responses do evince collective consciousness of, and consensus on, whom the Boom brought together, who best represented Latin America historically and intellectually.

Each has contributed—mightily, moreover—to the way outsiders still view relations between the United States and Latin America. They all have been critical of the political and social conditions that history, its fallen heroes, and its villains have produced in their own countries, and in the region they come from. They all have played a role in defining the culture of countries and region. The degree of consensus or dissensus evinced by their answers is appropriately representative of the region at the time of the quincentennial, just about when experiments with professional militarism and the (extended) Boom ended, and the New World Order began. Between their non-fictional lines a lot of historical thinking can be found. When juxtaposed with the words of Latin America's early-twentieth-century essayists (who wrote when markets for novels did not compare to those of recent times) they provide a rich source for the study of intellectual history through an entire century.[1] Their thought and self-perception ought to be taken seriously in contemplation of future relations between Latin America and the rest of the world and in future revisionist approaches to Latin American history.

Corsi-Ricorsi of Fiction, History, and Social Science

In *The Theory of the Novel* Georg Lukacs said that "the novel is the epic of an age in which the extensive totality of life is no longer directly given, in which the meaning of life itself has become a problem."[2] Put into a Latin American context this leads to a preliminary conclusion that for a while the novel may have been the revival of an epic-adventure form cut short in the sixteenth century with the establishment of colonial dominion and its unique Church-state relationship. In Latin America myth, epic, and tragedy evolved differently and experienced reflux at a literary pace different from that of the rest of the world.

Other writers, in other times and places, have been aware of the meaning of their own times and their pasts. Henri Barbusse was. He wrote that his own generation was living at the end of a specific historical era (*période de civilisation*).[3] And, Roland Barthes, in *The Pleasure of the Text,* dwelt on feelings about time and "dislike for the estranged past, for the past in and of itself."[4] Barthes, of course, went on to assert that beginning in the eighteenth century writers were more conscious of historical time than of cyclical time (a sign of structural weaknesses in European ruling dynasties, doubtless), and also commented on the "synchronism" of distinct times that may coexist with one another—that is, the overlapping of historical eras. Neither Barbusse nor Barthes vigorously affirms Vico's theories, of course, but their views do contribute to an understanding of the reasons behind fictional portrayals of history discussed in these pages. Time and history are distinguishable phenomena to the disciplinary scholar, less so to the author-commentator; they are more miscible for the writer of fiction than for the author-activist. Both time and history prove less understandable to those who live them than to those who look back on them. Latin Americans are no exception.

At the beginning of the past century Argentine essayist Carlos Octavio Bunge wrote that Spanish Americans lacked imagination, with the exception of a few, and did not write very good history at all. His suggested remedy was to "Europeanize ourselves."[5] Just a couple of decades later Uruguay's Manuel Ugarte would write that "hispano-americanism" would never exist unless Latin Americans took stock of all their problems, stopped relying on the past for their identity, and adapted the best of Spain, France, and Italy to their region.[6] The same year Ugarte wrote, Mexico's José Vasconcelos argued that Spanish Americans had created a civilization and culture unlike that of any other former colonial dominion.[7] In 1925 the Spaniard José Ortega y Gasset referred to novelists in general as sleepwalkers who were more interested in worlds they created than the ones they had left behind during their creative somnambulance.[8] Bunge, Ugarte, Vasconcelos, and Ortega—like essayists Cunha and Rodó before them and José Carlos, Mariátegui, and Argentine Ezequiel Martínez Estrada soon after—were as deeply affected by what had befallen Iberia and Latin America during the nineteenth century as novelists of the twentieth century were by the entire national period. Genres change, concerns prevail; writers are advocates as well as creators.

The arguments and challenges put forth by essayists of a century ago were carried forward by novelists of the late twentieth century who chose to collide with history in worlds they were unable or unwilling to leave behind. The direct link between the important early-twentieth-century essayists and the novelists whose fiction so dominated its recent decades is maintained as much by the thought and self-perception of the latter as it is by their fiction. Few of the writers who came in between—Paz, Asturias, Peru's José María Arguedas, Brazil's Jorge Amado, and a few others are exceptional rather than typical—can match intellectually those of the Boom or those of the era of the essay.

Over the course of the past century, literature, like the social sciences, became professionalized in Latin America. In recent decades one might actually make a full-time living as a writer or a sociologist, say, not just write and teach on the side. Literature as a discipline became more refined, both in its conception and its execution, at about the same time the social sciences were becoming dehumanized through excessive specialization of the disciplines. Latin American prose fiction became an "objective category of printed works of a certain quality," to borrow judiciously from Raymond Williams.[9] This is to say that the "novel in Latin America" became the "Latin American novel." The "dream of the soul's infinity," to borrow a bit less judiciously from Kundera, "realized its magic when the novel . . . took hold."[10]

Kundera once wrote that there was a strong tie between Cervantes and Descartes, two men of different cultures, different ages, with respect to history and fiction. They were, he thought, founders of two characteristics of the modern era: the world of wonder and ambiguity and that of the thinking self. Rather than the social sciences, Kundera cited the pure sciences as the fields of learning that had "propelled man into the tunnels of disciplines," that led people to forget the meaning of being.[11] More anent the social sciences anon, of course.

Suffice it to say that the novel of the Boom, more than the essay, ultimately would nurture and serve both Latin American "selves"—the thinking and the wondering—that scholarly history and social science could not, the former for its paucity of popular appeal, the latter owing to its novelty. That the social sciences ultimately would nurture and serve so ably will be discussed in the final chapter.

Novelists may be historians, politicians, social scientists, or scholarly writers as well. In Latin America, as Carpentier, Fuentes, García Márquez, and Roa Bastos revealed in their fiction and their public lives, the revising of history can no longer be a monopoly of Latin America's own historians and their few students. Bertrand Russell's admonition of 1954 that "history should not be known only to historians" certainly elicited eloquent responses in Latin America.[12] There history has been definitely deemed too important to be left to any guild closer to Clio than to Melpomene and Polyhymnia.

There the essay, then fiction, not scholarly history, would provide Latin America a place "within the framework of universal history" through the revisionist efforts of novelists.[13] Columbus, then others, "invented" Latin America (without naming it such); their descendants have been trying to define it. If this definition is imprecise still, then surely it means the task is both ongoing and still worth accomplishing by historians.

Those who wrote during the Boom, thought and perceived themselves from several standpoints, as will be obvious from what follows. Some would see themselves as part of a collective consciousness, as the only truly historically minded, as Latin Americans in the broadest sense. Some have seen a literary continuum in which they are the inheritors, the ultimate artificers of Latin American identity. Others express less lofty aspirations and opinions. These intellectual descendants of the conquering inventors of Latin America also debate in human terms Lukacs's assertion that bourgeois publishers are the real artificers, and their readers are unwitting tools in a capitalist scheme: the marketing and selling of others' works for the benefit of the few.[14] What could be a more unheroic, cogent argument for Latin American writers to make themselves at a time when heroes were expendable and traditional institutions oppressive?

In a dialogue of 1988, García Márquez and Vargas Llosa waxed eloquent on points like the ones just expressed.[15] The pair discussed the political and social role of fiction and its creators; the influences of history and early literary forms such as epic, tragedy, and novels of chivalry on contemporary writers; the same mix of real and fantasy that Descartes and Cervantes represented to Kundera; and the fact that they and a lot of their Latin American confreres had spent so much of their time abroad that they sometimes perceived themselves as no longer representative of Latin America. They debated the intellectual and ideological affinities (or lack thereof) between contemporary Latin American writers. That dialogue between the Colombian and the Peruvian is in fact a microcosm of what follows.

The four writers studied in this chapter all represent a generation of authors known as much for its absence from as for its presence in its homeland(s). Carpentier was born in 1904, in Havana, and died in 1980 in Paris, where he had spent much of his life. He also lived in Venezuela and Spain. From 1959 until his death he was associated with the Cuban government, both in Havana and in diplomatic posting to Paris.

Fuentes was born in 1928 in Panama, the same year Carpentier first went to Paris. He lived in Washington, D.C., Buenos Aires, and Santiago de Chile. He studied law in Switzerland and Mexico. He has served in the diplomatic corps—as ambassador to France while Carpentier was a cultural attaché there—and has lectured in England and the United States as well as in Latin America and Europe.

García Márquez was born in 1927 in Aracataca, Colombia. He

spent much of his youth there and in Bogotá, where he studied law. He has lived as a journalist in Colombia, Europe, Venezuela, and the United States. He has maintained residences in France, Spain, Cuba, and Mexico, as well as in Colombia, where at century's end he once again was active as a political journalist.

Augusto Roa Bastos was born in a small town in Paraguay in 1917. After serving in the Chaco War (1932–35) as a teenager, he became a journalist. Following the conclusion of World War II, which he had covered for Paraguayan publications, he went into exile for political reasons. In Buenos Aires he taught literature and published his first major work. He taught in France between 1975 and 1985, spending time back in Paraguay after the fall of Alfredo Stroessner in 1989.

Age differences notwithstanding, common life experiences, historical revisionism, travel, concurrent acquaintance with intellectuals, especially French and Spanish figures, and above all an appreciation of history, confer a group identity on these four authors. Here now are their responses to questions about themselves, their work, and their world(s).

Alejo Carpentier (1904–1980)

We begin with the Cuban, figuratively asking don Alejo if there might just be a collective consciousness defining the recent period in fiction, and if so, who constitutes the group associated with it. His initial, summary response would be simple: Yes, there is a consciousness. We are all part of a great sociocultural movement of liberation in which we are finally taking possession of our own history.

Latin American writers, Carpentier claimed back in 1967, had always identified with each other. Those who could afford it always traveled to Paris. Language was not the unifying factor in the region, "rather the existence of identical or similar problems."[16] Literature reflected this. Carpentier's chief examples of early symbols of latinoamericanidad were Andrés Bello, Domingo Faustino Sarmiento, Rubén Darío, José Martí, and José Carlos Mariátegui. Two years later he would name Bernal Díaz del Castillo and El Inca Garcilaso de la Vega as having played such a regional definition role earlier on.[17]

In a lecture given in Caracas in 1975, Carpentier asserted that change had accelerated the pace of Latin American history since mid-century. At last Latin Americans were becoming protagonists in, and chroniclers of, their own history.[18] Doing so they acted together whether conscious of it or not. Three years later, in an interview with Roberto Jaimes, Carpentier averred that the Boom was far more than a commercial phenomenon created by capitalist publishers and booksellers. It was a genuine literary movement. "Only the good merchandise sells; the bad stuff, no matter how much publicity you give it, yellows with age in the warehouse."[19] In this interview of 1978 he named Gabriel García Márquez and Mario Vargas Llosa as recent producers of "good merchandise."

What of the writer's sociocultural role and historical viewpoint? Here Carpentier's own words provide a response characteristic of someone of his age cohort: Latin American intellectuals had always played a sociocultural role—by positioning themselves well to do so. Had they not rubbed shoulders with dictators always? The Nicaraguan Darío was his example. Had not some of them stood up to the United States? Rodó and Martí figured here. Social revolution now provided them with new opportunities to express themselves and their role independently.[20] Intellectuals were Latin America's consciousness and its conscience. It was the novelist's role, he opined, to translate this consciousness into history for all to know.[21]

Latin American intellectuals were able now to see their history as "distinct from all others in the world," one that flowed differently across time and space, and one that had produced the greatest multicultural fusion of all time. No longer (and here both Carpentier's latinoamericanidad and his proximity to the Castro-led revolution comes through boldly) did Latin Americans see their past as the chronicle of a series of *golpes*, wars, battles, and corrupt presidents, or themselves as malevolently manipulated by foreign imperialist powers. Even though there was now so much more of it, their history was their own.[22] In other words the future was more promising than the present. Carpentier was both a Cuban and a Latin American in the fullest sense.

"There are still," said Carpentier in 1975, "people living in the times of [Mariano] Melgarejo or Francisco Solano López"[23]—that is, under archetypal South American tyrants of the later nineteenth century. Large landowners still had the mentality of manor lords of the colonial past. The great bourgeoisie lived and thought, although their clothing and material possessions betrayed them, like those of the French Second Empire, he noted in the same place. The past was omnipresent. His own dictatorial archetype, rendered in *El recurso del método*, was a "past-present" figure: 60 percent Gerardo Machado, 20 percent Manuel Estrada Cabrera, 15 percent Porfirio Díaz, 5 percent Antonio Guzmán Blanco[24]—archetypal Cuban, Guatemalan, Mexican, and Venezuelan tyrants also well known in history.

Like others before and after, Carpentier saw the Caribbean as a region with particular historical unity. There the Haitian hero Toussaint L'Ouverture, Venezuela's Bolívar, and Cuba's great man of letters Martí, had defined most history from independence to the twentieth century.[25] Carpentier's own novels portray that history quite well, all the while emphasizing the role of the common men and women, the nameless—outside fiction, that is.

In a collection of essays published after his death his words remind us that "all great novels of our time begin by forcing the reader to cry out: 'This can't be a novel!'"[26] This was so because novelists carried within them the consciousness and conscience of America. Their lives, their subjects, their characters, all served a sociocultural and historical purpose. Their work proved that Pan-Americanism was fraudulent, a U.S. creation, whereas socialism was the region's genuine salvation from chronic underdevelopment.[27] Where else could the likes of Darío and Martí, Bolívar and Henri Christophe share the same history? Only in a region where synchronism tied yesterday to today, where history had unique form as well as content. Carpentier's collisions with history occurred across time, but with the present a principal arena, owing to what he believed was America's propensity for *lo real maravilloso* (often rendered as magic, or magical, realism).[28]

What other genre but the novel to reveal this Carpenterian reality to readers of the present? "Since its modern conception in the sixteenth century," noted one of Carpentier's critics, "the novel has been considered a historical genre par excellence. Fiction was a mirror in which genuine, exaggerated . . . and artificial images were equally reflected."[29] Are the surreal and the baroque all that far apart, one wonders? Surely not in the fictional histories of Carpentier, nor in the Cuban's own commentary on history and the writer's role as historian.

Carlos Fuentes (1925–)

Carlos Fuentes could respond quickly to an interrelated question by saying that the Boom was part of a third great era (the Tragedy of the Recent Past?) in the region's history of relations with Europe and the Unites States, one in which he and others were engaged in an intellectual uprising against improper negation of the past, which characterized most historical writing about the region. From the times of Monroeism through those of Pan-Americanism, he said in 1960, Latin America had passed into the *etapa hispanoamericana*.[30] In this new age (a twentieth-century corso) Mexico, Venezuela, and Cuba—former tyrannies, let us not forget—had led the region toward a better understanding of the northern colossus by adopting nationalist positions on control of natural resources; writers throughout Latin America had become the region's spokesmen alongside political reformers and social revolutionaries.

Based on his familiarity with the Mexican Revolution, Venezuela's break with dictatorship following World War II, and Cuba's post-1959 Marxist regime, Fuentes believed that foreign influences could be historically both beneficial and pernicious. He personalized Latin America's situation through a grasp of American and European history unmatched by any other Latin American novelist. His observations are more than those of a writer, a journalist, or an ideologue. His commentary assumes the guise of reflections rather than advocacy or prescription. One does not have to squint to see it between the lines.

In a 1966 interview with Emir Rodríguez Monegal, Fuentes presciently compared Latin America to the Balkans, calling his region "the Balkans of culture."[31] The volatility of Latin American sociopolitical life meant that some of its most acute observers—Paz and Cortázar, for example—wrote from abroad. But Fuentes rhetorically asked in the same interview, Had not Henry James, Gertrude Stein, Ezra Pound, Ernest Hemingway, and F. Scott Fitzgerald flourished abroad too, and were they any less read for it?

The literature of its exiles distinguished Latin America as a cosmopolitan region where one day *Latin American* might mean as much as *Mexican* or *Cuban*. Literature allowed Latin America to define its own complex culture in relation to others—and this just might be the only way Latin Americans should hold their own culturally. Quality literature fomented production of more literature; would Latin Americans of the future be destined to read "Superman" or *Don Quijote?* he asked. "Without our own culture we will be mental colonies, prosperous perhaps, but in the end colonies."[32] Writers were clearly the chief agents of latinoamericanidad.

Interviewed in 1983, Fuentes responded to a specific question about the heterogeneity of Boom writers by saying that the generation in question was indeed eccentric. "It is a question that is not a question. In realty there is a profound coincidence at a specific moment in Spanish American literature; I would call it a grand arch beginning with [Jorge Luis] Borges yet without end."[33] As a term, the Boom, he added, was indeed an invention of critics and others, but contemporary literature, that was really something else: "The so-called Boom, in reality, is the result of four centuries that, literarily, reached a moment of urgency in which fiction became the way to organize lessons from the past." Fiction was providing Latin America a way to envision a civil society in which all could participate. Fiction provided identity, which in turn would empower Latin America with an ability to absorb the best of Europe and the United States—and to resist the worst. Fiction thus was doing for Latin Americans now what standard versions of history had failed to do.

Provision of historical identity through fiction came at no small cost. The novel, Fuentes wrote in 1960, had always competed with a "history more fantastic than any of Borges' stories; we children of Don Quijote really did become children of La Mancha, scions of a syncretic, baroque world."[34] Not all Boom novelists may have counted themselves as children of La Mancha, or scions of its most famous fictional inhabitant, but all were products of a rich, fantastic history.[35] They were all, according to Fuentes, involved in the grand struggle between tradition and change: the continuity of "Indo-Afro-Ibero-America" pitted against a modernity defined and enforced from without.

And whom did he see accompanying him in this great enterprise of rediscovery? Over the years in sources noted above he has mentioned Reinaldo Arenas, Asturias, Guillermo Cabrera Infante, Carpentier, Cortázar, Donoso, José Lezama Lima, García Márquez, Daniel Moyano, Juan Carlos Onetti, Nélida Piñon, Manuel Puig, Roa Bastos, João Guimarães Rosa, Juan Rulfo, Severo Sarduy, Osvaldo Soriano, Luisa Valenzuela, and Vargas Llosa as major contemporary figures. Fuentes, thus, has associated himself with the widest range possible of widely published and oft-translated Latin American novelists. He agreed with García Márquez's assertion that all were engaged in writing chapters in one great fictional history.[36]

Throughout Latin America's fantastical history—"abnormal history," as Fuentes termed that of Iberia and its former American colonies—the region had been plagued by vampirelike figures (some Mexicans he even compared with Frankenstein's monster): Trujillo, Batista, Pinochet. "Our interminable list of tyrants . . . depends on darkness." Writers struggled to bring light to reality, to end long nights with beautiful dawns—without a coup à la Alegría. The writer's sociocultural role, and involvement in historical revisionism and political action, "has its origin in that, denied normal channels for expression—political parties, trade unions, legislatures, the press, free electronic media—our societies seek and find in the work of poets, essayists, and novelists all that which is left unsaid about our past and present."[37] It will be enlightening to see how fictional history ultimately fares with the current revivification of "normal channels."

There were more than a few voices from the past to bring life to the present. Aleijadinho, Sor Juana, El Inca Garcilaso, José Joaquín Mora, Lastarria, Sarmiento, Bello, and Martí were not the only great figures of Latin American letters, Fuentes believed. Others, forgotten or purposely ignored, still needed the writers of the present to give them new life. "There is no living present without a living past," he said upon accepting the 1977 Rómulo Gallegos Prize for literature. The writer's sociocultural and political roles were inseparable, in other words, from his or her historical and political views and activities. The writer's work now represented Latin American reality better than that of the historian anywhere.

Language and words have always fascinated Fuentes: "There is no living past without a living language."[38] Latin Americans, he said, had a living language—and many perforce knew English, French, or German as well as their native Portuguese, Spanish, or Haitian Creole. Knowing their own language well would enable them to recapture their own history; lack of attention to language study could deter the people from reflecting on their past, a real problem, he thought, for

Latin America's neighbors north of the Río Bravo.[39] Ignorance of one's own language, in brief, was ignorance of one's own culture and history.

Ignorance bodes ill for those caught up in times of change. Certainly knowledgeable of past and present, perhaps even sensing what was abuilding, Fuentes noted in the late 1980s that the deaths of Franco and Salazar, the collapse of their regimes, and the fall of the Greek colonels in the mid 1970s (i.e., the onset of democratization) did not bring about sociocultural collapse in either Greece or Iberia. Rather, the unifying linguistic and cultural heritages of centuries exerted their influence over the disruptive forces of sociopolitical and economic change. (Fuentes could not have imagined the disruptive nature of culture and language in the late-twentieth-century Balkans.) Even emerging middle sectors had something of a history as well as a past to carry with them into the future, to put it Fuentes-style.[40] The future was brighter than the past will be.

Writing in 1990, Fuentes said the upcoming quincentennial (for which he created the television documentary "The Buried Mirror") would be both the end of an era and the beginning of a new one: an end to the age of encounter and the beginning of a reencounter. Fiction would be the vehicle, he said, for the *reencuentro* between Latin Americans and their historical past. Fictional history was rife with both main features of Latin American reality: the inconsistent regionalist and invertebrate, and the continuous, consensual, and corporate nature of the region. The novel, he offered, is the "watchdog of our history."[41] History was neither linear nor circular in Latin America; it was what might properly be called spiral. History was omnipresent *in* the present, change came through cycles, and no present could be entirely free from its past.

This is to say that corsi-ricorsi assured Latin American identity in the face of worldwide change. "Our first novelist," he said in *Valiente Mundo Nuevo*, was Bernal Díaz del Castillo, the "medieval and renaissance man" after whom savants and writers would fashion themselves until the present, for novelists still wrote in what in reality was epic form, so enamored were they of their past. Fictional history would support, certainly, the Mexican's assertion.

A "time of miracles" (1940–80) had ended, and just as the New World Order began, Fuentes insisted, democracy had to rely on tradition if it were to survive. Memory and imagination were inseparable; one recreated the past, the other created the future.[42] Both were necessary, different but inseparable, in order to make history real to all. Cataclysms made for closure, to be sure, but change was still evolutionary.

Differences between Fuentes and Carpentier abound; so do similarities. Both novelists saw the Caribbean as a unifying historical arena, a place that gave Latin America its earliest identity. Both recognized the inherent differences within that subregion. They saw greater Latin America in the same way. Europe's influence on their writing is obvious. Whereas Carpentier's youth was spent in a Cuba manipulated from without by the United States and from within by corrupt political elites and dictators, Fuentes's passed with him living well abroad or in postrevolutionary Mexico. Carpentier found the Castro experience a liberating one; Fuentes would find fault with his native land's revolutionary movement, and Cuba's too. In the 1990s Mexico's greatest modern novelist would even debate the venerable Octavio Paz over the historical legitimacy of La Revolución in the face of a Zapatista-style rebellion in Chiapas.[43] Differences notwithstanding, the first two fictional historians in our discussion had comparable views on the role of the writer and the significance of fictional history.

Gabriel García Márquez (1927–)

Gabriel García Márquez has shared Carpentier's and Fuentes's interest in differences and similarities. According to Vargas Llosa (and many others) the Colombian's fictive village of Macondo (site of *One*

Hundred Years of Solitude) is a metaphor not only for Aracataca, García Márquez's birthplace, and for Colombia itself, but for all Latin America.[44] If Vargas Llosa is correct (he likened *Cien años de soledad* to the saga *Amadís de Gaula*, no mean comparison), the Colombian's birthplace, Aracataca, represents a "world" (like Vargas Llosa's own childhood home, San Miguel de Piura) where all is possible, much is inevitable, where sadness, failure, and catastrophe prevail: all history's dark manifestations in microcosm.[45] If the metaphoric linkage is valid (and it is attractive), then Latin America becomes a grand designated target for the committed collisionist of the late twentieth century. Latin America is to Aracataca/Macondo for García Márquez what it is to San Miguel de Piura for Vargas Llosa, and what it is to the Caribbean and Mexico for Carpentier and Fuentes: something both local and continental, specific and general, familiar and wondrous, vulnerable and invulnerable to foreign influences.

García Márquez likened the literary outburst of the late twentieth century to an ideological movement more than would Carpentier or Fuentes. His initial response to questions about the Boom and those involved in it would downplay Macondo's significance and elaborate on that of foreign influences on the region's history. He would turn any response into a lecture with didactic intent.

He was more outspoken about Cuba's historical impact on the hemisphere and the rest of the world, even more than Carpentier. Indeed, he found the Castro movement's inspiration in the words of the writer-activist par excellence Martí.[46] The Cuban patriot's regional vocation, he thought, had been taken up by his own contemporaries from all over Latin America, not just Cuba. García Márquez's fellow writers now brought outsiders' attention to their countries and to the region as a whole (even more than Columbus had done, he offered.) Prior to the 1960s, he would say in 1978, Latin America could boast novelists, but not *Latin American* novelists. "Latin Americans need leaders, and believe they have found them among their writers."[47] This was more than a boast as long as the Boom prevailed.

Cuba, certainly, had become a lightning rod for writers and intellectuals, and like Carpentier and Fuentes, García Márquez acknowledged the United States as a pervasive and pernicious influence on the region, as important historically as Spain and Portugal. Because of the looming presence of the United States, Latin Americans had to struggle hard for a future they could call their own.[48] Their disunity and inability to communicate with each other was not their own fault (a Boom author would just about have to say this), it was an ideological and diplomatic problem, not a cultural one (someone who sympathized with the Cuban Revolution would have to say this emphatically). So would someone imbued with latinoamericanidad.

Politics and diplomacy had robbed Latin America of its past, denied it the benefits of nineteenth-century liberalism European-style. The Cuban Revolution, asserted the Colombian in 1982, was not a political and diplomatic extension of this robbery, nor was it a result of some perverse Soviet desires to deny Latin America its place in history.[49] García Márquez judiciously separated Cuba from any world Marxist-Leninist paradigm; what was going on there was just one variation on the Latin American response to political and diplomatic circumstances of hemispheric origin.

Writers, he claimed with equal consistency, had an obligation to help make life better for all, readers or not. He surely perceived his role as culture maven, for (like Vargas Llosa) he has had few kind things to say about most writers from his own country over the years. "Being a discerning reader is sufficient to prove that the history of Colombian letters since colonial times can be reduced to three or four worthy works."[50] His own reluctance to see Aracataca or Macondo as either metaphoric or microcosmic notwithstanding, this opinion of Colombian literature represents a statement on that of Latin America. Thus García Márquez belongs in the first rank of this generation of writers who found fault not only with history but with literature as well. Quantity of publication did not assure quality of literature over the course of a century and a half of national existence, he insisted.

Writers should not write novels just to get them published (or translated for that matter), they should above all write well, he argued: "This is my commitment."[51] Latin American writers were the only ones who could accurately portray their region. Few foreigners could ever grasp the complexities of Latin America's historicity. The French, for example—and here the Colombian master differs sharply from both Carpentier and Fuentes—appeared committed to fitting Latin America into a European mold, thus completely misinterpreting it. Europeans ignored the fact that it had taken centuries of struggles, war, bloodshed, and tragedy for their own continent to reach its current level of civilization and culture, after all.[52] Latin America's history was no more fantastic than Europe's; it was just closer to the present—creating an illusion that it was of short duration, newly constricted, as it were, through the dynamics of cataclysm.

The United States and its in-country lackeys throughout the region were no more acceptable than French intellectuals. Official national security policies, so popular throughout the Boom era, dictated that the real enemies of modernization and socioeconomic stability were none other than the people.[53] With friends like European intellectuals and U.S. policymakers, who needed enemies? he might have asked.

Needless to say, García Márquez's national-level exemplar for Latin America was Castro's Cuba. No remaking in a European mold there; no foreign-imposed national security-militarist tyranny either. Nor any undue restrictions on freedom of artistic or literary expression—despite the celebrated, enforced recantation of dissident poet Heberto Padilla in 1971. No, Cuba was far from an extension of Soviet influence.[54] What made Cuba different, exemplary for the rest of the region? Its immunity from outside manipulation—after the Castroite triumph of 1959, that is, made it, in theory, more sovereign than any other country of the region. So it seemed to the Colombian in the early 1980s, even though he allowed that same year that the Cuban Communist Party was beginning to resemble Eastern European counterparts.[55] This already had created problems for other writers, but should not be sufficient cause for anyone to openly criticize the Castro regime, he thought.

His responses to follow-up queries about the writer's historical and political views are more tightly intertwined than those of either Carpentier or Fuentes, and theirs are hardly compartmentalized. García Márquez may turn out to be to Latin American letters something like what José Maria Eça de Queiroz (1845–1900) was to Portuguese letters a century ago. Both were journalists, raconteurs. Carpentier's and Fuentes's diplomatic posts link them both to the Portuguese provocateur and iconoclast as well, but it is the journalist's touch that draws the Colombian closer to Eça.

As a journalist García Márquez has always reported what he sees, but his commitment to the writer's role has led him also to get on paper what he feels. He wrote, for example, in 1982 (in an essay on fellow Colombian novelist Alvaro Mutis), that "if we really were doing what historically corresponds [to our generation] we would be seriously investigating whether or not Bolívar really was a good general, if Santander really was 'the Man of Law,' as he was called."[56] *The General in His Labyrinth* can be seen in this light as investigative fictional history: a journalist's novel as well as a novelist's history.

García Márquez's ability to mix the fictive and the real makes it impossible to know where lies the line between the two, according to one critic.[57] This being the case, his work might be considered a long-awaited continuation of Spanish literary tradition interrupted following the publication of *Don Quijote,* the same kind of continuation alluded to earlier in this chapter. Corsi-ricorsi again becomes a construct to keep in mind when contemplating fictional history as revisionism effected through revitalization of old literary forms. Writing on García Márquez, Vargas Llosa would also insinuate pointedly that novelists are rebels out to correct, pillage, and assassinate reality, whichever suits their purposes.[58] So much for journalistic or historical objectivity, what a boon to fictional history, and what a comparison to postmodern revisionism.

Only an investigative novelist could report that Cuba's Angolan adventure of the 1970s was a great victory for the Cuban Revolution. Only García Márquez could claim with credibility that "inside information" had convinced him that Cuba's clamping down on dissident writers was justifiable, and that U.S. policy was the principal reason for domestic unrest in Central America. He did all these things in his journalistic writings.

His investigative bent (and, make no mistake about it, I do not view such as detrimental to the quality of his fiction, nor to the seriousness of his thought and self-perception), also induced him to comment even further on the reasons behind the writer's fulfillment of a political or social role. "Writing is a suicidal craft," he said in 1979. Time, effort, commitment—none of these could be measured on the basis of immediate rewards. Readers never pondered what writers went through, "what the cost in anguished hours and domestic calamities is to the author."[59] Only a perceptive reader or critic would be as interested in cause and effect as García Márquez.

The 1979 Sandinista victory in Nicaragua drew his journalistic attention there, just as it did Antonio Skármeta's novelistic interest. U.S. and Somocista causes of the Sandinista effect led the Colombian to question whether or not there could ever be any kind of national defense force that was not parasitically attached to its own population and dependent on foreign influence simultaneously.[60] He was not optimistic about such a change in civil-military relations occurring unless Latin Americans (e.g., Nicaraguans) could free both themselves and their military from dependence on a single source for military training and materiel (i.e., the U.S.).

García Márquez has been no less an assiduous devourer of others' fiction than Carpentier or Fuentes. The discerning reader will find in his works traces of *Oedipus Rex, Amadís,* and *El Lazarillo de Tormes,* of Daniel Defoe, Edgar Rice Burroughs, Joseph Conrad, Antoine de Saint-Exupéry, Arthur Rimbaud, Franz Kafka, Graham Greene, Ernest Hemingway, James Joyce, Virginia Woolf, and, of course,

William Faulkner. He would admit to none of these himself—except the last.

The Colombian claimed to have discovered analogies between his own works and Faulkner's, especially geographic ones, only upon traveling in the American South, after he had written about Macondo.[61] Elsewhere he also dismissed any identity of Macondo with the Garden of Eden or Latin America as fictions of critics' minds: no consciousness of revisionism for this collisionist, spontaneity and serendipity, rather. He also admitted to having few confreres in the effort to write any grand Latin American novel, allusions to which can be found in the nonfiction publications of most of the major figures of the era. Occasionally he has deigned to associate himself with Carpentier, Cortázar, Donoso, and Fuentes.

In order to create his Patriarch he readily admitted to less than spontaneity and originality in his quest to portray the quintessential strong man. Like Carpentier he combined historical characters. To write *El otoño del patriarca* he read up on the likes of Duvalier, Francia, El Salvador's Maximiliano Hernández Martínez, and especially Venezuela's Juan Vicente Gómez. His "ode to the solitude of power" represented the "only mythological personage produced in Latin America, and his historical era is far from its end."[62] Dictators, he would note in various essays and articles written in the 1980s, and anthologized in 1991, were caught in "traps of power," mesmerized "by their own existence," convinced that paralysis by terror meant peace, and that their own words automatically became the truth.[63] Writing about dictators, fictional or not, was indeed like writing "a story of generals who came to believe their own lies." Examples of such characters abound in Latin American historical scholarship well into the early twenty-first century.

The Colombian master's journalistic talents have made him no less a fictional historian than the Cuban or the Mexican diplomatists discussed here. His discussions of Macondo's lack of metaphoric stature make him no less a collisionist—if only because they make readers think long and hard. The epic qualities of his work place it alongside that of Carpentier and Fuentes as fictional history at its best. His commitment to writing well, educating his readers, and participation in the creation and molding of Latin American identity and opinion involve him deeply in collisions with history—whether or not his words lead us to believe he might want to stand alone.

Augusto Roa Bastos (1917–)

So much Latin American fiction draws its inspiration from epic and scripture. *The Iliad, The Odyssey,* and the Old Testament have had as much effect on modern writers as they did on sixteenth-century epicists and chroniclers. Along with Cervantes's great work, *Amadís,* and the fifteenth-century Catalan masterpiece *Tirant lo Blanc,* they surely have influenced the thinking of Augusto Roa Bastos, the Paraguayan. Of the four novelists considered in this chapter he alone lived abroad perforce, not by choice. And, like Julio Cortázar, discussed first in the following chapter, Roa Bastos would emphatically acknowledge exile as a creative, positive force equal, in its contribution to creative writing, to that of a more stress-free life at home.

His immediate contributions to our virtual inquiry would be couched in both historical and experientially political terms from the outset, and he would be blunt in his commentary on the historian's craft. There could have been no Paraguayan literature (little enough though there is) had there been no political exiles.

Present-day writers, he said back in 1965, had not only recognized their literature as atrophied, but they were taking notice of the reasons why.[64] He maintained an independent stand for himself on the Cuban Revolution (and recommended this for all members of his literary generation). Exiled Cubans were political orphans too, after all. His cautious stance on ideology and revolution places Roa Bastos closer to Fuentes than to either Carpentier or García Márquez. Writers were by nature revolutionary, he believed;[65] a writer of fiction should not have to swear allegiance to any movement or party to prove his adherence to an ideology—or to justify his efforts.

Along with Carpentier, Fuentes, and García Márquez, Roa Bastos believed that Latin American literature had begun with the epics and chronicles of the sixteenth century. Contemporary writers had inherited the responsibility of describing Latin America—through fiction. The novel had become "the literature of a society in formation," the only way in which history of indigenous peoples could be related,[66] and was the contemporary epic form to boot. Until recently, Roa Bastos noted in this same source, the novel had been the genre of the bourgeoisie; as such it had propounded a distorted vision of reality. The "new narrative" of the 1960s, however, revealed not only a change in literary approaches to dealing with societies in formation, but provided a more realistic view of history than any other activity of an intellectual nature.

Exile, travel, living abroad all gave a (politicized) writer the necessary distance from which to view Latin American reality through a prism. A "transcultural duality" made it easier for contemporary novelists to see reality. One of his favorite examples of this duality stemming from forced exile was the work of the Brazilian, Darcy Ribeiro, of whom more to come in the next chapter.

Economic and social underdevelopment and dependency had produced an underdeveloped and dependent literature in Latin America, the Paraguayan said in 1979. Nowadays Europeans were marveling at the "blooming" of Latin American literature—the Boom. "Critics see it [us] as revolutionary. It is accorded praise and distinction in bourgeois academic centers. We cultured Latin Americans boast of it with pride."[67] Roa Bastos warned that any tendency toward discreet identification or labeling of his generation was tantamount to the creation of an intellectual "mandarinate," something with which he did not want to be associated—but nevertheless is.

What distinguished contemporary fiction from the past was its content, he insisted. Its "mestizo character" revealed the most unpleasant aspects of the region and its history: domination from without and from above. Lest he be seen as entirely driven by a specific theory base, as portions of his increasingly comprehensive response to questions about the Boom and its participants might lead one to suspect, the Paraguayan denied any influence of the social sciences on his work.[68] Latin America itself dictated the manner in which a Latin American writer would see, hence write of the region. Fiction became to Roa Bastos the only genre through which to depict the real Latin America. Novelists of the present were "attacking and demystifying historiography, and taking it upon themselves to make history."[69] Even so, he admitted, the literature of the Boom generation still lagged behind the establishment of the objective conditions that cried out for depiction.

It is hard to imagine Roa Bastos being able to admit to a thoroughly satisfying relationship with history or the social sciences under conditions that obtained in Paraguay, at least until the fall of Alfredo Stroessner in 1989.[70] The necessary objective conditions, for him, would have to be those devoid of internal influences characteristic of authoritarian systems and external constraints of the capitalist world system.

Lest the reader (either of Roa Bastos's fiction, these pages, or both) wonder as to the possibility of a Marxist tinge to the Paraguayan's literary-political worldview, consider his statement of 1982 about the Boom. The phenomenon, he claimed, was all over, "dead."[71] The works of Cortázar, García Márquez, Fuentes, and Vargas Llosa did indeed constitute a flowering of literature, but the big multinational publishing houses had become intoxicated with their successes, and had begun to "discover" and promote lesser-known and lesser-talented authors indiscriminately. The Boom had been captured by entrepreneurs. It had become a capitalist endeavor. Established writers were being marketed as much as they were critically acclaimed; lesser known authors were encouraged to imitate, and were being treated as clones. Capitalism was prohibiting Latin American literature from realizing its full potential; individual writers could hope to become no better than those who had imitated European literature for decades. This is as much an attack on capitalism for its negative economic and social impact on the region as for its cultural impact.

Roa Bastos believed he was not alone in understanding the overarching effect of multinational publishers and their counterparts in the world capitalist system: The U.S. Department of Defense and the Central Intelligence Agency.[72] These forces corrupted both politics and literature, hindered the development of objective conditions for revolution (i.e., inevitably favorable to it), and kept Latin America underdeveloped and dependent. He knew he was not alone in championing the cause of a region and its history by writing works of fiction.[73] His own country's literature was without a past; without a past there could be no history; without a history there could be no future.[74] His country had no identity. Its linguistic and ethnic dichotomies denied it a literature of either the past or the present, thus kept it from establishing a historical identity. Paraguay's conflicting oral (indigenous) and written (Euro-Paraguayan) traditions (by extension, Latin America's) denied any sociopolitical cohesion. Only the establishment of truly national literature could give Paraguay's history the identity it needed for sovereignty and legitimacy to flourish there. Only a severe reduction of foreign influence could make for the establishment of a truly national literature and culture.

In one of his several published interviews, the Paraguayan commented to Carlos Fuentes (who, it will be remembered, alluded to such a comment coming from García Márquez, who, it will be remembered, virtually disassociated himself from such speculation) that Latin American writers were writing different chapters of the same grand novel all at the same time.[75] In this 1988 interview he added that the grand novel "is an amalgam in formation (. . . a nebula in gestation)." This nebula (either cause or effect of cataclysmic and spiral history?), this amalgam, ought to be considered as more than just *the*

Latin American novel in process. It may be considered Latin American history's Big Bang. For some it is still to be written, for others the necessary ingredients are still not clearly discerned.

Involved in the great enterprise of fictional history, according to Roa Bastos, were Fernando Alegría, Arguedas, Borges, Cabrera Infante, Carpentier, Cortázar, Donoso, Jorge Edwards, Fuentes, García Márquez, Lezama Lima, Onetti, Ribeiro, Rulfo, Ernesto Sábato, Sarduy, and Vargas Llosa.[76] As the names reappear in these pages, the contours of the Boom, and of its fictional history, as designed by novelists, become even more discernible to readers from beyond the region. So does the multifaceted configuration of the third historical cataclysm in Latin America, the recent past.

Given Roa Bastos's opinions on the nature of the Boom and its participants, his thought on the sociocultural role of writers and on history and politics should come as no surprise. It is already evident that he did not separate any writer's role from the politics and history of a homeland, much less from that of the region.

Mainly concerned as they were with the clash of culture and civilization, those who chronicled such momentous events as discovery and conquest had not provided readers with a history that gave equal weight to the indigenous populations affected by discovery and conquest. (Nor have novelists, for that matter.) Roa Bastos asserted that most historians also were more concerned with narrative history, as it was written until the eighteenth century, not analytical history as written (after Vico, this means), especially from the nineteenth century forward. Geography and events were more important than ideas, dynastic and chronological history more important than intellectual and cultural development, to most historians, he thought.

Once the land (read Paraguay) had succumbed to European invaders, a clash of cultures began, and social and economic dichotomies took form.[77] History and literature were the results, at first as one and the same genre, later to become distinct, but neither genre truly represented Paraguay. In Paraguay the result of invasion was a "phantasmagorical reality" comparable to that of any other Latin American country, but after five centuries of ethnic division more plainly the product of elitist government and politics.[78] Like Peru, Mexico, and Brazil, homelands of some of the writers discussed in these chapters, Paraguay had an "Indian problem." This was part and parcel of phantasmagorical history: Paraguayan *un*reality. It prohibited history and literature from flourishing as anything more than elitist pastimes.

Paraguay's "problem" meant that the majority of the population existed apart from the dominant culture, unable to read the creative works of a scant few Euro-Paraguayan literary figures. This problem kept reality marginalized and perpetuated unreality. Roa Bastos recognized this as a regional phenomenon too, problem or not. Only in Cuba, he claimed back in 1967, was literature really directed to the masses, thereby giving them a place within both the dominant culture, the hegemonic social sector, and the received history of the nation. Everywhere else in Latin America writers were still read only by the "bourgeoisie and petite bourgeoisie, for the most part, and to a lesser degree by the most advanced nuclei of the proletariat."[79] Nothing failed like success in Roa Bastos's literary universe. Unless writers directed themselves to the masses, their efforts, however critically acclaimed, fell short of quality and lacked legitimacy. Writing well (García Márquez's goal) was not enough. Nor were being translated, increased sales, or the notoriety of activism.

Writers and intellectuals who did direct themselves to defense of the downtrodden often found themselves in political trouble—and devoid of a market. They became exiles and had to communicate from afar. This gave them perspective, of course, but denied them their roots. In his own case Roa Bastos's residence in Buenos Aires was like a "double exile": both from Euro-Paraguay and from its Guaraní-speaking population. And it was to the last that he wanted to direct his work.[80] And they were a "problem," geographically and historically isolated from the rest of the world.

The dearth of Paraguayan (or Latin American) historical literature was rendered all the more a dearth owing to its neglect of the indigenous population's history. Valued from the onset of colonization for their physical stamina as laborers, the Indians of Paraguay were considered impediments to modernization half a millennium later: quaint, mysterious, primitive at best.[81] The dominant culture of the minority denied the subordinate majority culture historical and literary presence. Hence literature's dearth in Paraguay.

Writers and intellectuals of the past century had disdained themes and topics that might have hastened the onset of objective conditions, and foreign interests had abetted this disdain, claimed Roa Bastos. Paraguayans—all Paraguayans—lived in a cultural limbo between life and nonlife.[82] Capitalism and dictatorship had distorted both history and literature. "In my opinion," he told Alain Sicard in 1979, "history is not that history written by [cultural elites] and their scribes and notaries. Official historiography, legitimized by juridical guarantee of documentation, has always constituted a privilege of the conquerors and dominators. I have no respect for it."[83] If this reminds readers of Roa Bastos's fictional Dr. Francia, it should. Only in a legitimate literature could the reality of Paraguayan history be revealed objectively and equitably to the eyes of all. Paraguay's historians either could not or would not do this in their own work.

Roa Bastos found Dr. Francia to be more historically real than any other historical national figure. It comes as no surprise, therefore, that Roa Bastos should have so clearly spoken his mind on historians, lawyers, government functionaries, the clergy, and the military through Francia. No less surprising were his choices of the two novels that most correctly portray Latin America historically (and which ought to be read together): Conrad's *Nostromo* (1904), a reasonable choice, and Ramón del Valle Inclán's study of caudillism, *Tirano Banderas* (1926), both written by Europeans.[84] In a figurative if not literal sense were not those writers also exiles?

The essence of Paraguay's fraudulent history, its national nonlife, lay in the politics of state. Since the late nineteenth century the government had been controlled by an alliance of army and civilian leaders who ran the elitist, symbiotic Colorado Party. The latest representative of this unholy symbiosis was General Alfredo Stroessner, who presided over the riverine nation from 1954 until 1989.[85] U.S. interests, Roa Bastos thought, supported this military-civilian symbiosis in order to maintain a base of operations in case of social or political instability in Argentina, Brazil, or the Andes. Paraguay was a historical military outpost of imperialism, distorting its history to an even greater degree. It bears remembering that Paraguay remains a keystone state in U.S. security designs for South America, and that the Colorado Party is still a force to reckon with.

By the mid-1980s Roa Bastos's literary achievements had created for him an audience in both Europe and Latin America, and he was now urging his countrymen to take action against the symbionts: Stroessner and the Colorados.[86] Literature and those who created it could no more be neutral than could art, politics, technology, or science and their creators. All were instruments of change, even in Paraguay.

"I have fustigated the regime and its leader, and I will continue doing it without malevolence or rancor, for at stake are not personal matters, but rather the totality of collective life whose sovereignty has been usurped."[87] Democracy, Roa Bastos insisted, was surely as possible in Paraguay as it was in Spain after Franco, in Argentina following the end of the military government in 1983, or in Brazil after the devolution of leadership upon civilians in 1985. Fifty years after the end of the Chaco War was a good time to prove it in Paraguay. Until recently democracy had been only a "utopian aspiration" of the majority.[88] Their valiant efforts to establish national sovereignty and legitimacy notwithstanding, Paraguayans of the past had reaped few political or social rewards; those of the present were reaping fewer still. The troglodytic General Stroessner had no right to claim either Francia's or the Lópezes' mantle.[89] His regime was a parody of those of the nineteenth-century tyrant-nationalists, who, despite their excesses, Roa Bastos would have us believe, were nation builders. It was time for action.

Like Fuentes, Roa Bastos viewed the quincentennial as a "rediscovery" (*encounter* he considered a euphemistic attempt at camouflage). It was the most important event of the millennium owing to its geographical, economic, and historical implications for the entire world.[90] Its coming was auspicious for it might signal the beginning of an era of rediscovery (not re*encounter*) and integration, a "new order" in which Spain (now democratic, after all), Spanish America, Portugal (democratic as well), and Brazil might finally establish mutually beneficial relations.[91] Despite the stagnation of official history, a collective memory, increasingly shared dominant cultures, and democratization might just serve as the bases for intraregional cooperation for the benefit of the majority. What had begun badly back in the sixteenth century just might end well after all, Roa Bastos allowed.

The principal agent of historical change might just be, he posited strategically in 1986, the military. "It is reasonable to suppose that the military, responsible in the final analysis for the integrity and continuity of the nation, will assume, the moment having arrived, the appropriate stance at this historical crossroads for the country," he cautiously put it.[92] This cannot be taken as advocacy per se of a military role in future politics. Rather, Roa Bastos believed that the military's desire for self-preservation would guide the profession's leaders. They would find Stroessner expendable, he hoped. His hopes would be realized, but not without more than a decade of difficulties.

I know of no cogent argument that links Roa Bastos's writings to the ouster of Stroessner. Roa Bastos would not claim, as did the Ecuadoran writer Juan Montalvo (1832–1889), speaking about Gabriel García Moreno: "*Mi pluma lo mató.*" García Moreno's presidencies (1861–65, 1869–75) masked tyranny no better than did Stroessner's long tenure, and in the end (as with most tyrannies) a combination of elements brought them down, not anyone's pen. The Paraguayan author's exhortations did not fall entirely on deaf ears, though. He had assessed the 1980s correctly. "Writing is the instrument of power, and the spoken word is the instrument of the people," he said in a 1988 interview.[93] Both have had an impact in Latin America owing to collisions with history. Carpentier, Fuentes, and García Márquez would agree, I think.

THE FOUR AUTHORS discussed in this chapter, each of whose literary work is an important component of fictional history, are tacitly agreed that *something* called the Boom existed, that it was a quantifiable and qualitative phenomenon. Its cultural and commercial characteristics evoked no unanimity, but the naming of others involved in the flowering of fiction in the late twentieth century recognized by Carpentier, Fuentes, García Márquez, and Roa Bastos leads us further toward a conclusion that a generation did exist. Whether revolutionary or reformist, certainly didactic, distrustful of authority and dependence, these authors had a lot in common. The Boom was the vector for their commonality, collisions with history their intent, making history between the lines one of their legacies.

They all saw themselves as educators, communicators, ideologues, nationalists, revisionists, and rebels to one degree or another. The consensus on a sociocultural role for writers—intellectuals or no—is solid. Carpentier and Fuentes come across as highly sophisticated intellectuals owing to their composite responses in our virtual interrogatory; García Márquez and Roa Bastos reveal themselves as more ideological and spontaneously brilliant in theirs.

Each was committed—here the past tense is used to emphasize that they are seen as representative of the recent past—to the struggle against underdevelopment, authoritarianism, dependency, and undue ideological influence from outside the region. All were critical of the United States, singling it out as the dominant foreign influence on Latin American history (replacing the Iberian monarchies, thus assuming their negative historical status). Fuentes evinced a greater admiration for the democratic achievements of North Americans (always has done); Roa Bastos delivered the harshest, most consistent criticism.

All four viewed history as something that either needed to be revealed or revised, owing either to the way it had been written or to the control of its definition by foreigners and elites. All collided with history from between the lines, as here shown, just as they did in their fictional histories. Like those who follow, they saw something both tragic and of value in exile and familiarity with other cultures that enhanced their writing.

A question goes begging: Would they agree with this synthesis of their thought and self-perception? Clearly, their commentary as here recorded corroborates conclusions made in the first three chapters, so I think the synthesized conclusions reached here are just as sound. Fictional historians surely would agree with them as much as would any historical figures about whom conclusions are reached based on investigation, interpretation, and documentation.

Martí would have been gratified to know that literature would one day afford Latin American writers a pillory precisely when their nations needed it most. If doubts exist as to the intent of Boom novelists, their thought and self-perception directed to themes and topics of historical and contemporary import confirm it. The commentary of the writers discussed in this chapter and the next reads like a collective effort to displace intellectually the worst aspects of Latin America in favor of its best. It fortifies conclusions reached on cataclysmic history in the first three chapters, and it helps to explain why social scientists have striven to constrict history.

Chapter 5

The Commentary of Cortázar, Allende, Vargas Llosa, and Ribeiro

> There can be a "boom" in petroleum or wheat, but there can't be a
> boom in the novel and less still in poetry.
> —Octavio Paz, *Seven Voices* (1972)

SOON AFTER HE took power, Fidel Castro admonished Cuban intellectuals thus: "Within the revolution, everything; against the revolution, nothing."[1] What he meant was that writers had every right, indeed had an obligation to participate in the Cuban Revolution, but no right to deny its legitimacy. Criticism was one thing; opposition quite another. The revolution itself had rights, and to oppose it was to violate those rights. Being against the revolution was being outside the law and against the future.

In an island country long manipulated by the hemispheric superpower, definition of history and of culture were necessary to maintain power and assure the success of revolutionary programs. This was the revolution's own historical obligation. Had more governments in the region attempted with revolutionary zeal to define history and culture, the Boom would have been even more a historical phenomenon.

Castro's discourse of 1961 makes for fascinating reading in light of the present discussion. It came at a time when intellectuals in Cuba and throughout Latin America confronted Marxism-Leninism triumphant. The ensuing Boom was partially a result of this historical confrontation, for all its members professed to scrutiny, criticism, admiration, or active support of developments in Cuba as much as those in their own countries and across the region. It will be stimulating to watch Cuban affairs in light of the Cold War's end and the changes in international affairs in social science literature as well as in fiction.

In the 1960s and 1970s novelists had to come to grips with failed democracies and looming professional militarism. Castro's pronouncement came on the eve of both the Boom and the institutional *golpes de estado* of the 1960s. However the former is interpreted—as generational phenomenon, publishers' windfall, coincidence, or grand novel-in-the-writing—we can now see that fictional history will have a profound effect on the way the region's history is written in the future.

The Boom era's sharpened focus on history brought freedom of expression under more focused scrutiny across the region. In revolutionary Cuba, La Revolución was all: dissidents beware. In the authoritarian experiences of Argentina, Brazil, Chile, Peru, Bolivia, Paraguay, and Uruguay national security and "national values" were all: intellectuals watch out.

Castro said in 1961 that the only people who professed concerns about their creative liberties were those who were not yet sure of their commitment to the revolution. If one were not a revolutionary, one ran the risk of being labeled a counterrevolutionary (a little like being termed an antinationalist if one challenged traditional nationalistic views of independence, say). He received *aplausos* following his remark that "the most revolutionary artist would be he who was disposed to sacrifice even his own artistic vocation for the sake of the Revolution."[2] "He who is more the artist than the revolutionary is not capable of thinking as do we," he added. The revolution was the present—few would follow if it were just another movement promising only a better future. The revolution had rights that preempted those of individuals: the people and the nation had rights that preempted those of intellectuals. " 'What are the rights of the writers and the artists, revolutionaries or not? Within the revolution every [right]; against the revolution no rights' (APLAUSOS)."

The point here is that this same mentality (or something very close to it) prevailed among the South American professional militarists and Caribbean strongmen—with minor adjustments for ideology or dearth thereof. It helps to make even more clear the Boom's significance as a historical phenomenon, its appeal to a wide range of writers and readers alike. Throughout the region the individual, the dissenter, could be the enemy—of the state or the revolution, or of the standard historiographical status quo perpetuated by those in power. That Cuban artists and writers since the early days of the revolution have been able to get away with somewhat more than Castro's dicta would imply goes without saying. Only in revolutionary Cuba, let it be remembered, could a publication like *Casa de las Américas* have exerted the influence it obviously did, when it did, on writers from other Latin American countries.

Commentators dealt with in this chapter were writers every bit as concerned with history as the subjects of the preceding one were interested in politics. But I have chosen to deal more with the political and social science foci of Cortázar, Allende, Vargas Llosa, and Ribeiro in order to provide a continuity to lead readers forward to the discussion of social science's collisions with history in chapter 6. Cortázar, Allende, Vargas Llosa, and Ribeiro form a transitional set that enables the discussion of social science's constriction of history in the late twentieth century.

Nearly twenty years after Castro attempted to establish ground rules for artistic orthodoxy, a symposium at the Woodrow Wilson International Center in Washington, D.C., would address the phenomenon of the Boom.[3] Well-known authors and critics like David Viñas, Angel Rama, Jean Franco, Jacques Leenhardt, Jorge Aguilar Mora, Edmundo Desnoes, and Antonio Skármeta discussed many of the topics already mentioned in the present work. Tulio Halperín Donghi, a historian, claimed that Latin American participants in the "new narrative" movement had an easier time "navigating the rapids of a feverishly convulsed history" than had Latin American social scientists, with few exceptions.[4] History was in danger of being seen as irrelevant by those who sought solutions to contemporary problems. Within a couple of decades after Castro's address to Cuban intellectuals, this is to say, history was being viewed as the cause of these same problems by writers of fiction. The politics of democracy and civilian government were seen as causes, too, rather than solutions, in countries where La Revolución did not mean all things to all people.

According to Alain Touraine, a society that defines itself solely by its political identity and uniqueness (its legitimacy, its sovereignty?) cannot be a democratic society. Such societies are often characterized by oppressive state mechanisms that claim to be the expression of the nation. They can be as stiflingly nationalistic as they are stridently ideological. The most effective resistance to authoritarianism in Touraine's opinion is cultural resistance. This is as important as political resistance or class opposition.[5] Where culture manifests itself in literary form, it might follow, literature can be an effective form of resistance—lest that literature be proscribed, of course. In such a case writers (Roa Bastos certainly comes to mind here) must carry on their resistance from beyond the borders of their homeland, maybe even from beyond the confines of their fiction.

And this is what Latin American novelists were doing. In another place Touraine also noted that capitalism had come to be seen as the primary vehicle of cultural imperialism instead of being seen as just a vehicle for domination of the working class.[6] This permeated their thought and self-perception as well, we have seen, especially when it came to defining the Boom, thus assuring its legitimacy.

Working classes in developing areas have benefited only marginally from capitalism/imperialism in the way Víctor Raúl Haya de la Torre and Apristas thought they could: through imperialism as a first step of capitalist development. Following both on Touraine and Haya, capitalism (i.e., penetration by the U.S.) should be construed as either the alternative to socialism (*statism* might be a less charged word here) or as the agent for domination of entire societies and cultures. Experiences with institutionalized authoritarianism of Argentines, Brazilians, Chileans, and Peruvians, and the economic and cultural influence of the United States throughout the region, vividly colored the thinking of Cortázar, Allende, Vargas Llosa, and Ribeiro. Authoritarianism and the looming U.S. influence were not quite synonymous; socialism was only nearly a panacea.

"Fiction," in Derrida's words, "gives *in principle* the power to say everything, to break free of the rules, to displace them, and thereby to institute, to invent and even to suspect the traditional difference between nature and institution, nature and conventional law, nature and history."[7] ("Within fiction everything; outside fiction. . . .") Power, and freedom from rules, were claimed by adherents to Castro's regime in Cuba, by defenders of professional militarism in South America, and by intellectuals throughout the region: the first two groups in order to rule, the last in order to oppose. History really was up for grabs in the political arena now.

Conflicting if similar claims to political and philosophical legitimacy have characterized struggles for power throughout Latin American history. Literature's forces of opposition in exile, as noted in the preceding chapter, have at times been criticized themselves for being outsiders, for having lost touch owing to forced or self-imposed sojourns abroad. But outsiders, we know all too well, have always been agents of change, whether cultural, political, or social.

In his "Region and Class in the Novel" Raymond Williams pointed out that even "a class can indeed be seen as a region: a social area inhabited by people of a certain kind, living in certain ways."[8] A novelist with a mission, in other words, can indeed write about workers without having a book or story devalued owing to its bourgeois origins. English industrial novels of the nineteenth century were written by "visitors" to such "regions," just as the *indigenista* novels of Latin America would be. Novelists, as we are in the process of seeing, often have functioned vicariously as social scientists. Social scientists, as this chapter shows, can write novels.

Now is a good time to ask if literature (prose fiction, for our purposes) is a genuine reflection of sociocultural conditions, of history. Or were Boom novelists just making it up as they went along? Are their views contorted by their intellectuality, their social origins, their worldliness, their desire for sales? Is what they have left us a better view of history and contemporary conditions, or does it merely confirm our suspicions and prejudices? Does it distort? Were the Latin Americans really at war with their past and present, and are they still, or will they be again? Each of these chapters in part 2 adumbrates answers to such questions through their examinations of fictional history and the thought and self-perception of its writers. Definitive answers will come, both from the fiction and the commentary of the future.

Octavio Paz was perhaps the most intellectually optimistic Latin American of the twentieth century. He once spoke of his times as ones of "frenetic immobility" in which Latin Americans had "ceased to recognize ourselves in the future." The evolution of entire regions, he thought, was simultaneous in social and literary terms, but not at all synchronized in others.[9]

What Paz and the novelists who were both his contemporaries and coevals wrote about for decades is an Invertebrate America, an America whose historical corsi-ricorsi have been at odds—within the region and in relation to the rest of the world. "A literature is a history," Paz said, "within the vast history that every civilization, every language, and every society constitutes."[10] Perhaps it is for this reason he did not believe there could be any such thing as a boom in literature.

At the same time, Paz opined, literature is outside historical causality and cannot be entirely understood solely using economic, political, and social approaches. As a manifestation of culture, one is to infer from this, fictional history stands apart from, parallel to, but not wholly involved with, history. There is some substance to such an argument, as self-serving as it sounds, precisely because it is at odds with most of those offered here: Within intellectuality everything. . . .

Novelists are products of history and of their times, just as are historians and social scientists. I think it is more than some coincidences and market dictates that gave rise to something called the Boom. Just as there are no immutable laws of history, there are no monocausal explanations of why members of a generation have so much in common, yet are unique. Unless, that is, such a generation is a part of history's flux, has a historical consciousness, and its members recognize both their collective and individual significance. The commentary of the four novelists featured in this chapter supports this conclusion and supplements that of the previous chapter.

Julio Cortázar was born in 1914 in Brussels. Following the Great War his family returned to Argentina. He resided there until 1951, when he left for Paris, where he lived until his death in 1984. He was a militant defender of both the Cuban and Nicaraguan revolutionary movements. His inventive narrative forms have struck some critics as unrepresentative of Latin American fiction, and others as just the opposite. Cortázar needs no case made for his Latin Americanness, unless this quality can be defined more accurately than it has been to date.

Isabel Allende was born in Peru, nearly thirty years after Cortázar, in 1942. Like Carlos Fuentes's, Allende's father served in his country's diplomatic corps. In her youth she worked as a journalist in Santiago. Following the overthrow of her kinsman Salvador Allende Gossens, she left Chile for Caracas. She continued to work in journalism until she published her first novel, *La casa de los espíritus,* in 1982. Its success in translation (*The House of the Spirits*) and that of her 1984 novel, *De amor y de sombra* (*Of Love and Shadows*), in which she displays her journalistic expertise in a tightly written, moving portrayal of professional militarism in control of a fictional, thinly disguised Chile, elevated her to international stature. In 1989 she moved to the United States.

Mario Vargas Llosa was born in Peru in 1936 and spent much of his youth in Bolivia and the northern coastal city of San Miguel de Piura. He attended Colegio Militar Leoncio Prado in Lima, making of it a sociocultural microcosm of Peru in his first novel, *La ciudad y los perros* (1962). Known in English as *The Time of the Hero*, it established his reputation overnight. As a college student in Peru he involved himself in socialist activities, but steered clear of communism because of its restraining effects on creative expression. He traveled to France as a young man, and earned a doctorate from the University of Madrid with a thesis on the Colombian Gabriel García Márquez. In 1959 he moved to Paris and spent time in England and the United States as well. He lived in Europe again following his unsuccessful bid for the presidency of his native land in 1990, but returned to Lima in late 2000, following the resignation of Fujimori, his old foe.

Darcy Ribeiro was born in 1922 in the state of Minas Gerais. An anthropologist, he did field work in Amazonas, worked for UNESCO, and helped found the Indian Museum in Rio de Janeiro. In 1961 he became first rector of the new University of Brasília; a year later he was named minister of education and culture in the administration of João Goulart. When Goulart fell in 1964, Ribeiro left Brazil for Uruguay, where he was a professor of anthropology. He returned to Brazil a decade later, and by the time professional militarists left power in 1985, he was a senator for Rio. Ribeiro was better known as a well-published anthropologist than as a novelist. His best novel, *Maíra* (1978), evinces more social scientific than literary inspiration. He died in 1997. There are Brazilian novelists whose works are better known and appreciated for their literary merit; there is no Brazilian, let alone Latin American, whose works, fictional or no, better finalize the transition of collisions with history to the realm of social science.

Julio Cortázar (1914–1984)

Cortázar's immediate response to queries about his work, who figured in the Boom, the roles of the artist, and his historical and political viewpoints would contradict much of that already recorded in these pages. He spent so much of his life in Europe that he is often regarded as more French than Argentine, and admitted to uneasiness with the term *latinoamericano,* for he did not think Iberia or the Mediterranean had influenced the region's cultural development all alone.[11] His initial response also would be more stridently ideological than any of the novelists dealt with thus far, his responses to individual queries less discernible from each other—the distance between his fiction and commentary less than any other of the novelists discussed herein.

Cortázar claimed to have discovered himself, this is to say, by discovering his *other.* As for the existence of a distinct Latin American narrative style, he once opined that so many Latin Americans were involved in writing (in 1971 this was) that it was hardly worth consideration. But, he allowed, what was going on in the region might yet come to be compared with Spain's own protracted literary boom, the Siglos de Oro.[12] The Boom, he thought, was neither a product of publishers nor of editors out to make a profit, but a multinational phenomenon, more spontaneous than associated with a specific genre, authors, or specific works.

"Publishers and editors did not make the Boom, Latin American readers made it, and this in my opinion . . . was a revolutionary development in Latin America of the last fifteen years. It was a . . . formidable collective consciousness raising throughout the continent, concerned with our existence on the intellectual and literary plane."[13] Here didacticism is at work: readers respond to writers, the emerging consciousness of identity is a revolutionary synthesis, a teaching-learning experience. Far from serving the interests of capitalist publishers and booksellers, he added, translation of Brazilian and Spanish

American fiction was giving the world a better idea of "what we are, what we desire, and what we are searching for—even better, what we are going to accomplish." Fictional history, this is like saying, was serving a grand purpose.

Cortázar lamented his own fate. His voluntary exile from Argentina— he was not forced to leave Buenos Aires, and primarily aroused the ire of professional militarists there because of his pro-Castro and pro-Sandinista activities abroad—made him a cultural exile. He was a man cut off from his roots.

Like Roa Bastos and Vargas Llosa, he would miss his homeland, would resent his absence from it, and would blame both authoritarianism and lack of a learned and appreciative readership for his lack of popularity at home. He sympathized with those whose works were burned or banned, who could not return home, or who were kept from writing by state-sponsored intimidation.[14] Needless to say, he did not point any accusatory fingers at Cuba or Castro for censure or censorship in the name of revolutionary legitimacy.

Nonetheless, he claimed in 1978 that some of the Boom's best, most controversial works were written from abroad if not strictly from exile. Both Vargas Llosa and García Márquez could write effectively about South America from beyond continental confines, for example. Asked about his own case, he claimed to have learned much about Latin America from the Cuban experience. There a people had thrown off history's negative legacy (Spanish colonialism, U.S. influence, personalist authoritarianism).[15] He had learned much about his own country's experience from what was going on in Chile too. There cultural genocide marked the post-Allende years.

But the exile in him missed certain things, things that defined home in other than political terms. Family, pace of life, friends, smells, colors, architecture, street scenes, museums, newspapers, food, dogs: being deprived of these was analogous to the "the sudden end of a love affair" and to the ghastly experience that formed the basis for Poe's short story "The Premature Burial."[16] He rationalized his situation by comparing it to *una beca full-time* (a full-time grant) that allowed him to concentrate on his writing, and likening it to the classic Continental tour undertaken by intellectuals in the nineteenth and early twentieth centuries.

Cortázar's sympathy for Cuban and Nicaraguan revolutionaries led him to overlook their impositions on the freedoms of intellectuals, and to criticize professional militarism's denials of these same freedoms in Argentina, Bolivia, Brazil, Chile, and Uruguay (but not Peru).[17] In Cuba almost anything was justifiable in the name of revolution anywhere, for that matter. Speaking to a Cuban audience in 1980, Cortázar asserted correctly that competition for the Casa de las Américas literary prize was an ideal vehicle for writers from Latin America and the Caribbean. Because of this competition audiences everywhere were becoming familiar with writers who until recently had been praised paternalistically in the "shadow of colonialism."[18] The Casa, the preeminent arbiter of culture in revolutionary Cuba, should lead the way, he thought, to discovery of new writers, especially those from the Southern Cone, where the sinister forces of oppression had cut off cultural communications between intellectuals through exile, incarceration, denial of civil liberties, and worse.

Cortázar had little time for Latin American colleagues who opposed socialism because of its alleged economic failures, or who failed to recognize the successes it had achieved against overwhelming odds. Intellectual shortcomings like these, he told an audience of 1980, were tantamount to an outright embrace of imperialism and "neofascism." One was either with the revolution or against it. It was as simple as that for Cortázar.

"We live in an epoch," he wrote the next year, "in which the information and communication media present us with far more than the simple facts, situating us in a more complex structure, one more deserving of our presence."[19] Latin Americans were closer to the world beyond their region than ever before; the world beyond ought to return the favor by understanding the region, the Boom, the social and political revolutions taking place there. The Boom had brought Latin America to the literary forefront. Boom authors' ideas deserved airing beyond their fiction: García Márquez, Asturias, Vargas Llosa, Lezama Lima, Fuentes, and Roa Bastos were the names the Argentine cited as most worthy of being read and listened to by both Latin America and the rest of the world.[20]

Life abroad revised his historical view as well. Socialism was, he believed, inevitable. Cortázar's ideological commitment, expressed both continuously and constantly in his commentary, led to an experiment with fiction as a teaching device. *El libro de Manuel* (1973) can be read as both a work of fiction and a political documentary of violence, oppression, and exile. It is very much a part of the cataclysmic history of the recent past.

If Cortázar's critics faulted him for being a political activist, and if socialists criticized him for his creative flamboyance, well, he cared not. His literature was his "machine gun."[21] Fiction was to Latin America's revolutions (the term is used loosely by almost all writers), he insisted, what the *Encyclopedie* was to the French Revolution, what Mao Tse-tung's poetry was to China's.

The Argentine's participation in the Bertrand Russell–sponsored tribunals on U.S. war crimes in Viet Nam (1974–75) allowed him to call for investigation into the violence in South America.[22] Both he and García Márquez were outspoken in this endeavor. Meetings of intellectuals in Brussels and Rome led to condemnation by intellectuals of military rule and dictatorship, U.S. collusion with authoritarians, violation of indigenous peoples' rights, and environmental destruction.

The Colombian, we already have ascertained, demanded that writers write well; the Argentine demanded they innovate. Innovation was revolutionary; "original" works were only those that broke with tradition, and the more the better. An author's work should reflect an author's politics boldly. Cortázar also saw himself and his innovation as inseparable from history.[23] He was a part of history; history was a part of him. The setting of a story was not important.

The story was all. Readers worldwide identified with stories more than national settings; the telluric "cultural fascism" of authoritarian regimes could not prevent this.[24]

He always wanted all things all ways, did this Argentine. In terms reminiscent of García Márquez's he once claimed he was apolitical, no better a writer than any critic, devoid of theoretical base or religious convictions.[25] Yet in the very same interview he defended revolutionary socialism as the only possible historical road forward. The novel, he would say, was nothing more than a "big trunk" that had the capacity for holding a great number of ideas.[26] That which might be deemed fantastic was often something quite routine, and was more valuable if considered so. Like ideology, literature (the novel with its trunk full of ideas) should be useful to, but not serve politics: politicians take note. The best literature was that which was useful to revolutionary purposes: Castro, Sandinistas take heart.

Literature and revolution were interrelated because Latin American culture could not flourish under the conditions of the times (the 1964–89 quarter century). Asked once about his alleged lack of concern for Argentina's own political plight, for not involving himself in it, he replied that he was indeed concerned—but more so for all Latin America.[27] Exile from Argentina may have pained him but it also freed him from commitment to the national struggle against its oppressors.

"When Pinochet burns books in the streets of Santiago, he burns not only paper, he burns the readers of the books and those who wrote them."[28] Flames that burned literally in Santiago and throughout the Southern Cone, glowed figuratively in Cuba and Nicaragua, for in the Caribbean, state-supported mass literacy campaigns brought revolutionary literature to the people instead of denying it to them.

Vargas Llosa claimed on several occasions that writers were rebels; Julio Cortázar claimed that literature was a responsibility of those gifted enough to create it.[29] Those writers who had the gift were obliged to do so—for the sake of readers—in the Southern Cone and the Caribbean both. The *vox clamantis en deserto* that once had been the Latin American writer was now the voice of the people, the collective cry against the "internal exile" of people denied access to the literature of their compatriots.[30] Literature was more than a reflection of life, it had a life of its own—just like a revolution did.

The recent novel, thought Cortázar, consisted of "projections sui generis of history, they are like flowers of a plant that cannot be ignored, in that the plant is land, nation, people, *razón de ser,* and destiny."[31] Recent fiction constituted a mass interrogatory whose questions could only be fully answered by philosophy and science. The greater the quality (revolutionary, that is) of Latin American literature, the more significant that interrogatory. "In truth," Cortázar said in 1982, "a writer is always a sort of Christopher Columbus, that is to say, someone who sets out to discover with his ships of words . . . well, the great writers discover America, but not all can claim to be Columbus."[32] Voyages of discovery in novels found in trunks laden with words and revolutionary ideas, bound for homelands that needed a new beginning: The Boom can be seen to have meant to Latin Americans of the quincentennial era what the daring feats of the Genoese mariner had meant to Europeans five centuries before.

Just as the house of Aviz once had attracted an international collection of pilots, chartmakers, and master mariners to Portugal, political conditions in Latin America now made it possible for literary and political exiles to convene (sometimes literally) on the other side of the Ocean Sea.[33] Cortázar's and Roa Bastos's France and Vargas Llosa's and Fuentes's Spain were the encounter sites of the twentieth century. Exiles and sojourners would, Cortázar thought, ultimately rediscover Latin America, through both their fiction and their advocacy.[34]

Exiles constituted an intellectual vanguard whose sense of spiral history gained strength from the perspective of forced separation.[35] Onward and upward this spiral went, with intellectuals in the lead, for linear history would not obtain where foreign influences had prevailed for so long. Cuba and Nicaragua were not enough for Julio

Cortázar; the entire region needed revolutionary rediscovery. No more simple ricorsi for this writer-activist. Julio Cortázar comes through as the most militant novelist, the most political, and the most detached from history. Nevertheless he was as historical as he was talented.

Isabel Allende (1942–)

Isabel Allende's success is so recent, in comparison with that of her fellow authors, that little perspective or historical sense comes through in her response to questions from a virtual interrogatory. Her personal experiences, rather, are a greater influence on her thinking than is the Boom itself or her consciousness of it. Hers is a deductive, intuitive, rather than a learned or ideological approach to our queries. She is a product of the Boom more than one of its makers. She is personal and political in her worldview, not historic or historical—not yet anyway.

Her inspiration to write, she claimed in a 1985 interview, was the library in the house of her grandparents, where "there were so many books there was simply no time to count them, put them in order, or even dust them all off, and they just filled up the space like some great wild flower."[36] Reading as a child and having to leave the country when in her thirties were important motivations to write fiction. As awful as Chile's 1973 experience was, she noted in the same conversation, the tragedy was really Latin America's. Like Cortázar and others, Allende saw the plight of one country as linked to that of the entire region. If history had not made an impression on this Chilean, politics certainly would.

So would the economic state of Latin America. Others—outsiders—had benefited more from economic development than had the majority of Latin Americans. Many good works of fiction, she once said, were being published in Spain, because Spanish American publishing houses, until recently, had little incentive to publish works by writers from other countries in the region: "We have no Latin American consciousness."[37] These conclusions made in the mid-1970s are clearly at odds with those of other writers made at the same time. I think this is attributable both to Allende's feminist convictions and to her lack of historical perspective, but I do not imply a cause-and-effect relationship between the two.

There has always been hope in the mind of Isabel Allende, hope for the future. Women, unlike men, might be capable of unifying Latin America; women, she would say in the mid-1980s, were "sisters whose similarities are much more important than their [national] differences." Machismo divided, she continued. "Have you ever seen anything more machista than the military mentality? It is the synthesis, the exaltation, the ultimate exaggeration of machismo. . . . There is a direct line from machismo to militarism." [38] As much as one wants to read history into such commentary, Allende's worldview was not yet that full when she first put it into words. She already showed an ability to perceive with acuity, nevertheless, and from a social science vantage point to boot. Her militarism-machismo analogy is bang on.

Allende's Boom consciousness was clearly the result of her success as a writer, neither of intellectual reflection, nor historical sense. She agreed with Fuentes, García Márquez (despite the Colombian's disclaimers), Roa Bastos, and Cortázar, for example, that she and her contemporaries were engaged in "telling the same story . . . we speak with one voice, we speak for a people, a continent, we tell the real story, different aspects of the same story."[39] She and other novelists did this, she thought, because they were able to "assault" readers with information unavailable to them from other sources. Even if fiction did not display documentation, it was a valid source of information and inspiration. Such thoughts beg the question insistently: With whom did she associate herself in such a grand endeavor? Those who had influenced her own work, she said, were Pablo Neruda, García Márquez, Vargas Llosa, Jorge Amado, Borges, Sábato, and Carpentier. She also claimed inspiration from Jules Verne, Mark Twain, George Bernard Shaw, and Charles Dickens.[40] Allende's political sympathies, not her writing, forced her to leave Chile after the military rising of 1973. She later vowed not to return until democracy was restored to her country. Democracy, after all, was like women's rights, and like writing: slow to succeed in Chile and elsewhere in the region, but worth struggling for nonetheless. She likened critics and editors to authoritarians and militarists, for the former either had ignored women's literary works or degraded their significance the way the latter still ignored human rights.[41] Tenuous analogies notwithstanding, Isabel Allende's analogies make for stimulating commentary laced with convincing arguments, especially when compared to that of Roa Bastos, Cortázar, and Vargas Llosa.

She has been equally stimulating in her commentary on U.S.-Latin American relations as analogous to those between a dominant force (male?) and a subordinate one (female?). Cultural and technological discrepancies had kept Latin America subordinate to the U.S. and other industrialized countries the way authority and force still allowed the military to dominate civilians, and men women. This is a most appealing interpretation, as sophisticated for its potential applicability to social science research as it is for its candor. It is as appropriate to the study of Latin America as are Julio Cortázar's Gramscian perambulations about literature at the service of revolutionary cultural change.

Allende claimed she would allow neither the military, nor males, nor foreign influences to dominate her or her writing—but she did respond to market demands of the late twentieth century quite successfully. Nor would her exile keep her from her life's work, claimed long-time Chilean Marxist politician Volodia Teitelboim, based on a 1989 interview.[42] By this time, of course, both she and Teitelboim could think about returning home. She, at least, could consider the advantages of being a literary success, if not in Chile, in the United States and Europe.

Translation, a sign of having made it in the Boom, she saw as an opportunity to be read in another language: "something I'd never thought of before." Like Cortázar, Roa Bastos, and Vargas Llosa, Isabel Allende realized that intellectual exile did offer opportunities as well as challenges. Exile could be intellectual, professional, a "feeling of being marginal, the feeling that you are not accepted, like when people just can't find air to breathe in their own countries and they have to leave."[43] This commentary also comes from the late 1980s.

By now civilians and democrats were no longer excluded from government the way women had been traditionally denied important positions.[44] Editors were more disposed to publish female writers than they had been a decade before. The world of high culture no longer belonged solely to men. Neither history nor politics did, either. Women were no longer occupying "history's secret places." Allende's generation, she would say in 1991, was one that had "experienced more or less the same things," one composed of "individual voices that come together in a chorus."[45] At this juncture Allende admitted to identifying as much with Costantini, Skármeta, Soriano, and Puig, as with others named above. The Boom had grown, not diminished, according to its own voices.

Allende's minimalist historical perspective may be linked to her very measured reaction to her own success. Writing was not so much an obligation—as others insisted—but a "gift [don] from God, something that is within and just pours forth [like] a voice."[46] A writer should eschew institutionalized politics in order to be any good at her calling, she added. But women must not shirk their civic duty. In the quest for democracy, equality, and civilian control of politics and government women should naturally be "in the front line." Never again must they be contented just because a struggle for power had been won; they must continue to fight for their rights if democracy were to succeed.[47] The struggle would be won, of this she had no doubt.

There is a quality of inevitability in Allende's views on Chile and Latin America. The analogical relationship of women's rights, civilian government, and democracy, of male domination, military rule, and authoritarianism, of Latin America as subordinate, and the United States as dominant leads somehow to the conclusion that the triumph of women, democracy, and civilian control of Latin America is preordained. This may not be sound historical thinking, but it has been fortuitous politics. It is also political correctness. On the surface it leaves as little historical space for any more ricorsi as do Cortázar's militant stands.

Well between the lines, but clearly discernible to the assiduous reader, lies evidence that Allende may have a historical sense in the making. "History," she would say in 1987, "is measured in periods. But I suspect that time is [merely] a human convention. We have agreed to measure it, for we find it impossible to live with the idea of the infinite."[48] Chilean history proved just as vulnerable to periodization as the history of any other country of the region. This was not easy for Chileans to accept, especially those dedicated to civilian rule. It was Allende's "feeling of impotence, of fury about . . . what was happening in Chile," that caused her to write *De amor y de sombra*.[49] It was more to collide with politics and culture than to collide with history that she wrote.

"It is said that history repeats itself. To a certain extent it is true, but it never repeats itself in exactly the same way. I do not think we go in circles, rather in a slow spiral, each turn of which is a little bit higher,"[50] Allende said at the dawn of the New World Order. The moment had arrived in 1990 for a final turn of the Chilean historical spiral, one in which women would look to play a significant historical role. This was important, for they had played such an important role in resisting (but in supporting too, it must be noted) the Pinochet regime. It was important all over Latin America, where writers, resident or not, had assumed certain obligations because of their talents. The Boom encouraged a historical consciousness, even on the part of late comers, and even if their historical perspective was limited to a personalized recent past like that of both Cortázar and Allende.

Mario Vargas Llosa (1936–)

Mario Vargas Llosa considered himself one of a group. Like others in that group he lamented the dearth of opportunities for innovative and provocative writers prior to the late-twentieth-century discovery of Latin American fictional history by audiences in Europe and North America. His immediate responses to questions forming the interrogatory include every point made by the innovative and provocative writers discussed in these pages, but they are part of a highly personalized framework, more personalized even than Cortázar's or Allende's. He strikes listeners and readers as enjoying, more than any of the others, the role of outsider and rebel.

"Without publishers, without readers, without a cultural environment that stimulated and pushed him, the Latin American writer has been a man who fought battles knowing full well from the very beginning that he would lose them," he averred in 1967, at the beginning of his rise to a position of leadership in the Boom.[51] Some writers also knew they might lose their right to live in their native land if they ran afoul of authorities. Vargas Llosa was not one of these, but he knew that without his writing his life was empty.

Back in the 1960s, Vargas Llosa was as much a defender of Cuba as were Carpentier and Cortázar. The Peruvian equated Cuba's struggle with Latin America's much as did García Márquez, and as Isabel Allende would one day identify Latin America's struggles with Chile's. Vargas Llosa hoped that within a half century Latin America would have achieved that which Cuba had already surpassed in terms of social justice. The region would one day be free of "the empire that sacks her, from the castes that exploit her, from forces that today offend and oppress her."[52]

One reason for this was that committed novelists were now narrating tormented histories of social injustice that collectively "precede a universal deluge."[53] Novelists were like vultures, he would claim in this same place, feeding off the carrion of a decadent age and heralding the coming of a new one—when presumably a revolutionary deluge would provide more carrion. Novelists were perforce agents of change; fiction was the logical weapon of historical revisionism. Writers had an obligation to offer something new as well as to attack something old.

Until his own reputation was well established, this Boom novelist did not see foreign influences on Latin America in a positive light. By the time the presidential campaign of 1990 rolled around, though, Peru would have freed herself of military rule, civilians were back in power, and Vargas Llosa had some political ambitions of his own. Foreign influences in the form of neoliberal economic schemes were now beneficial, necessary to break the power of cultural nationalism or, euphemistically, "intellectual stagnation."[54] Writers of the Boom era who had achieved the greatest success, he now thought, were those who did not flinch in the face of alien cultural values, who had embraced cautiously and selectively European and U.S. culture. Were not Darío, Joaquim Maria Machado de Assis, César Vallejo, Paz, and Borges all cosmopolites? Modern communications media had brought the outside world into Latin America and broken the control of local and national media. At the end of the 1980s, Vargas Llosa could think of the empire as a model for democratization so that he, in contrast to most of his contemporaries, would end up a champion of neoliberalism. [55] He had come a long way since the 1960s. No other Boom figure evinced such an ideological volte face when confronted by success and fame.

Along the way from literary rebel to defender of established economic interests Vargas Llosa came to see himself in the literary and intellectual company of Amado, Carpentier, Cortázar, Cunha, Rosa, Lezama Lima, and Piñón—and he had written his doctoral thesis on García Márquez. He would do justice in full to the memory of his countryman Arguedas as well as to that of Darío. He would say that the principal influences on his writing were Joanot Martorell, Henry Fielding, Flaubert, Balzac, Dickens, Tolstoy, Joyce, Dostoyevsky,

Stendahl, Hawthorne, Melville, Hemingway, Fitzgerald, and Dos Passos—without ever seeming too presumptuous doing it.[56] His confidence in his ability to write, slow to be confirmed in Peru, bursts forth (in direct proportion to his publishing successes), over the years in commentary on the role of novelists and the relations between history, literature, and politics.

Painful childhood experiences led Vargas Llosa to personalize his view of Peru, of the world, in essentially the same way Allende's youth had influenced her. *La ciudad y los perros* is the fictional example of this deductive projection of self into society, specific into general, present into past. His comments in speeches, lectures, and interviews provide a better response to questions about the role of the writer and his politics than they help define the Boom itself.

Writers in Peru, he claimed back in the 1960s, suffered ostracism if they broke with tradition, if they provoked or innovated. They were in effect isolated, as Roa Bastos, Cortázar, and Allende would agree.[57] At best, writers were scorned, met with indifference. At the worst they incurred the hostility of critics whose tolerance for creativity was low. The bourgeoisie, he said in 1967, must discover that "books matter, that writers are something more than harmless madmen, that they have a function to fulfill among humanity." In the same place Vargas Llosa set out what would be his principal credo for the next decade and a half: "literature is fire, it signifies non-conformism and rebellion . . . the writer's very reason for being is protest, contradiction, criticism. . . . Literature's mission is to agitate, disturb, alarm, keep men constantly dissatisfied with themselves."[58] In this sense, Vargas Llosa's ideas are quite comparable to those of Fuentes and García Márquez as well as to those of Roa Bastos, Cortázar, and Allende. The bourgeoisie would certainly have to take notice of this writer.

This Peruvian's rebellion really was not so much against the bourgeoisie (although his fiction suggests it), it was against those segments of society, bourgeoisie or no, that resisted change and were supportive of institutions that perpetuated indifference to cultural pursuits.

"It is difficult to think of being an artist if one is born in a country where no one reads: the poor because they either do not know how or do not have the means, and the rich because they just do not want to."[59] The novel, he made the point bluntly, reveals the inner demons of its writer. A macro-level analogy might be that fictional history exposes the inner demons of countries and a region.

Vargas Llosa's first major literary achievement portrayed an institution—Colegio Militar Leoncio Prado—that, in his own words, "was a type of Peruvian microcosm within which all Peru was represented in miniature." Regions, races, classes were all there. And so, of course, was the novelist-to-be. While a student there he saw all Peru, and he would never forget the experience. There he discovered "the other face of my country, one very different from the one I knew." The purpose of this novel, he claimed, was to portray a greater reality, "Peruvian reality."[60] It was the genesis of a brilliant career in which Vargas Llosa has assumed a place in Peruvian letters easily and rightly comparable to that of José María Arguedas, César Vallejo, and Mariátegui.

"There is, then, I think, a relationship between the rise of the novel and the state of crisis and decay of a society."[61] He told José Miguel Oviedo, we know, that this decay was food for the "vultures" that novelists must become: "It is a fact that this is the sustenance they like best. All great epochs of the novel have preceded very closely social apocalypses."[62] The striving outsider of the 1960s became the successful predator of the 1970s; Vargas Llosa's own career of political activism followed closely the evolution of the Boom as historical phenomenon. His fame and its longevity led both to heights never before achieved by Latin American writers, either regionally or internationally.

And without need of any ideological determination, Vargas Llosa believed, the writer's sociocultural role was one imposed chiefly by virtue of membership in a community of intellectuals.[63] To eschew the role of carrion hawk, critic, and rebel was to let down one's countrymen and one's intellectual peers. Where else were Latin Americans

going to hear about the extent of its political corruption and viola-
tions of human rights? The electronic media in Argentina, Brazil,
Chile, and Peru (before the 1980–90 devolutions of political control upon civilians in any of these countries) were controlled by the
forces of authoritarianism. Fiction was not. Fiction "expressed a
truth that was neither historical, nor sociological, nor ethnological."[64]
Literature expressed a greater truth, in other words, and need not
hew to any line or follow any model. Writers reflected the drama of
their countries in their fiction: their moral, social, and political responsibilities, as well as the pressures they must confront.[65] Peru's
own drama was, he thought, better reflected in the works of Vallejo
and Arguedas than in any nationally generated historical or social science treatise. Until the 1990s Vargas Llosa probably was close to the
mark, Mariátegui's seminal work notwithstanding.

No matter how sweet or bitter the experience, how comfortable or
depressing the living conditions, this Peruvian's years abroad gave him
the opportunity to savor liberty and to observe free, developed societies in which everyone could read, speak, and act freely. Liberty to
do all these things, he believed well into the 1980s, "places upon the
shoulders of mankind a terrible responsibility, which no one bears
more intimately . . . than the creator."[66] Creative minds, whenever and
wherever, defended liberty; Latin America should be no exception.

Nearly a decade after the armed forces had left governance of Peru
to civilians in 1980, Vargas Llosa would observe that "in Latin America we have been, in one form or another, for brief or long periods,
subjected to . . . the intervention of the armed forces into politics,
which has been historically disastrous."[67] That he also criticized bureaucracy and excessive Church powers as well as the armed forces in
his novels makes one want to see him (perhaps even made him see
himself) as the intellectual and literary heir of Manuel González
Prada, as well as Vallejo, Mariátegui, and Arguedas.

Vargas Llosa's evolving ideological eclecticism (as opposed to political opportunism) allowed him to shift his political stance over the

years, hence his view of history, from one nearer Mariátegui's (in his youth) to a shockingly conservative 1980s and 1990s neoliberalism. He observed in 1989 that the forced recantation of Cuban poet Heberto Padilla back in 1971 had allowed him to see the difference between revolution and rebellion.[68] In terms Karl Popper could have understood, successful revolution led to an end to the need for literary rebellion, which just could not be. Better a *buitre* (vulture) than a *gusano* (worm), in other words.

By the late 1980s, political ambitions coloring his opinions on all topics, Vargas Llosa was more cautious in expressing his views on the armed forces. Nine years gone from power by 1989, Peru's military leaders were now capable of functioning for the benefit of a country under civilian control, he allowed. Their role under a civilian government now would be a positive one, for they would be following, not leading. Democracy, he believed, had now proved its worth by reviving after the failure of twelve years of military rule (1968–80) to ameliorate severe economic problems or alter the social order. A presidential candidate would have to say this, a fictional historian would not.

The end of military rule in Argentina and Brazil during the same decade, following the end of authoritarianism in Iberia, left only Pinochet and Stroessner to attack. For this reason Latin America was about to enter a new age, Vargas Llosa concluded. In this new age government had the obligation of proving that democracy was more than a palatable alternative to professional militarism. It had to provide "concrete benefits in those areas—jobs, health, education—where so much needs to be accomplished."[69] In Latin America democracy would also have to overcome the skepticism of outsiders[70] who believed that statism and some form of socialism were more suited to development there than were constitutional democracy and neoliberal economic policies.

The Peruvian's growing conservatism would lead him to see benefits for literature in a democratic setting that residence in Europe and the

United States had not made clear to him in the past. In free societies, he claimed in 1987, history and literature have their own realities, they exist side by side, "without invading or usurping the domain of the other."[71] Only in closed societies and polities would fictional history now need to figure in the struggle against present and past.

Latin America's new age of democracy would both permit freedom of inquiry to flourish in most parts of the region, and lead to a more objective and inclusive view of history, believed Vargas Llosa the politician. The days of book burnings and bannings were gone. Fiction, specifically the novel, was at last free to stimulate critical thinking about the past as well as the present in an atmosphere of freedom.[72] Popularly conceived authority need not suffer fiction's sting if it enjoyed the support of a majority.

However naive or self-serving all this may appear, it is consistent with the faith in popular sovereignty evinced by Latin American writers of this period. It certainly is at odds with Castro's view of the relations between art, literature, and politics. It certainly indicates that under conditions that prevailed in the last years of the twentieth century, fiction no longer collided with a history that had been characterized by authoritarianism in various guises.

The presidential campaign of 1990, in which Vargas Llosa both soared and tumbled as politician, allowed him to sum up and specify his most recently updated political views in a public forum. Democracy and economic development via the capitalist road were bound to stimulate confidence and make it possible for the armed forces and police to collaborate with the government instead of oppose it. Former wielders of power would see advantages in cooperation with former foes.[73] The novelist-candidate vowed to convert Peru into a peaceful land where all the people might prosper. "Thanks to the internationalization of ideas, technology, markets, capital, of life in general, any country, even the smallest and most devoid of resources, can be a modern and developed country," he maintained. This last point would attract the attention of social scientists at precisely the same time they were contemplating what was happening in politics and economic development throughout the region.

Vargas Llosa's sudden fall from a grace bestowed by presidential candidacy was not without any significant by-product, either paradoxical or positive. In most of the region the policies he advocated have been put into place and are proving of questionable long-term efficacy. If democracy is less than liberal in his own country, it is not his doing. If neoliberal policies have not made Peru prosper, it is not his fault. The novelist who played at politics for one brief historical moment is a stark ideological contrast to others discussed herein. His impressive literary endeavors and outspokenness on politics mark him as one of the major Latin American intellectual figures in both the Boom and the New World Order.

Darcy Ribeiro (1922–1997)

When is a novelist not a novelist? When he is a scholar? When he is not a big seller? The ideas of Darcy Ribeiro, the social scientist who wrote some fiction are contrastable to most of the novelists whose thought and self-perception thrust them into the realm of historical thought, then on into the realm of social science. The ideas of Ribeiro, the activist and intellectual who used fiction to portray sociocultural issues of his own country is comparable to theirs. His fiction evinced the scientific curiosity of the scholar. His social science writings displayed the subjective intensity of a novelist.

In these senses he is most comparable to Roa Bastos, whose fiction bears the unmistakable stamp of the social sciences. The Brazilian's tempered responses in our interrogatory and his follow-up commentary strike one more as those of a social scientist than a novelist. This is precisely why his ideas grace these pages, right here at the monographic meeting place of fiction and the social sciences.

Latin American intellectuals of earlier generations, Ribeiro claimed in 1972, had all been influenced from without. For this reason, and to achieve credibility in European and North American professional circles, social scientists and historians, unlike writers, often blamed their own societies rather than exogenous causal factors for the short-comings of underdevelopment.[74] Climate, miscegenation, and Iberian cultural heritage were often blamed when in fact they were only partially the causes for the state of Latin America.

Martí, Cunha, and Mariátegui were among the first to analyze Latin America's social and cultural conditions taking both domestic and foreign factors into account, and theirs were important works for all readers, he thought. The mimetic qualities of colonial and neo-colonial high culture were ill-suited to the contemporary scene. Latin Americans needed to find a synthesis of dominant and subordinate cultures. Doing so would enable them to construct political systems more amenable to economic advancement. It was up to the contemporary generation of intellectuals—scholars or novelists, it did not matter to Ribeiro—to abet the search for synthesis.

Only a thoughtfully conceived political typology would ever allow Latin Americans to flourish politically and culturally.[75] Such a typology should establish a definition of politics in Latin America that did not reek of *fatuidade* (Ribeiro's Portuguese seems so much more expressive than fatuity here). He found fault with almost all existing typologies, especially those conceived outside the region. Like Vargas Llosa, for example, he accused those who saw fascism and socialism as the only sociopolitical possibilities for successful government in Latin America of *"simplismo."* Elitism and antielitism produced revolution; no other synthesis had emerged so far to counter their effects. But that did not mean one would not. Indigenismo, so visible in places like Peru, should not be considered a menace to the status of established sectors and institutions, Ribeiro insisted.

Even the great Cunha could be faulted for his (albeit turn-of-the-century) racism. However illustrative it may have been, his juxtaposition of dynamic, coastal, elitist, republican Brazil with the stagnant, interior, egalitarian sertão had led many to relegate Brazil to a perpetual present, a status quo, based on its past as a "tropical" civilization and culture. "And tropical just does not count!"[76] On this level Ribeiro had something in common with Carpentier and García Márquez, representatives, after all, of other tropical cultures.

The Brazilian anthropologist did not leave us much evidence of his belief in a Boom identity or consciousness. He was too much a social scientist to spend his time and creative effort on that. He did not even believe in latinoamericanidad(e)—given the typologies perpetually used to frame it: "National substance has much more singularity and vigor than do those things in common that make us Iberoamericans." Indo-American, Afro-American, and Euro-American countries only had so much in common. "Even today," he added, "we Latin Americans live as if we were an archipelago that communicates less within itself than it does with international economic centers."[77] Internationalization, if properly evolved, might lead to Latin Americanness, he thought, above and beyond the economic realm. It remains to be seen just how close to, or far from, the truth Ribeiro the social scientist was in this last assertion.

In the 1980s "the idea of Latin America, of siesta and fiesta, of machismo and professional dictators, of rumba and indolence" prevailed.[78] There were, Ribeiro thought, still more economic and political connections between Brazil and Europe than between Spanish America and Brazil. What homogeneity there was, was based on language and culture, not (yet) on economic and political cooperation. The need for such cooperation was still not fully understood by Latin Americans.[79] It should come as no surprise that most of the opinions expressed by Ribeiro were formed during his years in exile (1964–68), in jail (1968–69), when he traveled in Latin America (1969–75), and when he was again in government service (1976–80).[80] His four fictional works come from the very recent past, when his life was less turbulent: *Maíra* (1976), *Utopia selvagem* (1982), *O mulo* (1987), and the invented autobiography *Migo* (1988).

From his fiction, especially from *Maíra,* and from his anthropological writings, indigenous and underprivileged populations emerge
as communal metaphors for all Latin Americans. Here again a deductive approach to historical thinking, more prominent in that of Allende and Vargas Llosa than in that of others discussed in these
pages, is to be seen clearly. As far back as 1962—just before the age of
professional militarism began in his own country—Ribeiro wrote
about three prevalent views of Latin American indigenes: the ethno-
centric, the romantic, and the fatalistic. Reminding us of typologies
employed by sixteenth-century clerics, nineteenth-century positivists,
and twentieth-century Hispanists from Spanish America, Ribeiro
wrote that the ethnocentrics believed Indians would survive by emu-
lation, the romantics that indigenous culture should be preserved by
isolating the Indians from the crush of civilization, and the fatalists
that the native peoples were redeemable only through programs like
those set up for poor people and charity cases.[81] It would be interesting to see how Ribeiro might have applied this 1960s typology to the
region in the late 1990s, just as marginalized sectors of the population
were being forced to cope with new internationalized forms of cultural invasion, economic conquest, and political exploitation simultaneously.

What he said back in 1972 still almost rings prophetic: "The new
decade starts out with innovations that begin to change the picture,
although government continues to reflect oligarchy and imperialism."[82] Then as now, foreign influences affected Latin America.[83] In
decades to come the effects will doubtless be felt by a greater number.

Ribeiro's tough line on shaky typologies and his commentary on
outside influences bespeak a pragmatic and clinical social science
approach—one that takes into account local reality as well as a theory
base engendered abroad. Ribeiro's work was quintessentially Brazilian, his doctorate was from the Sorbonne, and his references to
seventeenth-century figures like Gregório de Mattos and Antônio Vieira
made it plain that he considered them more Brazilianists than most

scholars of the postcolonial period and many contemporaries have,[84] except for novelists like Ana Miranda, one is prompted to suggest.

Latin America—only a term of convenience for Ribeiro—fit into a construct of world history and international affairs—terms Immanuel Wallerstein might appreciate—as part of a world system. Commercial and industrial revolutions each had changed Latin America, Ribeiro believed. So had the technological revolution of the early twentieth century.[85] And so will that of the late twentieth century, one is again prompted to suggest.

In Latin America the wealthy and privileged had reacted with mixed feelings to each of the revolutions (corsi?) mentioned by Ribeiro. There were profits to be made, but each time they were, a status quo disappeared. This was as true with regard to indigenista movements as it was with regard to social change within the capitalist framework.[86] In Latin America entrenched political and sociocultural interests sought to capture the essence of each revolution in order to survive. This was as true of Ribeiro's own Labor Party (Partido Trabalhista) as it was of more conservative groups. Liberal democracy and free-market economics still had to be tested rigorously, thought Ribeiro in the late 1970s;[87] socialism still had to be proven incapable of fomenting development before being permanently dismissed as passé.

And Brazilians still had to prove themselves worthy of being in charge of their native land. Soon after both the restoration of civilian government in 1985 and his own return to political life, Ribeiro lashed out at his compatriots for their despoliation of the environment, especially the Amazon basin. "As a rule," he said, "around the world people know the names of their trees; not here. To Brazilians all trees are pieces of wood, no more important than any other live creature. What a contrast there is between Brazilians and Indians."[88] Brazilians—Euro-Brazilians, that is—cared little for the environment, they polluted and logged off their birthright; Indians lived with theirs, only to see it destroyed by others. The metaphoric allusion solidified in this comment is that of a national-level authority-subordination relationship based on government as Euro-Brazilian (dominant) and society as indigenous (passive). It warrants comparison with Allende's discussion of military-civilian and U.S.–Latin American relations, Vargas Llosa's use of a military prep school as microcosmic Peru, and Cortázar's own allusion to internal exile.

"The experience of being a novelist is among the most important of my life. To create personalities and make them live and love and suffer is, to put it mildly, moving." None of the readers of his social science works, Ribeiro went on to say, had ever asked him the same kinds of questions that readers of his novels had put to him: "Will there be a war at the end of the world? Is there life after death? Do Indians really know how to love? To these and many other questions I have had to respond in many countries. I believe, for this reason, that in the novel the same degree of communication can be reached with readers that can [otherwise] be experienced only through love."[89] However much Darcy Ribeiro accomplished in a life of politics and government service, academic leadership and anthropological research, I think he surely understood the power of fiction as metaphor for social science and history, and the potential of the author as a sociocultural activist.

THE FOUR WRITERS whose thought and self-perception grace this chapter are comparable among themselves and with those discussed in the preceding one. All are contrastable with each other as well. Individually and together they represent their region, whether according to typologies à la Ribeiro, as part of the Boom as defined by some of the others, or simply as voices from individual countries. Afro-America, Indo-America, mestizo-America, neocolonial America, Latin America, Ibero-America, authoritarian America, democratic America, socialist or corporatist America, Invertebrate America, and neoliberal-capitalist America—all are given new form and features by more than one of those who once collided with history in works of fiction or by other words, deeds, and activism.

All found fault with traditional historical interpretations of their country or region; all were critical of authoritarian schemes and putatively democratic systems—Carpentier and Cortázar less so of the Cuban variety of authoritarianism, to be sure. Vargas Llosa, Roa Bastos, and Allende most firmly condemned professional and personalist militarism. Fuentes and García Márquez have been most consistently and, I think, most persuasively critical of the United States. But none figures alone in any category.

Most shared some positions on Cuba, the United States, outside economic interests, and military political action. All had the advantage of viewing their homeland and their region from the other side of the sea. Whether travelers or exiles, they knew the outside world well. Cortázar, Allende, and Vargas Llosa, while concerned with history, have evinced in their commentary a personally, politically, and ideologically motivated worldview. Carpentier, Fuentes, García Márquez, while politically and ideologically literate and experienced, evince a more historically and philosophically influenced outlook. Roa Bastos, the author-ethnologist, might well have been discussed in this chapter, and Vargas Llosa in the one preceding; Ribeiro, the anthropologist-author, might well have been a part of the next chapter.

The thought and self-perception of each in sequence moves this work further toward its conclusion, wherein social scientists depict their own collisions with what remains of Latin American history. Ribeiro's adumbrates this quite well. It is thought-provoking to compare and contrast the arguments and opinions of chapters 4 and 5 with those of chapter 6. The eight novelists featured in the previous two chapters sounded very much like social critics when given opportunities to comment on the state of affairs in Latin America. The advent of the New World Order has brought their collisions to an end, but collisions will occur, nonetheless.

This may mean that fiction as genre is now in a synchronistic relationship with other genres that explore the past, however it be marked off. It may mean that fictional history is (temporarily?) unnecessary;

or it may mean that causes and effects stemming from the distant past are no longer worth the time it takes to collide with them. The next chapter addresses this possibility.

For the time being in Latin America the most pertinent attention being paid to the past—re its relevance to the present—is that by the region's social scientists. Disguised among their theories and prescriptions I do not yet see the kind of ideation that characterizes the cataclysmic history of fiction. More akin to history between the lines, it is a constricted history, a mindset and an activist worldview disguised in the literature of the social sciences and applied to some of the very themes that abound in the commentary we have just examined. Contrary to Paz's opinion, there surely can be a boom in fiction, even more in social science.

Part Three

History in Disguise

Chapter 6

Social Science and the Constriction of the Past

> There is nothing more difficult to take in hand, more perilous to conduct, or more uncertain in its success, than to take the lead in the introduction of a new order of things.
>
> —Niccolò Machiavelli, *The Prince* (1513–14, printed 1532)

GEORGE SANTAYANA SURELY was not the first to warn that ignorance of the past could lead to its repetition. Negation of, and disdain for, the past, which leads some to see history as in its final stages, however, also leads to misinterpretations of the present. Disguised within Latin American writings from the social science disciplines is something close enough to a constricted view of history to negate long-count cause-and-effect relationships' responsibility for current problems.

Bearing in mind the waves (dare I invoke again corsi-ricorsi?) of scholarly emphasis by European, North American, and Latin American social scientists on things like bureaucratic authoritarianism, corporatism, dependency, developmentalism, modernization, monism, organic statism, et alia, it should surprise no reader that their strains are present in discussions of this chapter's themes. Not until the last quarter century or so have sufficient numbers of Latin American social scientists been able to address problems theoretically with sophistication, and had so many opportunities to apply their expertise at the same time. The various theories represent the consensual realization that the causes of the region's economic, political, and social problems are systemic. What we saw as causal factors attacked by novelists in the first three chapters we saw as effects in the fourth and fifth. In this chapter the transition runs its course: It is as if contemporary economies, polities, and societies are simultaneously root causes and dire effects of contemporary Latin America's situation in the world, not its history. Contemporary causes and effects, this means, call for contemporary solutions, not ones grounded in historical thinking.

By colliding with history Latin American intellectuals from the disciplines of economics, political science, and sociology arrived at a synthesis of theories to assess blame for underdevelopment. Social science literature of the 1980s and 1990s evinced a remarkable grasp of just what the domestic and foreign causes of long-term Latin American problems had become in combination. The bulk of this literature is dismissive of much of the unpleasant past; it constricts history and looks to the present or only the recent past for solutions. Chronologically we are now about as close to the present in these pages as we can get without losing historical perspective entirely. Theoretically we are at a point where regional approaches to economic, political, and social problems take precedence over national ones. This is what latinoamericanidad has become.

I do not intend by any means that this chapter be a definitive discussion of the state of the social sciences in Latin America, nor of outsiders' scholarship (any more than I intended earlier chapters to be essays on historiography or literary theory and criticism). Rather I want to show how their conscientious and contentious discussions of five related themes represented the historical mind-set of late-twentieth-century Latin American social scientists, and thus led to constricted history.[1]

The selected themes are: internationalization, democratization, the state and governability, civil-military relations, and the concept of the continual or permanent present. With regard to collisions with history for revisionist purposes, social science literature replaced fiction at the historical juncture of the Cold War's end, the Columbian quincentennial, and the onset of the New World Order.

A decade after the Boom began and novelists had initiated their revisionist activities, social scientists themselves had already begun to constrict history. In contrast to fiction, the social sciences in Latin America, until the 1960s, could boast little formal identity, much less widespread academic tradition, organizations like Argentina's Instituto Torcuato di Tella (now a prestigious university) notwithstanding. Because of this, the historical viewpoint of most Latin American social scientists is disciplinarily limited. They are applied and theoretical scholars concomitantly. In writings examined in this chapter, World War II is the common beginning point for matters of historical import that economists, political scientists, and sociologists deal with most urgently. The present, this is to say, is more a product of the very recent past than of history.

The agglomeration of issues drawing social scientists' attention coincides neatly with the initiation of a professionalization process. The historical position of late-twentieth-century social scientists is thus analogous both to that of first-generation professional militarists of the early twentieth century and that of Boom novelists. They perforce profess, theorize, and apply their expertise at the same time. The issues that have drawn social scientists' attention are very close to those that attracted Boom novelists. Historical breezes became whirlwinds of the present; Immanuel Wallerstein's late-eighteenth-century "political whirlwind of a kind that had never been known before"[2] blew again as *torbellino* and *furação*. It is not uncommon beyond the developed world, these pages reiterate, that artistic and scholarly achievement outpace, in terms of sophistication, economic, political, and social developmental successes. In Latin America, as noted in the preceding chapter, an equilibrium is slowly in the making.

Latin American social science literature of the 1980s and 1990s constitutes a scholarly monographic dialogue among colleagues as significant as the one carried on between novelists by means of commentary elicited through the virtual interrogatories of chapters 4 and 5. In their own dialogue social scientists refer and respond to each other frequently. Selected articles from widely circulated journals, edited works, and monographs by internationally known Latin American scholars focus on Cold War origins of the region's problems with the same intensity that fictional history once dealt with discovery and conquest. Discussions of the transition from authoritarianism to putatively democratic rule are comparable to what novels did for the independence saga. And their opinions on the alluring and frustrating New World Order might be compared with fictional treatments of the recent past—the tragedy-filled authoritarian experiments from 1964 to 1990.

Stretching history to its utmost social scientific limits, Latin America's present, in this context, would be no more than a massive end result of the East-West split following World War II, the ascendance of the United States to hemispheric hegemonic (in a non-Gramscian sense) status in economic and military matters, professional militarism, the international debt crisis of the 1980s, and the beginnings of democratization. Although these are historical causes of some magnitude, their effects help to circumscribe history severely, for they come so soon. One day their historical qualities may be more appreciated than they are now.

In a December 1996 interview with David Streitfeld, Argentine novelist Tomás Eloy Martínez (*The Perón Novel*) commented that "the border between reality and fiction is very weak in our literature."[3] Martínez was referring to two things: his most recent novel,

Santa Evita, and the contrasts between conduct of scholarly research in Latin America and in the United States. Politics, fiction, and history are still inseparable in Latin America, in short.

No wonder, then, that social scientists should mark out their own historical paradigm, their own intellectual space. No wonder that someone should fill the void. Journalists-cum-novelists like Martínez are no less revisionists (García Márquez combined the two fields, let us not forget) than are social scientists-cum-novelists like Darcy Ribeiro, or novelists turned social commentators and historians like Roa Bastos. The (perpetual) immediacy of Latin America's cultural, economic, political, and social dilemmas still forces intellectuals to wear more than one cap. It has been this way, we know, since the essayists of the nineteenth and early twentieth centuries confronted their own realities and tried to fashion from them their own historical paradigms.[4] What else could be expected from a new breed confronting immediately the whirlwind of its own century?

If the Boom included rejection of a certain historical worldview—of Latin American history since 1492, to put it more pointedly—may not social science writing of the 1980s and 1990s constitute ultimately a rejection of the recent past through a different medium? If ambiguities of the 1960s produced dynamism in fiction, and frustration, conflict, and regeneration in social science, then what will the ambiguities of the 1980s and 1990s produce?[5]

The answer may be forthcoming for a long time. But critics and scholars were ever so quick to see the fictional outpouring of the 1960s and years following as Boom. So we would not be reaching too far to assess the work of social scientists at the end of the Cold War as something akin to a boom in that field. With less tradition to fall back on, but just as much to collide with, Latin America's social scientists seized the day from the novelists. We already have at hand a good case study: Chile, a country still in search of consensus at the end of the millennium. In what follows, the Chilean case will be cited as an example—not a model, for most social scientists think more inductively than some novelists when it comes to defining Latin America.

Jeffrey Puryear has pointed out the critical role played by intellectuals in the demise of the Pinochet regime and the revival of civilian-led government.[6] The social science intellectuals he portrayed as *intelectuales comprometidos* (*intelectuels engagés,* Sartre called them) and their work are products of the second half of the twentieth century. Their careers, and those of their counterparts elsewhere in the region, have been molded principally by confrontations with their times, more than by their reflections on the past.

However theoretical some of their work appears, it is first and foremost applied social science. Until the professionalization of the social sciences in Latin America—much of this through the efforts of North American foundations and international organizations, for instance, the Economic Commission for Latin America (ECLA; in Spanish, CEPAL) and the Latin American Social Sciences Faculty (better known by its Spanish acronym, FLACSO)—nineteenth-century positivism in various post-Comtean adaptations served as the essential framework for social science ideation in the region. Professionalization introduced modern methodologies and the latest theory bases from the United States and Europe via postgraduate specialization. Whatever their disciplinary specialty may be, social scientists discussed herein routinely thought and wrote interdisciplinarily. This and their activism serve to magnify their impact.

Methodology and theory have been applied vigorously and immediately to the economic, political, and social crises that beset Latin America from the 1970s forward. This has happened because social scientists became personally and professionally involved in the processes of economic, political, and social change. They participated in government, state agencies, and international organizations, taught, and exchanged ideas though scholarly writings and dialogues, both nationally and internationally. Here are the collisions that result in constricted history. Here is history in disguise.

Internationalization

Midway through both the Boom and the age of professional militarism, one of ECLA's pioneer figures wrote that East-West détente might be entering a new era, one analogous to the Latin American independence experience.[7] He meant that the relative international calm of the mid-seventies as well as the resurgence of representative, civilian political regimes in Iberia and Greece were part of a movement that might directly influence Latin America. He clearly saw the region as a community, not merely as a collection of disparate states. He saw its problems as interrelated with current worldwide issues and events, as part of a world system.

Before too long others would not only grapple with continual thawing of East-West relations and democratization, they would have to confront the debt crisis of the 1980s. Economies that had expanded, however modestly, during the quarter century or so following World War II were now in deep trouble. Latin America was not competitive industrially. Its markets had not grown enough. Commodity prices still fluctuated too much. By the time Latin America—not just a collection of disparate states, but a region—proved noncompetitive with other developing areas, such as East, Southeast, and South Asia, a technological revolution hit the region.[8] Chile's Carlos Ominami called this the beginning of a "new technological paradigm,"[9] referring pointedly to the internationalization of telecommunications that was making Latin America even more susceptible to foreign influences.

In the opinion of Brazil's Hélio Jaguaribe, Latin America's most serious dilemma of the late 1980s, the debt crisis, was the result of a protracted struggle between two "strategic empires."[10] The entire Third World was vulnerable to this conflict, for the United States and the USSR had virtually parceled out access to resources after the end of World War II. Only unilaterally could Latin American countries effectively deal with superpowers because the extant world paradigm of regionalisms and developmental categories hindered regional generation of identity by the vulnerable themselves. Jaguaribe published this opinion just prior to the pulling down of the Berlin Wall. It is worth comparing with opinions of Darcy Ribeiro on typologies. Jaguaribe already had foreseen some change. In a 1988 essay he opined that the current "state of indetermination" could not last much longer.[11] Before the decade ended, he continued, "and what is more probable, within a couple of years," profound changes were going to occur, altering the relationship of Latin America to Europe. If they did not, Latin America would continue to exist as a satellite region of the United States.

What happened late in 1989 in Berlin, before the decade ended indeed, touched off a series of events and heightened the significance of some earlier happenings, which in concert ushered in the New World Order—a euphemism for the still positively viewed present of the early 1990s. Seen in historical context, what resulted from the collapses of the German Democratic Republic and Eastern European regimes, the Soviet Union, the redefinition of Europe, and the quincentennial of Columbus's first voyage was a new kind of independence experience.

Immediately Latin American social scientists accelerated their struggle with both present and past—at almost precisely the same time novelists were ending theirs. Independence from the "strategic imperialism" of the Cold War meant worldwide *inter*dependence. Still industrially underdeveloped, now feeling the initial impact of transnational free-market capitalism, Latin Americans readily understood that without some statist-nationalist regulation (anathema to neoliberal economic theorists, after all) a lot more decisions affecting their countries were going to be made in boardrooms far, far away.[12] In short, this new kind of independence meant to some the internationalization of capitalist manipulation, to the point of full transnationalism, as much as it did Latin America's freedom from authoritarianism and Cold War geostrategic marginalization. It was a mixed historical blessing. The new independence did not mean (as independence had not meant in the 1820s) automatic improvement of economic or social conditions.[13] Nor would it mean, for the next decade, improvement of conditions for all citizens as long as foreign interests continued to play determinative roles in domestic economies and national-level economic policymaking. The analogies abound.

Was internationalization preferable to continued economic dependence (used both in a neutral and theory-based sense) on U.S. and other markets and sources of capital? There can be no clear answer to this question yet. Just as novelists had seen both sides of the United States in its world and hemispheric roles, so would social scientists. The United States certainly had been chiefly responsible for Latin America's relative isolation from the world between World War II and 1990, thought many from both intellectual sets.

Even if the economic hegemony of the North Americans already had begun to wane by the 1980s, their political and military influence endured. By the time economies weakened during that same decade, U.S. influence, if one reads the likes of Chilean Luciano Tomassini carefully, was being perceived as becoming increasingly negative rather than positive re development. Indeed, he thought, U.S. policy was being expressed incoherently now, owing to political shifts ongoing in that country itself.[14] Goals of the Inter-American Treaty of Reciprocal Assistance were not (obviously) compatible with those of the Alliance for Progress, for example. What was U.S.–Latin American policy anyway?

For one thing, U.S. policy toward reformist political parties and coalitions was historically inconsistent. Economic problems, manifest by the time the Viet Nam conflict ended, made the United States appear an undependable and inconsistent partner for Latin American countries and blocs. For another, the United States, now somewhat less than omnipotent, ceased to be the sole source or market for Latin American economies by the end of the decade. Free-trade policies would accelerate the transnational integration of other economies with Latin America's. Like Jaguaribe, Tomassini had it about right: This new independence was not altogether a blessing.

Mexico's Carlos Rico had it about right too. "The United States," he said in 1988, "feels threatened whenever a poor nation fights for national and social liberation, but that liberation is necessary and inevitable."[15] Rico referred specifically to Cuba's propensity for assembling a defense system with the blessings of the USSR, but "national liberation" was ever a red flag for U.S. policymakers. So, too, might be economic liberation.

That the developed North (a.k.a. First and Second Worlds) exploited the less developed South (then synonymous with the Third World) in strategic and economic struggles, remained a widely accepted paradigm for Latin American social science thought right up to the end of the 1980s.[16] The capitalist center now included Europe and Japan, of course. Would the new independence brought about by internationalization mean their influences diluted or merely replicated those of the United States? Would it mean much more than independence from Iberia had meant?

Osvaldo Sunkel saw this problem another way. Raúl Prebisch's original center-periphery thesis held that technology, hence both development and modernization, spread slowly from the developed parts of the world to the less developed: from Western Europe and the United States, then Japan, to Africa, Asia, and Latin America. In the peripheral areas development was manifestly uneven. It moved at a different historical pace. Urban and rural Latin America were not developing at the same rate. The influence of transnational corporations meant that urban areas might end up having more in common with each other than they did with their own hinterlands.[17] Seen in the context of the new independence this means that unevenness was increasing domestically, while superficial development was becoming more comparable internationally. Put another way, Caracas, Lima, Buenos Aires, and Rio de Janeiro now reflected the center as much or more than they did the periphery. Rural Mexico, Honduras, Chile, and Paraguay were more peripheral than centric, and this made them more alike. All this did not bode well for the historical record at all. It encouraged social scientists to apply more than theorize. Internationalization had drawbacks. It could be associated with dependency. It still can, and this encourages constriction of cause and effect.

Democratization

A major drawback to internationalization and its spawn, transnationalism, was their association with democratization. In the immediate aftermath of authoritarian experiences, social scientists of the 1980s and 1990s had to interpret, as well as participate in, the reconstruction of democratic systems. It did not take long for reality to set in. "Enough of the reality, we want promises!" one Uruguayan political scientist recalled reading in a Lima graffito of 1988.[18] Reestablishment of political legitimacy soon became more difficult than optimists had foreseen. If jobs were lost or state-funded entitlements were abolished, just what did democratization stand for? Questioning of democratization's association with internationalization showed no signs of abatement in the early years of our own century.

Elections were not enough—not for social scientists anyway. Brazil's record of 1985–88 was not an altogether lustrous one, for example.[19] Nor would it be further on into the 1990s, in Paraguay, Peru, and Venezuela, say. The process had its critics in Argentina, Chile, and Mexico too. Old faces with new labels, transnational penetration of weak economies, and growing gaps between domestic centers and hinterland peripheries demanded attention from all those leaders who claimed to represent the will of the majority and from ecomomic planners who claimed that everything was fine at the macro level. Social scientists already were calling for action to counter negative side effects of the very things they had so long advocated: liberal democracy and economic development.[20] Years, in some cases decades, of suppression or inactivity had left the forces of democracy in a weakened state, and infusions of capital were not helping much to spread income widely and deeply enough.

For some social scientists the late 1980s and early 1990s became a time of "low intensity democracy," to borrow from Guatemala's Edelberto Torres-Rivas.[21] "On the brink of the twenty-first century," to paraphrase a Mexican writer dealing with the complexities of economy and society, "political parties look more and more like parties designed in the past, before the modernization they helped to implement."[22] If authoritarianism's greatest challenges were legitimacy and mechanisms of succession,[23] democracy's were reestablishment of its own legitimacy and finding mechanisms for implementation. Identity and sovereignty were not sufficient. Moreover, stability, long linked to civilian democracy (in theory if not in practice), does not always figure among the goals. Ecuador's Amparo Menéndez-Carrión, writing in the same journal with the scholars just cited, questioned the value of stability itself, for authoritarianism had shown itself capable of imposing, if not maintaining, stability per se.[24] It took more than stability to insure the success of democratic political systems, especially with the rise of transnational economic practices.

Nevertheless, democracy remained the consensual choice as best agent for the kind of economic and social change that should benefit all sectors of the population.[25] In the face of a transnational economic system that was polarizing already fragmented societies because of the unevenness of development patterns,[26] democracy was still the last, best hope. Only democracy contained within its theory base concepts of equity, participation, and full citizenship that would militate against the onslaught of unregulated internationalism.[27] Only democracy's intrinsic qualities would militate against the Africanization of Latin American economies—their condemnation to a permanent periphery of backwardness, far from commercial and financial centers. Democracy may light the way out of a labyrinth of marginality, but not without difficulty.

Coupled with the end of the Cold War, Jorge Castañeda wrote, democratization might just be the vehicle for accomplishment of something hitherto only dreamed of: "latinamericanization" of the left and the incorporation of Marxist-Leninist theory into mainstream politics (the way Cortázar and García Márquez may have wanted?).[28] History now had less to do with ending something than it did with beginning something else, hence it could be reduced to the dimensions necessary for present purposes.

From the onset of a perceived shift in world paradigm, professionalized social scientists of Latin America saw economies, polities, and societies as products of the same historical forces. They debated the merits of free-market economic structures; they championed (with few exceptions) liberal democracy; they worried a lot about uneven social development as the result of economic and political models adopted in concert. They also debated the ideal relationship between state and economy, and did so increasingly as the new paradigm took form.[29] Whatever their specific take on economics, politics, and society, social scientists could agree with Enrique Ottone's conclusions of 1991, that the "new situation . . . demonstrates the need to keep an eye on the future, thinking of it not as an extension of the present, and to remember that everything that obtains now is manifestly tenuous."[30] Social science debates of this era are analogous to those carried on by Spaniards of the sixteenth century, who confronted their own paradigm shift.

Democracy would not bloom spontaneously upon the recession of authoritarianism. It could not immediately assure social justice to the majority of Latin Americans. That which we call democratization (sometimes *re*democratization), has occurred throughout the region at a national level with little international coordination or vision. It has been far more a political success than an economic or social one. Social scientists clearly understood this and still do. Only some of their conclusions based on national experiences, therefore, can be appropriately applied to the region as a whole.

History was in danger of becoming something contemporary owing to the alleged orthodoxy of the internationalization-democratization equation. Mexican Héctor Aguilar Camín wrote in 1988 that his country now lacked a sense of history. "Our present turns into our past with increased rapidity," he said in an essay on Mexico's perceived transition toward a more truly participatory electoral process.[31] The Mexican journalist's comment on the waning of the PRI's grip on, and the revolution's appeal to, Mexicans can be applied to Latin America—carefully. Perceived change, at least, gave social scientists much to think and write about. It induced them to see history (i.e., the recorded past) as something less than a positive legacy but more than a transitory one. So much had changed, it seemed, in such a short time, just how important was the past anyway? Such musings remind one of speculations on history by the likes of Fuentes.

The most recent past became the important one, and this is why constriction of history has continued to characterize Latin American social science as much as any developmental theory base. By this I mean simply that what past there is to take into consideration is the short term—as long as it has a positive aspect. For to the social scientist this is where the significant historical cause-and-effect relationships play out. Direct (applied) historical causation is more important than indirect (theoretical). Little need, then, for economists, political scientists, and sociologists to look for origins of issues or problems in the early national period, much less the colonial centuries. Or so the disciplinary literature would lead the historically minded to believe.

Despite arguments to the contrary, endings, in such a historical view, can still count as much as beginnings: "The end of a historical cycle has a higher social cost than the beginning of another," two scholars agreed in 1990.[32] The costs of all phases of transition, thus, are high. There can still be a blurring of ending and beginning. Transitions are not necessarily all that new or unique, moreover. They are part of history's corsi-ricorsi, after all. As Lorenzo Meyer pointed out in 1988, Mexico's first steps toward democracy were taken when democracy was "more theoretical than real, even in the central or dominant countries."[33] Meyer placed democratization in a wide historical context, but his remark begs the question whether or not democratization takes place now in a context similar to any of the past. Central countries are themselves in the throes of theoretical struggles over the economic and social meaning and content of democracy. Transitions are important to social scientists who have to apply theory to what is still in the process of change.

Do democratization and internationalization actually militate against latinoamericanidad as it was perceived and described by novelists? Or do the two processes really latinamericanize national experiences? Finding common experiences, according to FLACSO's Norbert Lechner, has not been easy for Latin Americans.[34] If the last half century now constitutes the recent past (for as long as it can), what sort of regional-historical legacy can such a short span of time ever bestow? Will the most recent past render a more accurate view of Latin American history than have five hundred years of recorded and revised history? Here again are questions whose answers are still forthcoming.

Diversity, often thought of by novelists as the region's unifying, identifying factor, may be interpreted quite differently now, and for the foreseeable future, in clinical, applied terms. Seemingly, once within grasp both in the pages of fictional history and in the thought and self-perception of its advocates, Latin America as a historical entity, hence latinoamericanidad, is being redefined by economists, political scientists, and sociologists. Perhaps this is an intellectual paradigm shift of historical proportions, perhaps it is not. This redefinition may result in erasure of the historical past, the one so artfully collided with in fiction.

If independence was indeed a process of negation as well as affirmation,[35] something that led right up to a break with the past but never quite achieved it culturally, democratization might be seen as a double negation, not only in Spanish America but in Brazil as well. Neither the authoritarian nor the putatively democratic long-term pasts have a place in social science's historical construct. They serve no positive purpose. They are not applicable. Both are to be rejected.[36] Social science of the late twentieth century condemned both to history's dust bin, made them useless artifacts of a past that is better forgotten than considered a legacy. Acknowledgment of their significance makes democratization a more difficult process—especially if something goes wrong. But that same acknowledgment would serve to remind Latin Americans of what aspects of internationalization should be avoided in the future.

Such an acknowledgment might serve Latin America well, for lessons learned from the past can make it easier to maintain internal order and international peace, develop economies and social policies without allowing the new transnational economic models to perpetuate peripheral status for the region. It also might allow Latin Americans to enjoy something more than "democracy of low intensity."[37] The past—recent or distant, authoritarian or putatively democratic, peripheral or marginalized—must not be allowed to mutate and survive. This is the social science consensus on democracy and development, and their social consequences in the early New World Order.

The State and Governability or, The Politicization of History

One question that found its way boldly into social science literature of the 1980s was, Whither (Wither?) the state? This question begs others. Will the state be the agent that guarantees by its actions evenness, or condones by its inactions unevenness of development because of its action or inaction? Or will peripheries and centralities become even more internationalized than they were in the 1980s?[38] Will the state cease to be relevant? In Alain Touraine's words, the state has always been an agent of "historical change."[39] Will decline of the state as economic regulator and social balancer foment or retard change—all in the name of democracy? Without a state can a people claim to have a history? Without a state can there be democracy? Yet again, only forthcoming answers will approach definitive status.

In the late 1980s, there still were plenty of social scientists who believed the state crucial to the success of social democracy.[40] Without social democracy, economic democracy appeared a dream, political democracy a mere mutation of past experiences to be avoided, something akin to man's fate as treated by Carpentier. Nevertheless, diminution of the power and responsibility of the state accelerated in the early 1990s.[41] This process of reversal of all historical trends in the region is widely perceived as fundamental to democratization and economic development. Let us now turn to a topic that allows us to see how some social scientists saw the recent past and their own present in applied political terms as they planned for the future.

The ending of the Cold War paradigm did not mean to all social scientists that erasure of the past was a foregone conclusion. Reasoning of which Vico would have been proud, led Atilio Borón to say in 1988 that coetaneousness of past and present was responsible for a number of disagreeable phenomena.[42] As events have shown, the 1989–91 break with the past was in reality an end result of changes in train since the end of World War II, certainly events of the mid-1970s. In Latin America it was part of the third great historical cataclysm. Borón cautioned against thinking that the present would endure as it was. Uncertainties should be considered normal, not aberrant, echoed a Guatemalan political scientist the following year: the unexpected and the possible were as likely as the predictable and the unlikely.[43] The status quo, this is to say, cannot be permanent.

The perception of ebb and flow of recent past into present led some social scientists to warn against the reappearance of partisan politics lest bureaucratic authoritarianism itself reemerge as a kind of "partisan bureaucratics" equally capable of neglecting the past.[44] A rush to adopt any model of democratic politics without recognition of possible variations in form and content would be little improvement over the dogmatism of the recent past. A consensus in favor of pragmatic approaches to democracy, coupled with better synchronization of socioeconomic development, would provide the ideal environment in which *gobernabilidad* (in the sense of legitimate governability) could flourish. Without it the future would be bleak.

Governability—acceptance, decisiveness, effectiveness, responsibility, responsiveness, communication, efficiency, and coordination—was what Latin America needed.[45] The state still had a role in assuring an environment for both governability and democratization.[46] Unless civic culture, economic growth, and social harmony could be coordinated, democracy had little hope, thought Rolando Franco, writing in 1989.[47] Violence, the narcotics trade, stagnant political parties, demagoguery, and U.S. interference all militated against democracy in its fullest meaning and governability in its most beneficial. They all challenged the authority and viability of the state. If there were no state could there be governability? If governability were lacking, could there be development?

Several Latin Americans who contributed to an influential edited work of 1991 made it clear that there never had been a simple formula for either democracy or development—something five centuries of history should have been able to provide them with, but never had. No system was perfect nor applicable to all locales; no rules applied all of the time. Liberal democracy was neither prerequisite to implementation of neoliberal economic policies nor a panacea for social problems. Authoritarianism was not necessarily antithetical to socioeconomic development.[48] Political parties that did not undergo thorough change in leadership could not expect to regain much of the legitimacy they had once enjoyed. Nor could their old programs. Democracy was not "partocracy." Unless politicians and planners took such points into account, governability, let alone democracy, would be difficult to achieve, asserted a consensus in that volume. Unless civic culture, and economic and social development were shared responsibilities of the public and private sectors (i.e., national and international), could either promote the cause of social justice?

Mexican researcher Germán Pérez Fernández del Castillo added to a widening dialogue of dissensus created whenever the role of the state was mooted, asserting that in Mexico the polity confronted an uncertain present with its cadre of politicians who wanted to govern but had little ability, and others who had ability but no real taste for politics or government. Guatemala's Torres-Rivas warned his own readers to be wary of U.S. influence, for it might taint their own efforts on behalf of democratization and governability.[49] Ecuador's Menéndez-Carrión put it even more bluntly: revival of the democracy of the past and wholesale adoption of neoliberal economic policies would lead to perpetuation of a "bankruptcy of solutions emanating from the peripheral past, dependent on imported solutions, and a present of transnationalization of the world economy."[50] The transition to democracy was going to take more than a little time and much effort to avoid continual relegation of Latin America to the periphery. The role of the state needed a lot of attention.

This periphery, as opposed to that of the Cold War, was one of a fragmented Latin America, according to Chile's Ignacio Walker. As of 1992, at least, he saw little prospect of the future being any better.[51] Perhaps the present was permanent after all. If it was, the forces of constricted history played an important role still, in more than one country, in more than one sphere of political and economic activity.[52]

Governability obviously meant consensus on the part of political, professional, business, military, and intellectual elites, on their willingness to make democracy more than putative. It meant consensus among those whose status desperately needed improvement too. That governability depended on legitimacy of new leaders and organizations was a regionwide, not simply an isolated belief; that some aspects of old systems and isms might serve in new forms was another. That governability was not sustainable without some way of tying the state to the majority of the population was obvious. What from the past might be useful in sustaining such ties, the state?

As a case in point, Colombian Francisco Leal Buitrago would

point out in 1988 that a thicket of interlaced family trees had provided a good share of national leaders and chief executives in his country.[53] A look at the leadership cadres of some other countries of the region—Chile is a fine example—would show the same characteristics. A certain stability might indeed be provided by a "ruling class" (in the form of the state, not a dynasty), but it would not do so unless leadership championed new policies from which large numbers of the citizenry benefited.[54] This prescription contrasts vividly with Roa Bastos's diagnosis of Paraguay's ruling class. Continuity, though, must not mean perduration of failed alternatives to democracy, lest corporatism (and its attendant involvement of the armed forces) again rear its ugly head in the region.[55] This was a universal conclusion.

Ethnic conflict certainly raised its head(s) again in the initial stages of the struggle to establish governability. From Mexico and Central America to the Andes, and into the Amazon basin, it threatened the stability of national institutions and made clearly manifest the weaknesses of diminished states and reformed political systems.[56] Coupled with new economic policies, ethnic conflict threatened to minimize the efforts of the democratization process by perpetuating marginality of large sectors of national populations. Latin America's "new" democracies simply had to be "much more than a restoration of the democratic regime[s] previously in power."[57] There is enough continuity and consistency in expressions of priorities for, and concerns about, democracy to warrant a conclusion that as a generation, late-twentieth-century Latin American social scientists were fully cognizant of the tough roads that lay at a fork they had not yet reached.

However much some social scientists may have disguised their opinions, others knew history simply did not "end." Writing in 1988, Enzo Faletto made the point that the end of the century's great ideological conflicts ought not be cause for unmitigated jubilation—yet. Neither Marxism-Leninism, corporatism, nor what had passed for democracy had proved sufficient to the task of serving Latin America very well. The only theory base for progress that had ever come close to doing so had been positivism, and it too had proven less than perfect.[58] History's own failures, social scientists seemed to be saying, just could not be repeated by democracy and capitalism in their newest guises. Something had to work or governability was out of the question. Something had to provide both continuity and stability.

History did not cease to be simply because some popular writers so decreed, thought social scientists. The "end of history" was nothing more than a poorly conceived theory designed to make it easier to forget past mistakes and to accept new realities at face value. Jorge Castañeda put it succinctly and ominously: "the hypothetical end of the idea of revolution represents in no way the end of history, but it does represent what might be called the end of a certain idea of history, an end to the idea of the future."[59] I think this means that some scholars worried that the continual present was approaching permanence owing solely to its perceived and superficial successes.

The rush of events, the perceived rapidity of significant change, the apparent demise of old orders, and the allure of internationalization, democratization, and their new transnational economic structures were beguiling Latin Americans and bedeviling them at the same time. Social scientists were warning against trusting illusions of the past and variables of the future; in so doing they were both rebuking and constricting history to make it suit what they thought were the needs of the times. They were also searching for agents of continuity and stability. The very term *end of history* had been misinterpreted owing to illusions of definitive change.

Across the region the illusion of military withdrawal from the political scene, for example, was ever so popular. Military government failures in Argentina, Brazil, Chile, and Peru, as well as in Bolivia, Guatemala, Paraguay, and Uruguay, coincided with the wave of democracy that crested in the late 1980s. Across the region social scientists warned against believing too much in illusions. Armed forces had "bunkerized" in the face of civilian ricorsi,[60] and had guaranteed themselves specific kinds of power, thought one Chilean. Military presence in whatever form militated against gobernabilidad and establishment of a prerequisite consensus, thought colleagues from other countries.[61] Having survived other bouts with civilian political leadership, can Latin American military organizations coexist with internationalization and democratization? Can they contribute to governability?

The Militarization of History or, Whither Traditional History?

If one does see history as flux and reflux, the answer to the questions just posed is a guarded yes. Latin American military social scientists and civilians who study military-civilian relations have a lot to say about the military presence now, and will for some time, I think. Witness the relatively privileged position enjoyed by most Latin American armed forces today. Even in Argentina, where post-Falklands War civilian administrations have denied the military much of what was once reserved to it (including a good portion of its budget), prestige is rebuilding through peacekeeping activities and domestic actions. Elsewhere constitutional and statutory guarantees protect armed forces from severe budget reductions and civilian intrusion. This is true despite recent reversals of amnesty laws, reversals that may threaten the comfortable retirement of former authoritarian leaders. *Reflux*, according to one Brazilian, is the best term for the status that can be accorded the military's position during the region's latest return to civilian rule.[62] At most, military influence is rebuilding, at least it is holding steady. If there is any substance to this view, then the military may play a behind-the-scenes role in the future potentially as significant as any overt one of the past. Can democracy be realized in this context? Yes, it can, if one accepts modified definitions of that system of government and allows for the ability of the state to play a role in all processes.

National defense by any other name is still security driven. Once referent to protection of the fatherland against hostile neighbors and internal threats to stability, it became, officially or unofficially, national security doctrine during the Cold War. Enemies did not need to come from limitrophe states or be citizens in rebellion. The most pernicious attacks against national values (as defined all too often by the armed forces) could come from within and without—in the form of ideas. Now, again, much of Latin America is perceived as beset by potential threats to national well-being from without: fluctuations in international markets and interest rates, competing sources of capital, alienation of blocs of voters because of downsizing of the state and privatization of social services, decision making in absentia by transnational corporate boards, terrorism, the narcotics trade, changes in national culture. Latin America's new independence may only have increased the number of potential threats to security and sovereignty, and national values. These are threats to the legitimacy of all that has been going on in the New World Order.

Civilian and military social scientists often have faulted the United States for having forced Latin America from its historical course, owing to its cultural and economic influence. Following World War II a new Pan-Americanism—regional solidarity against the ideological foe—replaced the old cultural, diplomatic version of the interwar years. One Chilean general went so far as to write that Cold War Pan-Americanism had deprived a generation of intellectuals of the opportunity to discover the "cultural roots" and the "historical continuity" of their own region.[63] By means of this line of reasoning Pan-Americanism becomes the nemesis of latinoamericanidad, Pan-Americanism becomes the most tragic aspect of the real past. At once denied access to their past and disdainful of its historical constriction, military social scientists may engage in the process of delineating their own cultural roots and their own historical continuity, the way novelists once did. It is conceivable that they revive traditional history for purposes yet to be determined, but linked, in theory, to a wish to erase the stigma of their Cold War roles.

If history's constriction means, as it seems to for most social scientists, that the causative past is limited to the post–World War II era, it follows that the role of the United States as principal foreign influence becomes predominant, more than just important. How much the new age of transnational economic growth will mitigate the perceived international role of the United States—analogous now to that of the Iberian monarchies in the colonial centuries—remains to be seen, but professional military resentment of treatment by the United States (as ungrateful ex-ally in the East-West confrontation) will endure for a while.

Whether in uniform or not, many social scientists once held that military political actions in the second half of this century were largely results of U.S. Cold War policies and priorities. Stability of Latin American countries and access to their raw materials had to be assured. No longer, some officers now maintain, need national security be inextricable from U.S. influence. But national priorities still are no less affected by decisions taken by foreigners.

Thought of by some as little more than apologists for occupying forces preventing communist subversion, Latin American military intellectuals resent being cut loose by their former ally and benefactor.[64] No longer in need of surrogate armed forces, the United States now champions democratization and civilian rule, while at the same time it strives to cement partnerships with military organizations that are paradoxically trying their best to show their independence from the Pentagon.[65] Until and unless the military ceases to maintain a privileged position, it is going to remain a significant, if not overtly so, player in democratization. Until and unless the United States recognizes this, its Latin American policy will be as invertebrate as the region itself.

In the 1990s the military found its new status as tenuous as that of the democratization process.[66] "At the same time some leaders complain about the inability of the armed forces to defend," wrote one Brazilian social scientist, "they are not capable of articulating logically an argument that convinces other political forces that more financial resources should be [forthcoming]."[67] Some professional leaders remain convinced that armed forces can indeed still play the role they traditionally championed. In one Chilean's opinion, as "permanent and fundamental institutions of the state, [they could still] contribute to development, provide advice, maintain security in order to make such development possible. And, just like their European peers [their] permanent contribution to the peace of their land is the highest objective."[68] Somewhere between these contrasting views—civilian and military, in that order purposely—is there some ground from which armed forces might launch a successful argument for their future worth as history's agents of defense and development—and democracy? Will the career still have the appeal to officers like those described by Allende?

Despite evidence to the contrary, the new international ambience may provide this ground. As the last bastion of traditional, continental European-style military professionalism (however great the distance between theory and practice may always be, as Vargas Llosa cogently pointed out repeatedly), some armed forces still bind themselves permanently to both the state and the historical past. Privatization and downsizing of state functions may not in the long run provide the kind of environment needed for social and economic development that appeals to all sectors, as has been posited. Nor can a weakened state assert itself against international threats or foreign influences for very long. These resemble, at once, arguments once used by fictional historians and those perpetually employed by military authors.

Under the proper circumstances foreign policies of downsized states might benefit from geopolitical and technological expertise gained over the decades by military professionals. Defense of national patrimony and sovereignty (in their full senses) might be facilitated by the utilization of such expertise.[69] Should more social scientists see substance in this argument, which validates old professional military claims, they might find ways to bind the military profession to the democratization and developmental processes in a new and significant way. Their writings will have an impact the further these processes continue in future corsi.

Long a leading member of Latin America's military intellectual elite, Peru's Edgardo Mercado Jarrín has stressed in most of his writings that during the Cold War the major threat to national security was not ideology but underdevelopment. It was the inability of civilian political leadership to respond to this threat that led to the South American institutional golpes in the 1960s and 1970s.[70] This (as well as ambition) clearly was the rationale behind his own involvement in Peru's 1968 military movement and the regime that ensued from it. Should uneven socioeconomic development accompany democratization and transnational economic expansion, might not a few military leaders play supportive or opposition roles in the century ahead? If they do, historians, novelists, and social scientists will be under additional pressure to revise formulaic views of military-civilian relations, to see them as historically diachronic rather than politically synchronic, say.

They will have to take into account seriously the arguments of some civilians that there are significant linkages between the rise of the military profession, the redefinition of the nation-state, and the assumption of tutelary roles in twentieth-century Latin America.[71] Never have specialists in military-civilian relations agreed with so many other social scientists so strongly on this.

Until democratization proves that governability (however one chooses to define each) is sustainable in the new transnational economic framework, military wariness and goodwill remain just as important as is popular support for the process.[72] Exclusion invites opposition and alienation; neoliberal economic policies may foster exclusion through uneven development and modifications of sovereignty. Constitutional democracy may hang in the balance. It may be associated with the less attractive side of laissez-faire capitalism, the one that shows insufficient concern for human welfare. And that could be ultimately cataclysmic.

Power vacuums have always caught the attention of political observers. Without either a U.S. presence akin that of the post–World War II era or an institutional military role, can Latin American political systems democratize fully in the face of the new economic policies? Is a multipolar or "apolar" world more conducive to democracy and economic development? In the face of instability who or what will assure national survival? Will the military be the ultimate repository of traditional, national history to be employed to justify this survival? Here again are questions whose answers can be but adumbrated.

History's Future or, The Continual Present

"Man lives and dies, governments change, empires fall; but the vital interests of the nation do not disappear, they just adjust to new situations," wrote a Chilean admiral in 1993.[73] The state and the nation are permanent; history dictates that eternal vigilance assures permanence and security. Perhaps never before has the gist of such an argument caused so much discussion. The transcendence of the nation-state as opposed to the transitory nature of government and politics is an old professional military stand. For some, history continues to flow and ebb, resembling more the tides than the course of a stream.

Agreement and disagreement pending, civilian and military social scientists as a "generation" seem to concur that old-fashioned international geopolitics has given paradigmatic way to neoliberal transnational geo-economics.[74] Despite the effects of the New World Order, this means, Latin American thinkers may have more in common intellectually now than ever before. This commonality may shape the way Latin American history will be shaped in the future. If this is the case, it means outside forces will continue to define the region's history— and be blamed for its legacy—as much or more as they always have.

The essence of history will then be its constriction, and constricted history has only a very limited legacy.

Chilean Francisco Rojas Aravena wrote in 1992, "looking to the future we need to heed the lessons of the recent past. Latin America is not a unity, but contains competing interests capable of reconciliation."[75] The struggle between Latin America's disparate and competitive interests may be exacerbated by the new state of affairs to a point where the region's history becomes one with that of the rest of the developing "internationality." This irony would be hard to ignore, for it would mean the denial of latinoamericanidad and the internationalization of constriction. Both the content and form of history would cease to be Latin American in essence as well as in appearance.

Another Chilean described the region's historical present as a series of events and connections—cause-and-effect relationships—incapable of becoming a "duration." In other words, he saw historical events as insignificant to the definition of a structural past, present, or future: a paradigm. "We live," he wrote, "in a continual present."[76] Without a past, any present lacks definition and any future lacks attraction. History disappears unless somewhere it is appreciated, needed. If the only repository of appreciation and need for undisguised history as an explanatory and defining device for the present lies within the boundaries of professional military thought and self-perception, collisions with history are bound to recur in Latin America for a variety of reasons, most of them unpleasant. These collisions may continue to reflect cataclysm, but they will not occur between anyone's lines, and it will be impossible to disguise them.

Without history, Latin American social scientists may find one day that they have a lot in common with historians who look back from some future decade upon the late twentieth century, when collisions were the norm. They may already be finding themselves in a situation not unlike that in which Karl Mannheim saw intellectuals at mid-twentieth century: writing about the past "with a false sense of participation—the illusion of having shared the lives of people without knowing of their toils and stresses."[77] Intellectuals of the right who have social science credentials express their support for transnational capitalist structures as collective sine qua non of the democratization process, but they do it cautiously lest they be branded reactionaries mired in the past. Those on the left express their concerns more pointedly. Their anti-U.S. stance, their thoroughly justifiable skepticism about neoliberal economics, and their demands for social justice indicate that reformism and extremism are not totally out of the question for the future. Like their colleagues on the right, they are wary of the new paradigm.[78] Military social scientists stand somewhere between caution and pointed criticism. In all cases it is the social science disciplines that shape the dialogue, not history, and most certainly not its fictional variant. That they do this interdisciplinarily refines the dialogue; it does not confuse it.

Early on in the now classic *Capitalism, Socialism and Democracy*, Joseph A. Schumpeter asked and then answered himself thus: "Can capitalism survive? No. I do not think it can." Schumpeter went on to argue that capitalism's very excesses undermined it, for they did not redound to the benefit of all citizens. Uneven development, in short, is nothing new. "Can socialism work? Of course it can," he added. "Socialism in being might be the very ideal of democracy. But socialists are not always so particular about the way in which it is brought into being," he concluded. Upon reflection, both a paraphrase and an invocation of historian's license are in order—for a final time: Could socialism survive? No. I did not think it could. Can capitalism work? Of course it can. Capitalism in being might be the very ideal of democracy. But capitalists are not always so particular about the way in which it is brought into being.[79]

This applies to Latin America in the aftermath of the Boom and on into the New World Order. As long as the United States maintains a high profile in the spread of transnational capitalism and the campaign for democratization, and despite the growing presence of European and Asian interests in the region, Latin American critics and commentators will have a significant and easy target—one with an undisguised historical identity, both long- and short-term. As long as economic and social policies do not produce opportunities for increasing numbers of citizens with growing expectations, socialism will have opportunities to revive politically. The present may be continual in the minds of some, but it is not permanent in the minds of most.

This recalls an exchange (not altogether unlike Carpentier's fictional one described in chapter 2) between John Dos Passos and Rómulo Gallegos in which the North American reacted strongly to criticisms of his country's policies by Latin American colleagues during an international meeting of writers. The Venezuelan novelist and statesman responded to Dos Passos's views, allowing that Latin Americans had indeed created conditions propitious to authoritarianism, "but you exacerbated them and turned them to your advantage."[80] Can Latin Americans, social scientists or no, see analogous relationships now between democratization and neoliberal transnational capitalism? Yes. I think they can.

For nowadays, as Chile's Bernardo Subercaseaux would have it, "it is politics that will be contemplated [through the lens of] culture."[81] If true, this finalizes the break with a traditional Latin American mind-set in which the definition of culture has been an object of political interest and activism. Latin American social scientists will prove constant in their scrutiny of politics and economic policy. Latin America will be the better for this even if it takes history's constriction to accomplish it.

Latin American social scientists have had lots of support for their position(s). Pope John Paul II, Subcomandante Marcos, the Economic Commission for Latin America, and other institutions and individuals, all in their own way, have recognized the unevenness of development, the dichotomy between macro- and micro-socioeconomic successes.[82] Following the macro-level mandates of the World Bank, the International Monetary Fund, and the World Trade Organization does not automatically lead to *pan, techo, y abrigo* for all Latin Americans, not this soon at the micro level.

EXCISION FROM THE historical record of a past that does not neatly coincide with an intellectual, or disciplinary, or even a pragmatic view of the present is no response to Latin America's own massive collision(s) with its past(s). It serves only to perpetuate an ahistorical present and a misunderstood past. Civilian intellectuals cannot ignore five centuries of frustration any more than professional militarists can erase their recent failures and abuses. Dogmatic rejection of alternative definitions of theory and practice of democracy and capitalism is no less folly. Relegation of socialism, democratic or authoritarian, to any of history's figurative dustbins is a mistake, for the injustices of the past have not yet been erased from the historical record. Such actions serve to constrict and disguise history, not to reveal its essence, nor to preclude its reflux.

"The mere fact that communism didn't work," said a contemporary novelist midway through the 1990s, "doesn't mean that capitalism does. In many parts of the world it's a wrecking, terrible force."[83] Collisions with history were necessary. Constriction of history may be a grave error. Excision of portions of history smacks of despair. To have to relive the past would be a terrible future for Latin Americans. Those who understand all this will not fight their distant past, they will learn from it about their present, however unattractive each may be. Those who remember the past will use their memories to create a better future.

Attempts by Latin American social scientists to constrict history—in order to make it more understandable, utile, and applicable to an understanding of the present—have proved as successful as did the efforts of fictional historians to revise through collision—so far. Constriction may not even be a conscious motive of Latin American social scientists, but it pervades disciplinary literature that currently sustains a significant intellectual exchange among economists, political scientists, and sociologists. History's constriction merely disguises it in the garb of the recent past. This collision stands in stark contrast to the conscious revisionist efforts of Boom novelists in their fictional histories and resembles conclusions reached in their commentary.

All three modes of discontent with past and present—cataclysmic history, history between the lines, and history in disguise—are subject to question, for each lends a distinct hue to time's passage, to cause and effect. No one can claim a monopoly on accuracy, much less truth, certainly neither fictional historians nor social scientists. History is not finite, surely, regardless of temptations to see it solely as the years between the beginning of the Cold War and the advent of the New World Order. Intellectuals will have to face this fact soon. A constricted history may make it easier to introduce a new order of things, as Machiavelli meant, but it may not help sustain it.

After all is said and done, contemporary phenomena remain but history's echoes, reverberations of the past up and down the corridors of time. These echoes will continue along future corridors. Elevation of expectations for the future based on the allure of the continual present may prevail, and the past may remain unnecessary to explain the present for a while, but neither fiction nor social science will be able to ignore for long the uncertainties bound to attend all that transpires in Latin America. The efforts of late-twentieth-century novelists and social scientists to find meaning in the present by confronting and redefining the past have not diminished Clio's importance to Latin Americans. Indeed, those efforts have served the interests of scholarship by giving the region's own historians, not to mention Latin Americanists from elsewhere, much to think about.

Conclusions

We have seen, then, how a mere curiosity about the past could develop in the course of a century into an elaborate and all-inclusive philosophy of history.
                        —George S. Fraser, *The Modern Writer and His World* (1951)

ON THE MEANDERING path to the present, history and literature meet in various places, and at various times. In Latin America the path that began in 1492 has been the scene of many encounters in which standard versions of history have found themselves challenged. In late-twentieth-century fictional histories epic heroes tumbled from pedestals, human sagas turned into studies in failure, and tragedies became surreal horror stories. In scholarly writings Latin American history has been reinterpreted as cycles and spirals, it has been circumscribed and subjected to deconstruction and quantification.

Fictional history popularized revisionist views of discovery and conquest, and independence and early nationhood. It put the authoritarianism of the recent past in greater perspective for a wider audience than historians had ever reached. Novelists of the Boom themselves evinced a sophisticated grasp of their genre's ability to depict parallel and alternative history. And they actively participated in the cultural and political debates of the region that questioned the very meaning and worth of history. By the end of the 1900s, after novelists had curtailed their interest in historical problems, the social sciences had constricted history to the recent past. History was barely recognizable as such, either in fiction or social science literature, owing to its disguise as an essentially twentieth-century phenomenon.

Historians in Latin America have a lot of repair work to do, for collisions have resulted in very serious damage to the idea of history. Despite the very considerable accomplishments of the region's own historians, answers to most of the historical questions asked herein are now being more effectively proffered by social scientists. These social scientists are applying their expertise to the resolution of problems that are popularly perceived as the results of the constricted history of the recent past. Latin America's professional historians are only gradually reaching audiences comparable to those reached by novelists or affected by the doings of social scientists.

The fictional histories discussed in chapters 1 and 2 attacked, for popular readers, icons of a written and received history of nearly half a millennium that had contributed little to the enlightenment of most Latin Americans. The great men and the caudillos finally got what they deserved in fiction, whereas in scholarly works by Latin Americans they had only been exposed to a limited and self-selected clientele. Foreign influences, *others,* the Church, Latin America's fantastical, magical qualities—these all were vividly portrayed for popular audiences.

By the end of chapter 3 it should be clear that, in the course of the Boom, the fantastical and the magical had failed Latin America, except as literary devices. Latin American history was like an exotic old man, less interesting for his exoticism than for his age. Dictatorship and institutional authoritarianism had been exposed as effects not causes, institutions prevailed over individuals, foreign influences had come to mean the United States specifically, and the military profession had been successfully attacked. In fiction cause-and-effect relationships had been reversed. Cataclysmic history was seen as negative history. If not nationally, surely regionally novelists had done to their history what outsiders had been doing for decades, and what the region's own revisionist historians could still only envy. Novelists literally and figuratively had sold their vision of Latin America to a mass readership at home and abroad.

In chapters 4 and 5 the commentary of selected Boom figures provided us with more evidence that the meaning and worth of history—the recorded past—to the present was highly debatable. Fictional historians made it clear, in their works, that they were aware of Europe's and North America's historical scholarship as well as of their literature. If the recent past, as described in chapter 3, was no more than the end result of a worthless and disposable past, then traditional versions of history had not led Latin Americans very far at all. In these chapters on history between the lines the virtual interrogatories elicited commentary that evinced the collective consciousness of a literary generation of historical proportions. Combinations of motives motivated its members: revolution in Cuba and Mexico, authoritarianism in South America, personal convictions regionwide.

Some sharp differences of opinion notwithstanding, writers of the Boom perceived themselves as fulfilling significant public roles. They played these roles concomitantly, either in their fiction or as activists, or both, by elaborating on contemporary themes and debating topics associated with traditional history and its legacy. They were attacking past and present in their fiction, providing alternatives and proffering solutions in their commentary—all at the same time. Literary metaphors sell; clinical procedures do not. History between the lines shows just how inextricable were fiction, history, and social science to the region's premier novelists. History between the lines informally ties present to past in ways more comparable to modern historical and social science methodologies, thus allowing us to connect cataclysmic with constricted history, fiction with social science.

The past became more regional and thematic in both importance and structure as fictional history moved toward the present. It became less locally and nationally focused. Latinoamericanidad took on a shape comparable to what essayists had advocated decades before just as the New World Order set in. Then, the commentaries of chapters 4 and 5 bridge the intellectual gap between fiction and social science by providing us a vantage point from which to view collisions with history. History between the lines shows also how inseparable were novelists from social scientists when it came to dealing with history.

The constriction of history described in chapter 6 disguises it as a set of cause-and-effect relationships occurring in the second half of the twentieth century. Social scientists collided with the same past novelists did in their commentaries, but in addition to being highly critical, they were boldly clinical. Like committed novelists, Latin America's social scientists have a greater impact on their fellow citizens than historians. They apply as well as theorize and revise. If people do not read social science literature, they can be made to think they are benefiting from its content. The art of the possible is compatible with the possibilities of art. History in disguise is that of modern institutions, problems, and policies. Internationalization, democratization, the role of the state, civil-military relations, and the continual present all have counterparts in the earlier chapters, but to Latin American social scientists their very essence is contemporary, not historical; it is as applied as it is theoretical.

CONCERN FOR OUR past bespeaks the same for our future; disregard for our past leads to the reduction of our future, to a continual present. History is not just belief in the past, it is recognition of the future as its ultimate product. Ignorance of the past's importance signifies a lack of interest in anything but the present and its perpetuation to the detriment of cultural, economic, political, and social change. We can see all this more clearly owing to collisions with history. I hope history becomes the object of Latin America's own forces of fictional and academic contentiousness in the future the way it did in the second half of our century.

A book about the historicity of ideas expressed in fiction, commentary, and social science is perforce a voyage of discovery. It is an essay in the less-known, a revelation of what is, what might have been, what might still be. A book that deals with dissent is like a voyage on which anything might turn up on the horizon, beyond which, of course, one cannot see.

In the process of writing these pages a lot of things turned up that were entirely unexpected. "Charts" helped part of the way; "fair winds" did the rest. The charts and winds of scholarly inquiry took me where they would. I think readers will see where charts became less than definitive and where winds of speculation picked up: somewhere between fiction and social science, somewhere between the lines in both. These are the same places to which the urge to collide led fictional historians and applied social scientists of the Boom and the early New World Order.

Fiction is to history what lyrics are to music—adaptable and changeable. Will this ever be true for the social sciences? Latin American fiction and social science scholarship have a lot in common, as I have pointed out. In the last part of the twentieth century they both achieved world status. These intellectuals collided with and rebutted standard versions of national and regional history far more effectively than any generation of Clio's Latin American cohort had ever been able to do. A rebuttal to history does not have to be entirely accurate to be successful. To have a lasting effect it only has to provoke thought.

Fictional and social science views of Latin America's distant and recent pasts—and only future historians will be certain of this—may be even less accurate than previously accepted versions. Or they may prove to be as accurate, which means future historians will have all that much more to work with when they undertake a rewriting of Latin America's past according to their own scholarly criteria. It bears mention over and again that the approaches chosen by social scientists—and those that pervade novelists' commentary on their work and their world(s)—do resemble those of state-of-the-art professional Latin Americanist scholars of the late twentieth century in purpose if not in means.

Taken as generations, novelists and social scientists of varying ages have been faithful to their times: the late 1900s. Their views of the past reflect their reaction to the present ever so strongly owing to their times. Their creativity and disciplinary methodology show through impressively owing to the heights their genre or discipline reached. That the glaring subjectivity of the Boom and the utilitarian objectivity of the New World Order guided the intellectuals who have represented each is impressively evident. So is the diminution of interest in a metaphysical latinoamericanidad among social scientists in their practical approaches to contemporary problems.

Until recently Latin America had been defined by outsiders as much or more as it had been by Latin Americans themselves. Essayists of the last hundred years or so made an impressive start toward defining latinoamericanidad, though personally they might have been concerned more immediately with *mexicanidad, peruanidad, argentinidad, brasilidade,* or *chilenidad,* say. It was not until the Boom and the rise of the professional social science disciplines, however, that writers—and readers—had a chance to define their region based on what it never was as well as what it had not become. What these savants have to say is sophisticated, perceptive, sometimes downright perplexing.

The end of the Cold War, a phenomenon that aided insiders and outsiders alike in defining Latin America, put an end to the Boom as I have defined it herein. It also led social scientists to question the theories and solutions they and their predecessors had offered for decades. Portents of the 1980s convinced social scientists that something new was in the making. And then it happened, most of it in the space of three years. The Berlin Wall came down. The military ceded power to civilians in Chile, completing a regional process that had begun in 1980 in Peru. The Cold War was declared at an end. Europe redefined itself. The New World Order was proclaimed. The USSR fell apart. The Columbian quincentennial came and went. The rest of the world that had defined Latin America as much or more than the doings of Latin Americans ever had was no more. But neither was the Latin America that fictional historians had so forcefully attacked.

What had the third cataclysm wrought? Neoliberal economic policies took hold and democratization proceeded apace. If one sees merit in the concept of cataclysmic history, the events of 1989–92 can be construed as the ending of Latin America's third historical cataclysm—the recent past—and the beginning of what may end in a fourth. All this will need placing in historical context some day. In disguise currently, will the history of Latin America have to be "hatched o'er again" in another cataclysm?

It will if it continues to represent the tedious, but those who find need to collide and revise may again discover new historical regions to explore. Latin Americans may be less reluctant to pillory their historical and political leaders, as Martí suggested nations do—especially if the present does not lead to a better future for a lot of people. Paz's dictum notwithstanding, there was a Boom in literature, all right; it was a phenomenon not at all unlike those associated with Chile's Generation of 1842, the Portuguese Vencidos da Vida of the late nineteenth century, Spain's Generation of 1898, or the Parisian Lost Generation of the 1920s. As these examples show us, few things are more perilous—or more exciting—than creating a new order of things.

THERE ARE PLENTY of historians in Latin American countries, all right, but there currently is no cadre of Latin Americanists among them to rival either novelists of the Boom, the region's social scientists, or

Latin Americanists from Europe and North America. Until such a cadre exists, the region's own history will be in the minds of national historians and in the hands of social scientists in countries south of the Río Bravo. Fictional history may still be written, but its appeal may be limited in Latin America and beyond. Who and what else is to be collided with? That is the question that will determine where and why future collisions will take place—and how well they will sell.

If it is to be written in the immediate future by Latin Americans, history is likely to be less national than regional, for it will be even more dependent on social science approaches. Were there more anthropologists among the ranks of those who both construct and apply social science theory to contemporary problems with historical roots, this might not be altogether a bad thing. Anthropologists would doubtless be able to exchange ideas on culture as much as economists, political scientists, and sociologists did in chapter 6. Their ideas would provide an antidote to constricted history, alternatives to cataclysmic history. A few more Augusto Roa Bastos and Darcy Ribeiro types would not hurt.

What Europeans and North Americans have contributed to the historiography of Latin America, especially in the last fifty years, demands immense respect and admiration. The views of Latin American intellectuals of the historical impact of the outside world on the region demands equal respect and admiration. Knowledge is power, power defines knowledge, whether these are thrown together within the context of a personalist dictatorship or a totalitarian one. We have seen that this is so under professional militarism. We are currently seeing what the relationship between the two is like within the contexts of participatory democracies. Would that the efforts of social scientists result in a democratization of both power and knowledge that allows Latin Americans to rethink their history. Historians of Latin America have greater opportunities, thanks to their colleagues, the region's fictioneers and problem solvers.

In chapters 4 and 5 the thought and self-perception of intellectuals also convey to readers commitments to activism: government service, ideological faithfulness, journalism, teaching, participation in electoral struggles, public protest, "active" exile. The most successful novelists (in terms of world recognition through translation, travel, and number of publications) carried on activities outside their writing rooms. Other Latin Americans had written and acted in the same ways; intellectuals from other regions have done the same. There are few instances of so many accomplishing so much, however, as in late-twentieth-century Latin America.

What distinguishes ideas flowing from the pens of late-twentieth-century writers as much as their regional quality is their sharp focus on what had made Latin America the way it was. Latin American history began with discovery and conquest, but the region's past(s) already existed. Independence and early nationhood gave the region something of an identity, but the legacy of the colonial era could not be shaken off. The recent past lent a regional tinge to history only through the responses of fiction and social science to politics and government. But this did not make the legacy any more palatable.

Iberia, Europe, and the United States constituted the major foreign influences. Cultural, economic, and social influences of a domestic nature combined with foreign ones to produce three epochs of cataclysmic history and their principal political legacies discussed herein. The thought and self-perception that emerge from between the lines of their nonfiction constitute a joint declaration of regional identity by novelists that could not have been made by contemporary historians from Latin America. The historical mindset disguised in the writings of social scientists could not have been generated by historians either.

Had the Columbian quincentennial and the millennium come and gone unaccompanied by the end of the Cold War and its attendant events, fictional history might have continued to be the principal vehicle for collisions with history. The quincentennial would have been cataclysmic, all right, but it would have been associated fictionally, if not historically, with the tragedy of the recent past—not with the beginning of the New World Order as well. It would only have been an ending.

Owing to this, the historical past is being viewed increasingly only as that part of it that counts most. This has become a constricted regional, not a long-term national past, and this is going to pose problems for the region's historians. Latin Americans perforce still see their past as one dominated by foreign influences, rather than one in which blendings of long-term foreign and domestic causes produced contemporary effects. In the recent past it is the United States that has played the role of pervasive foreign influence in all spheres. In the transnational economic framework of the New World order the United States will still be the single hemispheric power, and this poses a problem for the region's historians because it will legitimate the belief that Latin Americans were hapless victims, not participants in the tragedy of the recent past, and that material gains achieved then do not count as valid historical gains. The wealth and influence of the United States assure it a status once ascribed by fictional historians to Iberia. It takes both prosperity as well as grandeur of thought and feeling to make a civilization, no matter what Rodó would have had us believe. The tragedy of the recent past as rendered in fictional history is the effect of institutions gone wrong because of a single foreign influence not that of combinations of foreign influences over time. And this poses a problem for the hemisphere's policymakers.

Independence, the second cataclysmic epoch (or corso, in the context of this book), really should be seen much as depicted didactically by fictional historians. Their renditions of what Bolívar and San Martín, Hidalgo and O'Higgins did, or failed to do, compare favorably with recent historical efforts of scholars. Fictional history vividly went further, though. Heroes really did become all too human. The founding fathers were every bit as villainous as the worst of the conquerors and the foulest of the postindependence tyrants. It is not so much what they accomplished as what they failed to accomplish that defines them in fiction. It is not that they failed, it is that they failed in so many ways historically. Independence did not mean the same things to all. It did not mean freedom for all; it allowed economic and social neocolonialism to flourish in new guises. Independence was less cataclysmic than it was transitional for the vast majority. For most of the people the nineteenth century was not all that different from the eighteenth. This is why there were culture wars among the intellectuals; this is why these wars continued on into the Boom. And it is why there will be culture wars in the future.

These culture wars will take place, it would appear, within the multiple processes of democratization and internationalization, and within the several contexts of authority and subordination discussed in chapter 3. Not all Latin Americans prosper because of internationalization. Not all benefit directly, yet, from liberal democracy. Not all see latinoamericanidad the way creative intellectuals, most of them male Euro-Latin Americans, did. Not all understand the macro-level alternatives proffered by social scientists to the macro-level strictures of international financial agencies. However much more they be aware of their history, the problems of most Latin Americans are micro-level, local problems: day-to-day survival, to name just one. For most Latin Americans hope for the future is much more important than disdain for the past.

When it came time to commemorate the quincentennial of American-Portuguese contact, in late April 2000, for example, the folk did not share their government's enthusiasm for what happened over the half-millennium since that day in 1500 when Cabral first saw the shores of what was to be Brazil. The poignant photograph of Indians holding a "march of the excluded" in Porto Seguro, and press coverage of Hã Hã Hãe chieftain Naílton Pataxó's march on Congress in Rio de Janeiro testify to the fact that for most Latin Americans history still has a role to play locally.[1] Fictional history, by provoking further revisionism, may serve the interests of democratization.

Among those who are not scholars, activists, or intellectuals there may be, paradoxically, a greater sense of resignation about what has been and is, and hope for what will be. In a recent essay a historian of the American West reminded us of the great continuity of that region's history, for the majority of its inhabitants, despite what appear to be watersheds for its leaders.[2] Continuities evinced by scholarly cultural and social history—and prominently manifest in history between the lines—may prove more meaningful to most Latin Americans than either cataclysmic or constricted history.

Continuing in retrospective steps, consideration of discovery and conquest by fictional historians was as serious a challenge to traditional views of the origins of Latin America as was that posed to the chronicle-style historiography of independence. It certainly was as outspokenly thoughtful as were the attacks made on late-twentieth-century authoritarianism. In chapter 1 we saw that novelists went somewhat beyond what their contemporary scholarly compatriots were doing; they went beyond revisionism—the new historical standard of their era. The anti-Iberian tone of most of these works, as I have pointed out, was the result of hostility to Portugal and Spain before 1974-75. The hostility directed toward the powerful of the past indirectly serves the interests of the downtrodden of the present and future.

Certainly the fictional histories of each cataclysm debunk the historical roles of former untouchables, be they cloaked in the garb of gods, heroes, or mere humans. Great men, dynasties, battles, and such all come out of fictional history as far less historical than hitherto portrayed. If the collisions discussed herein accomplished only this they will have served their purpose. If our knowledge of Latin American history has not expanded exponentially owing to the number and popularity of works, in translation or no, our perception of that history has been enhanced owing to their quality and timeliness.

I AM CONVINCED that the continual presence of the status quo alluded to in chapter 6 will run its course, will prove to be illusory. The tightening of the historical spiral may result in another cataclysm—the fourth referred to above. The Viconian progression in which Latin America finds itself at the millennium may prove to be a ricorso (Vico thought in terms of threes, let us not forget), or it may be little more than another corso. (Allow me to iterate: however powerful the influence of his historical thinking on fictional historians was, this was not a book about Vico and Latin America.)

Many have seen history as waves, cycles (within cycles), eddies, and spirals; there is as much room for such interpretation as there is for insistence on linear history. There is a lot of history to come; plenty of opportunities for authoritarianism and democracy to confront each other, especially the ways they did in Venezuela and Peru during the final years of the old millennium and early in the new one. Economic and social indicators of these years did not bode well for endless improvement of socioeconomic status for the majority; gaps between production and consumption, highest and lowest per capita income figures did not portend a utopian future for all. Dystopia seems more likely from Mexico south. When will this occupy historians' time? Only when it is history. Curiosity about the past did not produce an all-inclusive philosophy any more than collisions with history produced "better" history or a history acceptable to all. But curiosity may continue to provoke collisions

To think that the capitalist-democratic-international framework of the New World Order is permanent is tantamount to thinking that discovery and conquest would never occur, that independence never happened, that professional militarism was an ahistorical phenomenon. There were signs aplenty that what went on economically and politically in the recent past was not synchronized with cultural and social conditions. Why else would novelists have written what they did? There are signs aplenty that gaps still yawn between theories and practices of democratization and transnational economics. Why else did social scientists say what they did? Why else is history not written the way it was once upon a time?

Notes

Full information for the novels cited by short title in the first three chapters can be found in the bibliographic lists at the end of those chapters.

The following abbreviations appear in the notes for chapter 6:

CEPAL	*Revista de la CEPAL*
NS	*Nueva sociedad*
PE	*Política e estrategia*
PI	*Pensamiento iberoamericano*
RBCS	*Revista brasileira de ciências sociais*
RCP	*Revista de ciencia política*
RICS	*Revista internacional de ciencias sociales*
RLCS	*Revista latinoamericana de ciencias sociales*
RMS	*Revista mexicana de sociología*
ROEL	*Revista occidental: Estudios latinoamericanos*
RPS	*Revista paraguaya de sociología*

Introduction

1. See Lionel Gossman, *Between History and Literature* (Cambridge, Mass.: Harvard University Press, 1997).

2. See *Casa de Las Américas,* October 1964, esp. the introduction by Angel Rama, "Diez problemas para el novelista latinoamericano," 3–43. Owing to errors that occur in volume numbers, I have limited most periodical citations to date of issue.

3. For a full definition of the term and stimulating discussion of the subgenre see Seymour Menton, *Latin America's New Historical Novel* (Austin: University of Texas Press, 1998). In a useful "prepandix" (1–13),

Menton provides chronologies of the historical novel from 1949 to 1992, and claims that others are in the writing. The book also has a superb bibliography.

4. Jay Parini, "The Memoir versus the Novel in a Time of Transition," *Chronicle of Higher Education,* July 10, 1998.

5. I refer, of course, to Vico's *Principi di una scienza nuova d'intorno alla comune nature delle nazioni* (1725 and various editions), in English known as *The New Science,* sometimes simply *New Science,* esp. book 4, "The Course Nations Run," and book 5, "The Resurgence of Nations." The most useful English version of *The New Science* is that translated and edited by Thomas Goddard Bergin and Max Harold Fisch (Ithaca: Cornell University Press, 1984).

6. By Richard M. Morse in "Towards a Theory of Spanish American Government," *Journal of the History of Ideas* 15 (1954): 71–93.

Chapter 1

1. Latin Americans were by no means alone in a quest to take a hard look at the history of Latin America on the eve of and during the quincentennial of discovery and conquest. See, for example, Richard M. Morse, *New World Soundings: Culture and Ideology in the Americas* (Baltimore: Johns Hopkins University Press, 1989); Kirkpatrick Sale, *The Conquest of Paradise: Christopher Columbus and the Columbian Legacy* (New York: Knopf, 1991); Xavier Robert de Ventos (a Spaniard), *The Hispanic Labyrinth: Tradition and Modernity in the Colonization of the Americas* (New Brunswick: Transaction Books, 1991); Stephen Greenblatt, *Marvelous Possessions: The Wonder of the New World* (Oxford: Clarendon Press, 1991); Fredrick B. Pike, *The United States and Latin America: Myths and Stereotypes of Civilization and Nature* (Austin: University of Texas Press, 1992); David Stannard, *American Holocaust: Columbus and the Conquest of the New World* (New York: Oxford University Press, 1992); Hugh Thomas, *The Real Discovery of America: Mexico, November 8, 1519* (Mt. Kisco, N.Y.: Moya Bell, 1992); Hugh Thomas, *Conquest: Montezuma, Cortés, and the Fall of Old Mexico* (New York: Simon and Schuster, 1993); and Stephen Greenblatt, ed., *New World Encounters* (Berkeley: University of California Press, 1993).

2. Milan Kundera, *The Art of the Novel* (New York: Grove Press, 1986), 9. No one interested in Latin American literature's roles should fail to read

Jean Franco's *The Modern Culture of Latin America: Society and the Artist* (Baltimore: Pelican Books, 1970).

3. They were, after all, already predisposed to wonder and fantasy, owing to the literary tradition they brought with them. Spanish literature (Portuguese as well) was well endowed with tales of mystery, magic, and chivalry, and proscription would not prevent their continued popularity among conquerors and colonists. See Irving Leonard, *Books of the Brave* (Cambridge, Mass.: Harvard University Press, 1949).

4. See Tzvetan Todorov, *The Conquest of America: The Question of the Other,* trans. Richard Howard (New York: Harper and Row, 1984). See also, Germán Arciniegas, *America in Europe: A History of the New World in Reverse,* trans. Gabriela Arciniegas and Victoria Araña (New York: Harcourt Brace Jovanovich, 1986); and Frederick M. Nunn, "*Latinoamericanidad* from *Encuentro* to Quincentennial: The 'New Novel' as Revisionist History," *Revista interamericana de bibliografía/Inter-American Review of Bibliography,* no. 2 (1994): 219–50.

5. *Harp,* 9.

6. *Witness,* 9.

7. *Terra Nostra,* 492–99.

8. *Dogs,* 174.

9. Edmundo O'Gorman, *The Invention of America: An Inquiry into the Historical Nature of the New World and the Meaning of Its History* (Bloomington: Indiana University Press, 1961); Todorov, *Conquest,* esp. 14–33; *Harp,* xiii. And see José Rabassa, *Inventing America: Spanish Historiography and the Formation of Eurocentrism* (Norman: University of Oklahoma Press, 1997).

10. *Harp,* 55–75.

11. *Dogs,* 136.

12. *Harp,* 118; *Dogs,* 223–24.

13. *Lentils,* 122.

14. *Harp,* 158, 164–65.

15. See, for example, *Dogs,* 157.

16. *1492,* 99.

17. *Harp,* 104.

18. *Dogs,* 295.

19. *Terra Nostra,* 24.

20. See Octavio Paz, *One Earth, Four or Five Worlds: Reflections on Contemporary History,* trans. Helen R. Lane (New York: Harcourt Brace Jovanovich, 1985).

21. *Terra Nostra,* 265.

22. *Lentils,* 12.

23. *Dogs,* 301.

24. See esp. Thomas, *Real Discovery of America.*

25. Ilan Stavan, "Autumn of the Matriarch," a review of Luisa Valenzuela's *Bedside Manners* (London: Serpent's Tail, 1995), *The Nation,* March 6, 1995, 316–19.

26. *Lentils,* 32.

27. *Daimon,* 23, 117, 159.

28. Ibid., 65.

29. Ibid., 122.

30. *Harp,* 119; *Dogs,* 223–24.

31. *Harp,* 126.

32. *Terra Nostra,* 450. See Díaz del Castillo, *True History of the Conquest of New Spain* (many editions), *Historia verdadera de la conquista de la Nueva España* (1632); and Carlos Fuentes, *The Orange Tree,* trans. Alfred Mac Adam (New York: Farrar, Straus and Giroux, 1994), *El naranjo, o los círculos del tiempo* (1994).

33. *Terra Nostra,* 507.

34. Ibid., 612.

35. Ibid., 738.

36. *Lentils,* 39.

37. *Terra Nostra,* 224.

38. *Daimon,* 95.

39. See Hermann von Keyserling, *South American Meditations: On Hell and Heaven in Man's Soul,* trans. Theresa Duerr (London: Jonathan Cape, 1932).

40. *Dogs,* 188.

41. For example, *Terra Nostra,* 132, 142; *Dogs,* 208, 229.

42. *Dogs,* 298.

43. Ibid. Keyserling, of course, would have concurred.

44. *Daimon,* 33; see also 31–43, 51–59 for a glimpse of the epic span of time and its impact on the "hero."

45. *Witness,* 124–25, 128–31. For a twentieth-century source expressing the same degree of wonderment re American inhabitants and their culture, see Claude Lévi-Strauss, *Tristes tropiques,* trans. John and Doreen Weightman (New York: Atheneum, 1974).

46. On this epic voyage see Napoleón Baccino Ponce de León, *Five Black Ships: A Novel of the Discoverers,* trans. Nick Caistor (New York: Harcourt Brace Jovanovich, 1994), *Maluco* (1990).

47. See *Daimon*, 43, 80, 115, 241.
48. *Dogs*, 7.
49. Ibid., 30.
50. *Lentils*, 27, 34, 45, 151, 153; *Terra Nostra*, 95.
51. *Lentils*, 157.
52. *1492*, 158.
53. Ibid., esp. 89–90.
54. *Nation*, 110–11.
55. See *1492*, 98–99, 106–7, 114–15, 116–17, 130–31. The cited passage appears on p. 158.
56. See esp. *Nation*, 111–20.
57. *Terra Nostra*, 450. And see n. 32, this chapter.
58. *1492*, 128.
59. See *Lentils*, 14, 157.
60. *1492*, 130, 149.
61. *Lentils*, 178.
62. *Harp*, xiii.
63. *Dogs*, 204.
64. For an example of what this means see Osman Lins, *Avalovara*, trans. Gregory Rabassa (São Paulo: Melhoramentos, 1973; Austin: University of Texas Press, 1990).
65. Such corsi-ricorsi-like history is also portrayed in *Terra Nostra*, 302–3, 387, 392–93, 771, and is the dominant theme of *The Orange Tree*.
66. *Terra Nostra*, 614.
67. *Daimon*, esp. 95, 216–17.
68. See *Nation*, 110–17.
69. Ibid., 139–99 passim.
70. *Daimon*, 101, 175.
71. *Witness*, 132, 133.
72. *Terra Nostra*, 771.

Chapter 2

1. Sor Juana Inés de la Cruz, *The Answer/La respuesta*, trans. and ed. Electra Arenal and Amanda Powell (New York: Feminist Press of the City University of New York, 1994), 47 (par. 6, ll. 179–80).
2. Paz, *One Earth*, 142–47.

3. Recent studies of independence that complement this presentation re history and literature are David Bushnell and Neil Macaulay, *The Emergence of Latin America in the Nineteenth Century*, 2d ed. (New York: Oxford University Press, 1994); and Doris Sommer, *Foundational Fictions: The National Romances of Latin America* (Berkeley: University of California Press, 1991).

4. *General*, 37.

5. Ibid., 240.

6. Ibid., 4.

7. Ibid., 267.

8. Ibid., 124.

9. *Campaign*, 172.

10. Ibid., 174–75.

11. Ibid., 166.

12. *General*, 193.

13. *Campaign*, 168.

14. Ibid., 169.

15. *Supreme*, 370.

16. Ibid., 370–71.

17. Ibid., 38.

18. Ibid.

19. Ibid., 32.

20. Ibid., 40. See also p. 156 for further comments on the army.

21. Ibid., 330.

22. Ibid., 32.

23. *Relations*, 106.

24. Ibid., 110.

25. *Peregrinations*, 137.

26. *General*, 184.

27. On this subject see Edward Said, *Beginnings: Intention and Method* (New York: Columbia University Press, 1975, 1985), esp. ch. 3, "The Novel as Beginning Intention," 79–188.

28. Said, *Beginnings*, 83.

29. *Campaign*, 41–42.

30. Ibid., 42.

31. Ibid., 225–29.

32. Ibid., 68.

33. Ibid., 100–1.

34. See *General*, esp. 188ff., 223–40.

35. *Relations,* 108.

36. See *Relations,* 70, 116, 167–71.

37. *Explosion,* 146. See also Fuentes's remarks on the French Caribbean in *Relations,* 123–24.

38. *Relations,* 24.

39. *General,* 222.

40. *Explosion,* 32–33.

41. I refer, of course, to Edward Said's *Orientalism* (New York: Vintage Books, 1979).

42. *Concierto,* 116–17.

43. *Explosion,* 154.

44. *Kingdom,* 175.

45. *Peregrinations,* xvi–xvii.

46. *Concierto,* 114–15.

47. *Explosion,* 58.

48. *Kingdom,* 184–85.

49. *Campaign,* 142.

50. Ibid., 134–35.

51. Ibid., 129.

52. *Relations,* 88, 100, 106, 110, 183–84, 197.

53. See, for example, Carlos Fuentes, *The Buried Mirror: Reflections on Spain and the New World* (New York: Houghton Mifflin, 1992), based on the five-part television documentary produced for the Columbian quincentennial.

54. *General,* 18.

55. Ibid., 71.

56. Ibid., 193.

57. *All Saints,* 37.

58. Ibid., 184.

59. *Supreme,* 32.

60. Ibid., 96.

Chapter 3

1. Recent treatments of modern and contemporary Latin America useful to readers of these pages are Alfred Stepan, ed., *Americas: New Interpretive Essays* (New York: Oxford University Press, 1992); Peter Winn, *Americas:*

The Changing Face of Latin America and the Caribbean, updated ed. (Berkeley: University of California Press, 1999); Thomas E. Skidmore and Peter H. Smith, *Modern Latin America*, 5th ed. (New York: Oxford University Press, 2001); and Howard J. Wiarda, *The Soul of Latin America: The Cultural and Political Tradition* (New Haven: Yale University Press, 2001).

2. I refer to the title and subject of my own work, *The Time of the Generals: Latin American Professional Militarism in World Perspective* (Lincoln: University of Nebraska Press, 1992).

3. *House*, 187.

4. Ibid., 286.

5. Donoso's portrayal of lackeys as go-betweens brings to mind French social scientist François Bourricaud's perceptive description of duplicitous intermediaries between landowners and capitalists, and peasants and Indians in twentieth-century Peru. See Bourricaud, "Notas acerca de la oligarquía peruana" (previously published as "Remarques sur l'oligarchie péruvienne"), in *La oligarquía en el Perú*, ed. José Matos Mar (Lima: Francisco Moncloa Editores, 1969), 13–54. See as well François Bourricaud, *Pouvoir et societé dans le Perou contemporain*, Cahiers de la Fondation Nationale des Sciences Politiques (Paris: Presses de la Fondation Nationale des Sciences Politiques, 1967), esp. pt. 1, "La mobilization d'une societé dualiste," 13–112. In both these works Bourricaud uses fictional depictions of social relations to document his conclusions. He also claimed that fiction was well ahead of the social sciences in this regard.

6. *Rebellion in the Backlands* was first published in English translation by Samuel Putnam (Chicago: University of Chicago Press, 1940). Publication data on Vargas Llosa's novel appear in the list at the end of the text of this chapter.

7. *War*, 83.

8. Ibid., 500.

9. Miguel Angel Asturias, *El señor presidente*, trans. Frances Partridge (New York: Atheneum, 1980), *El señor presidente* (1946), cited as *Presidente;* Gabriel García Márquez, *The Autumn of the Patriarch*, trans. Gregory Rabassa (New York: Harper and Row, 1976), *El otoño del patriarca* (1975), cited as *Autumn;* Roa Bastos's magnum opus was first published in 1974. See also Alejo Carpentier, *Reasons of State*, trans. Frances Partridge (London: Victor Gollancz, 1976), *El recurso del método* (1974).

10. *Presidente*, 97. See also, pp. 254–76, passim.

11. *Autumn*, 168.

12. *Rain*, 191.

13. See *Lizard,* 80–103, passim. The Southern Cone countries are Argentina, Bolivia, Brazil, Chile, Paraguay, and Uruguay. Peru may be included based on intraregional criteria.

14. *Lizard,* 103. Valenzuela's emphasis.

15. *Conversation,* 53.

16. *Insurrection,* 55.

17. *Night,* 27.

18. *Snow,* 51.

19. *Winter,* 33.

20. Allende's first novel, *The House of the Spirits,* trans. Magda Bogin (New York: Alfred A. Knopf, 1985), *La casa de los espíritus* (1982), is a time-sweeping work, comparable, say some, to García Márquez's magisterial *One Hundred Years of Solitude,* trans. Gregory Rabassa (New York: Harper and Row, 1970), *Cien años de soledad* (1967). Allende's early work should also be consulted for its treatment of women's changing roles. García Márquez's can be read with the entire history of Latin America in mind, disclaimers of its author like those noted in the following chapter notwithstanding.

21. See *Song,* 260–61.

22. Ibid., 379–83.

23. *Death,* 261.

24. *Curfew,* 94.

25. *Silence,* 158.

26. *Spring,* 28.

27. The term *mili-tech* is Ignácio de Loyola Brandão's. See *Earth,* 16.

28. The term *antipolitics* is defined and studied in depth in Brian Loveman and Thomas M. Davies Jr., eds., *The Politics of Antipolitics: The Military in Latin America,* rev. and updated (Wilmington, Del.: Scholarly Resources, 1997).

29. *Infierno,* 189.

30. *Curfew,* 110.

31. *Celebration,* 143.

32. *Festival,* 63.

33. *Zero,* 313

34. *Tower, 131.*

35. *Song,* 426–27.

36. See *Insurrection,* 139–40.

37. *Cuzcatlán,* passim, esp. 4–5, 34–35, 104–5.

38. Ibid., 4–5.

39. See *Life,* 62–63, 92–93.

40. *Love*, 103.

41. Ibid., 134.

42. See *Conversation*, esp. 383–85.

43. Louis Hubert Gonzalve Lyautey (1854–1934) was the French officer whose time in southeast Asia and Morocco resulted in expansion of the French empire and inspired generations of officers to see hinterlands and frontiers as natural destinations for armies. Most of the French officers who served in Peru from the 1890s, and in Brazil from 1919 until World War II, were disciples of Lyautey, hence the adaptation of France's *mission civilizatrice* to Peruvian and later Brazilian military usage.

44. *Gods*, 168.

45. *Night*, 82–123, passim.

46. See Frederick M. Nunn, "The Latin American 'New Novel' in Translation: Archival Source for the Dialogue between Literature and History," in *Translating Latin America: Culture as Text*, ed. William Luis and Julio Rodríguez Luis, Translation Perspectives 6 (Binghamton, N.Y.: Center for Research in Translation, State University of New York, 1991), 67–77.

47. The Argentine and Brazilian masterworks are referred to elsewhere in these pages. Lastarria's *Literary Memoirs* appeared in English for the first time in 2000 (trans. R. Kelly Washbourne; intro., Frederick M. Nunn) (New York: Oxford University Press, 2000).

Chapter 4

1. Very useful studies of the essay include William Rex Crawford, *A Century of Latin American Thought*, rev. ed. (Cambridge, Mass.: Harvard University Press, 1961); Martin S. Stabb, *In Quest of Identity: Patterns in the Spanish American Essay of Ideas, 1880–1960* (Chapel Hill: University of North Carolina Press, 1967); and Ilan Stavans, ed., *The Oxford Book of Latin American Essays* (New York: Oxford University Press, 1997).

Similarly useful descriptive and definitional studies of the Boom, and that place it in historical perspective, are Luis Harss, *Into the Main Stream: Conversations with Latin American Writers* (New York: Harper and Row, 1967); Julio Ortega, *La contemplación y la fiesta: Ensayos sobre la nueva novela latinoamericana* (Lima: Editorial Universitaria, 1968); Carlos Fuentes, *La nueva novela hispanoamericana* (Mexico City: Joaquín Mortiz, 1969); Emir Rodríguez Monegal, *El boom de la novela latinoamericana* (Caracas:

Editorial Tiempo Nuevo, 1972); José Donoso, *The Boom in Spanish American Literature: A Personal History* (New York: Columbia University Press and the Center for Inter-American Relations, 1977); David Viñas, *Más allá del boom: Literatura y mercado* (Mexico City: Marcha Editores, 1981); Yvette E. Miller and Raymond Leslie Williams, eds., *The Boom in Retrospect: A Reconsideration*, special issue of the *Latin American Literary Review* (January–June 1987); Renato Martínez Torres, *Para una relectura del boom: Populismo y otredad* (Madrid: Pliegos, 1990); and Raymond L. Williams, *The Modern Latin American Novel* (New York: Twayne, 1993).

2. Georg Lukacs, *The Theory of the Novel: A Historico-Philosophical Essay on the Forms of Great Epic Literature*, trans. Anna Bostock (London: Merlin Press, 1978), 56. Three recent, highly significant (and superbly documented) works placing the Latin American novel in a historical and political perspective are Roberto González Echevarría, *Myth and Archive: A Theory of Latin American Narrative* (Durham: Duke University Press, 1998); Doris Sommer, *Foundational Fictions: The National Romances of Latin America* (Berkeley: University of California Press, 1991); and Raymond L. Williams, *The Postmodern Novel in Latin America: Politics, Culture, and the Crisis of Truth* (New York: St. Martin's Press, 1996).

3. Henri Barbusse, *Manifeste aux intellectuels* (Paris: Les Ecrivains Réunis, 1927), 9–10.

4. Roland Barthes, *The Pleasure of the Text*, trans. Richard Miller, intro. Richard Howard (Oxford: Basil Blackwell, 1980), 33.

5. Carlos Octavio Bunge, *Nuestra América* (Barcelona: Henrich, 1903), 87–99.

6. Manuel Ugarte, *El destino de un continente* (Madrid: Editorial Mundo Latino, 1923), 394–401.

7. See José Vasconcelos, *La raza cósmica: Misión de la raza iberoamericana: Notas de viajes a la América del Sur* (Paris: Agencia Mundial de Librería, 1923).

8. José Ortega y Gasset, "Ideas sobre la novela," in *Meditaciones del Quijote* (Madrid: Revista de Occidente, 1960), 139–92.

9. Raymond Williams, *Marxism and Literature* (Oxford: Oxford University Press, 1977), 48.

10. Milan Kundera, *The Art of the Novel* (London: Faber and Faber, 1988), 8.

11. Ibid., 3–4.

12. Bertrand Russell, *History as Art* (Ashford, Kent: Hand and Flower Press, 1954), 8.

13. Edmundo O'Gorman, *The Invention of America: An Inquiry into the Historical Nature of the New World and the Meaning of its History* (Bloomington: Indiana University Press, 1961), 138.

14. Georg Lukacs, *Studies in European Realism: A Sociological Survey of the Writings of Balzac, Stendahl, Zola, Tolstoy, Gorki, and Others* (London: Merlin Press, 1972), 97.

15. See Gabriel García Márquez and Mario Vargas Llosa, *Diálogo sobre la novela latinoamericana* (Lima: Editorial Perú Andino, 1988).

16. Alejo Carpentier, "Literatura y conciencia política en América Latina," in *Cuba: Una revolución en marcha* (*Suplemento 1967 de Cuadernos de Ruedo Ibérico*), ed. Francisco Fernández and José Martínez (Havana: Ediciones Ruedo Ibérico, 1967), 283.

Following is a select list of works conveying ideas of the novelist pertinent to this chapter: Alejo Carpentier, *Ensayos* (Essays, selections) (Havana: Editorial Letras Cubanas, 1984); Alejo Carpentier and Virgilio López Lemus, *Entrevistas : Alejo Carpentier* (Havana: Editorial Letras Cubanas, 1985); Alejo Carpentier and Roberto González Echevarría, *Historia y ficción en la narrativa hispanoamericana: Coloquio de Yale* (Caracas: Monte Avila Editores, 1984); Alejo Carpentier, *Literatura y conciencia política en América Latina* (Madrid: A. Corazón Editor, 1969); and Alejo Carpentier, *La novela latinoamericana en vísperas de un nuevo siglo y otros ensayos* (Mexico City: Siglo Veintiuno, 1981).

17. Alejo Carpentier, "Papel social del novelista," *Casa de las Américas,* March–April 1969, 14–15. Carpentier named Sarmiento in this source, but given the chance, failed to include Sor Juana Inez de la Cruz.

18. Alejo Carpentier, "Conciencia e identidad de América," in *Razón de ser (Conferencias)* (Caracas: Universidad Central de Venezuela, Ediciones del Rectorado, 1976), 17–25.

19. Alejo Carpentier, "Habla Alejo Carpentier de los novelistas latinoamericanos," interview with Roberto Jaimes, in Carpentier and López Lemus, *Entrevistas,* 432–34.

20. Alejo Carpentier, "La actividad cultural en Cuba," *Sur,* March–April 1965, 60–67.

21. See Alejo Carpentier, "La novela y la historia," in *Letra y solfa,* ed. Alexis Márquez R. (Caracas: Síntesis Dosmil, 1975), 118–120. See also *Razón de ser,* 75–96.

22. See esp. "La novela y la historia," *Razón de ser,* and López Lemus, *Entrevistas.*

23. Alejo Carpentier, "Problemática del tiempo y el idioma en la moderna novela latinoamericana," in *Razón de ser*, 75–96. The citation is from p. 93.

24. Ibid., 112–14.

25. Alejo Carpentier, "Sobre su novelística," *Conferencias* (Havana: Editorial Letras, 1987), 90–101.

26. Alejo Carpentier, "Problemática de la actual novela latinoamericana," in *Tientos, diferencias, y otros ensayos* (Barcelona: Plaza y Janés, 1987), 7–28. The quotation is from p. 12.

27. Ibid., 49–57.

28. Ibid., 66–77.

29. Graciela Maturo, "El recurso del método de Alejo Carpentier: La novela como lectura de la historia," in *Fenomenología, creación y crítica: Sujeto y mundo en la novela latinoamericana* (Buenos Aires: Fernando García Cambeiro, 1989), 71–94. The cited passage is from p. 71. For similar comments see Hermann Herlinghaus, ed., *Romankunst in Lateinamerika* (Berlin: Akademie-Verlag, 1989).

See also the following selected sources for further information on the thought of Alejo Carpentier: Donald Leslie Shaw, *Alejo Carpentier* (Boston: Twayne, 1985); Bobs M. Tusa, *Alejo Carpentier: A Comprehensive Study* (Chapel Hill: Albatros Hispanófila, 1982); Frank Janney, *Alejo Carpentier and His Early Works* (London: Tamesis Books, 1981); Roberto González Echevarría, *Alejo Carpentier: Bibliographical Guide* (Westport, Conn.: Greenwood Press, 1983); Roberto González Echevarría, *Alejo Carpentier: The Pilgrim at Home* (Austin: University of Texas Press, 1990); Sally Harvey, *Carpentier's Proustian Fiction: The Influence of Marcel Proust on Alejo Carpentier* (London: Tamesis Books, 1994); Mercedes Rein, *Cortázar y Carpentier* (Buenos Aires: Ediciones de Crisis, 1974); Oscar Velayos Zurdo, *Historia y Utopia en Alejo Carpentier* (Salamanca: Universidad de Salamanca, 1990); Esther Mocega-González, *La narrativa de Alejo Carpentier: El concepto del tiempo como tema fundamental: Ensayo de interpretación y análisis* (New York: Eliseo Torres, 1975); Marcia Hoppe Navarro, *O romance do ditador: Poder e história na América Latina* (São Paulo: Icone Editora, 1990); and Simon Gikandi, *Writing in Limbo: Modernism and Caribbean Literature* (Ithaca, N.Y.: Cornell University Press, 1992).

30. Carlos Fuentes, "América Latina–Estados Unidos," *Política* (Caracas), August–December 1960, 51–72.

Following is a select list of works conveying ideas of the novelist pertinent to this chapter: Carlos Fuentes, *Geografía de la novela* (Mexico City:

Fondo de Cultura Económica, 1993); Carlos Fuentes, *High Noon in Latin America* (Los Angeles: Manas Publishing Company, 1983); Carlos Fuentes and Jorge Bernal, *Integración y equidad: Democracia, desarrollo y política social* (Bogotá: Corporación S.O.S. Colombia, 1993); Carlos Fuentes, *A New Time for Mexico* (New York: Farrar, Straus and Giroux, 1996); the aforementioned, *La nueva novela hispanoamericana* (Mexico City: Joaquín Mortiz, 1969); Carlos Fuentes, *Tiempo mexicano* (Mexico City: Editorial Joaquín Mortiz, 1971); Carlos Fuentes, *Valiente mundo nuevo: Épica, utopia y mito en la novela hispano-americana* (Mexico City: Fondo de Cultura Económica, 1990); and Carlos Fuentes, *Whither Latin America?* (New York: Monthly Review Press, 1963).

31. Carlos Fuentes, "La situación del escritor en América Latina," *Mundo nuevo,* July 1966, 5–21.

32. Carlos Fuentes, *Premio Internacional de Novela "Rómulo Gallegos":Discursos de Carlos Fuentes y Luis García Morales* (Caracas: Ediciones de la Presidencia de la República y del Consejo Nacional de Cultura, 1978), 23.

33. Carlos Fuentes, "Entrevista a Carlos Fuentes (1980)," by José Anadón, *Revista iberoamericana,* April–September 1983, 621–30. The citation comes from p. 621.

34. Carlos Fuentes, *Valiente mundo nuevo,* 280–81. This book comprises lectures given when the novelist held the Simón Bolívar Chair at Cambridge University and the Robert F. Kennedy Professorship at Harvard University.

35. See Carlos Fuentes, "Los hijos de don Quijote," *Nexos,* January 1991, 43–51.

36. See Anadón, "Entrevista," 630.

37. Ibid.

38. Ibid.

39. See Anadón, "Entrevista," passim; and Carlos Fuentes, "Palabras pronunciadas por Carlos Fuentes con motivo de la entrega del 'Premio Miguel de Cervantes, 1987'" (Alcalá de Henares: n.p., 1988), typescript, 15 pp.

40. See Carlos Fuentes, introduction to George Konrad, *The City Builder,* trans. Ivan Sanders (Harmondsworth, Middlesex: Penguin Books, 1987), vii–xxv.

41. Fuentes, *Valiente mundo nuevo,* 27.

42. Fuentes, "Hijos de don Quijote," 45–48.

43. As an example of interest in this debate outside Mexico, see Walter Boeheich, "Ein Brüderzwist in Mexiko," *Die Zeit* (Hamburg), *Feuilleton,* January 21, 1994, 41.

See the following sources for further information on the thought of Carlos Fuentes: Elena Poniatowska, *¡Ay vida, no me mereces!* *Carlos Fuentes, Rosario Castellanos, Juan Rulfo: La literatura de la onda* (Mexico City: Joaquín Mortiz, 1985); Daniel de Guzmán, *Carlos Fuentes* (New York: Twayne, 1972); Wendy B. Faris, *Carlos Fuentes* (New York: F. Ungar, 1983); Robert Brody and Charles Rossman, eds., *Carlos Fuentes, A Critical View* (Austin: University of Texas, 1982); Georgina García-Gutiérrez, *Los disfraces: La obra mestiza de Carlos Fuentes* (Mexico City: Colegio de México, 1981); Jorge Ruffinelli, *La escritura invisible: Arlt, Borges, García Márquez, Roa Bastos, Rulfo, Cortázar, Fuentes, Vargas Llosa* (Mexico City: Universidad Veracruzana, 1986); Francisco Javier Ordiz, *El mito en la obra narrativa de Carlos Fuentes* (León: Universidad de León, Servicio de Publicaciones, 1987); Aída Elsa Ramírez Mattei, *La narrativa de Carlos Fuentes: Afán por la armonía en la multiplicidad antagónica del mundo* (Río Piedras: Editorial de la Universidad de Puerto Rico, 1983); Liliana Befumo Boschi, *Nostalgia del futuro en la obra de Carlos Fuentes* (Buenos Aires: F. García Cambeiro, 1974); Martín Ramos Díaz, *La novela mexicana en Estados Unidos, 1940–1990* (Mexico City: Universidad Autónoma del Estado de México, 1994); Yolanda Osuna, *Tres ensayos de análisis literario* (Mérida, Venezuela: Universidad de los Andes, Consejo de Publicaciones, 1980); and Raymond L. Williams, *The Writings of Carlos Fuentes* (Austin: University of Texas Press, 1996).

44. See Mario Vargas Llosa, "*Cien años de soledad*: El Amadís en América," *Amaru*, July–September 1967, 73–74. See also José Miguel Oviedo, Hugo Achugar, and Jorge Arbeleche, *Aproximación a Gabriel García Márquez*, Cuadernos de Literatura 12, 2d ed. (Paysandú, Uruguay: Fundación de Cultura Universitaria, 1970); and Rosa Fortuna Boldori, "*Cien años de soledad* y la novela latinoamericana," *Universidad*, September–December 1979, 21–106.

45. See Mario Vargas Llosa, "García Márquez: De Aracataca a Macondo," in *La novela hispanoamericana actual: Compilación de ensayos críticos*, ed. Angel Flores and Raúl Silva Cáceres (New York: Las Américas Publishing, 1971), 157–75; and Mario Vargas Llosa, *García Márquez: Historia de un Deicidio* (La Paz: Difusión, 1971). The Colombian, it should be noted, staunchly resisted depictions of Macondo as a microcosmic Latin America.

On the Colombian's blending of fiction with history, and its significance to the writing of recent history, see Eduardo Posada-Carbó, "Fiction as History: The *Bananeras* and Gabriel García Márquez's *One Hundred Years of Solitude*," *Journal of Latin American Studies*, May 1998, 395–414.

46. See, for example, Gabriel García Márquez, *Operación Carlota: Los cubanos en Angola* (Lima: Marca Azul, 1977).

The following works also convey ideas of the novelist pertinent to this chapter: Gabriel García Márquez, *Cuando era feliz e indocumentado* (Esplugas de Llobregat [Barcelona]: Plaza y Janés, 1974); and Gabriel García Márquez and Mario Vargas Llosa, *La novela en América Latina: Dialogo* (Lima: C. Milla Batres, 1968).

47. See Gabriel García Márquez, "La literatura colombiana, un fraude a la nación," *Eco,* September 1978, 1200-7; and Gabriel García Márquez and Alfonso Rentería Mantilla (comp.), *Gabriel García Márquez habla de García Márquez en 33 grandes reportajes* (Bogotá: Rentería Editores, 1979). The quotations are from the latter work, pp. 33-39.

48. Gabriel García Márquez, "Conversaciones con Gabriel García Márquez," by Omar Prego, *Cuadernos de Marcha,* September 1981, 69-77.

49. See Gabriel García Márquez, *El olor de la guayaba: Conversaciones con Plinio Apuleyo Mendoza:* (Barcelona: Editorial Bruguera, 1982), 142-43.

50. García Márquez, "Literatura colombiana," 1201.

51. Rentería, *García Márquez,* 33.

52. See García Márquez, "Conversaciones," 76.

53. Gabriel García Márquez, Eduardo Galeano, Carlos Fuentes, Octavio Paz, Julio Cortázar, Juan Carlos Onetti, Ernesto Cardenal, Alán García, Belisario Betancur et al., *La democracia y la paz en América Latina* (Bogotá: Editorial El Buho, 1986), 15.

54. García Márquez, *Olor de la guayaba,* 142.

55. Ibid., 142-45.

56. José Miguel Oviedo, "Macondo: Un territorio mágico y americano," in Oviedo, Achúgar, and Arbeleche, *Aproximación,* 11.

57. Ibid., 3-15.

58. Mario Vargas Llosa, *García Márquez: Historia de un Deicidio,* ch. 2, "El novelista y sus demonios," 85-213. However one interprets either of the two novelists, their work, or their interpersonal relations, this book remains one of the best examples of criticism by one Latin American writer of another.

59. Gabriel García Márquez, "Desventuras de un escritor de libros," *Eco,* June 1979, 113.

60. Gabriel García Márquez, "Entrevista a los Sandinistas," in García Márquez et al., *Los Sandinistas* (Bogotá: Editorial La Oveja Negra, 1979), 135-67.

61. García Márquez, *Olor de la guayaba,* 50. See also Juan Gustavo Cobo

Borda, *Para que mis amigos me quieran más: Homenaje a Gabriel García Márquez* (Bogotá: Siglo de Hombres Editores, 1992).

62. García Márquez, *Olor de la guayaba*, 89.

63. Gabriel García Márquez, "El cuento de los generales que se creyeron su propio cuento," in *Notas de prensa* (Madrid: Mondedori España, 1991), 33–34.

See the following sources for further information on the thought of Gabriel García Márquez: Mario Benedetti, ed., *Nueve asedios a García Márquez* (Santiago: Editorial Universitaria, 1972); José Miguel Oviedo, *Aproximación a Gabriel García Márquez* (Montevideo: Fundación de Cultura Universitaria, 1969); Graciela Maturo, *Claves simbólicas de Gabriel García Márquez* (Buenos Aires: F. García Cambeiro, 1972); Gustavo A. Alfaro and Germán Arciniegas, *Constante de la historia de Latinoamérica en García Márquez* (Cali: Biblioteca Banco Popular, 1979); George R. McMurray, *Critical Essays on Gabriel García Márquez* (Boston: G. K. Hall, 1987); Juan Manuel Marcos, *De García Márquez al postboom* (Madrid: Editorial Orígenes, 1986); Lucila Inés Mena, *La función de la historia en "Cien años de soledad"* (Esplugas de Llobregat [Barcelona]: Plaza y Janés, 1979); George R. McMurray, *Gabriel García Márquez* (Bogotá: Carlos Valencia Editores, 1978); Hans-Otto Dill, *Gabriel García Márquez, die Erfindung von Macondo* (Hamburg: Kovac, 1993); Michael Bell, *Gabriel García Márquez: Solitude and Solidarity* (London: Macmillan, 1993); Gabriel García Márquez and Robin W. Fiddian, *García Márquez* (London: Longman, 1995); Oscar Collazos, *Garcia Marquez, la soledad y la gloria: Su vida y su obra* (Esplugas de Llobregat [Barcelona]: Plaza y Janés, 1983); Gene H. Bell-Villada, *García Márquez: The Man and His Work* (Chapel Hill: University of North Carolina Press, 1990); and Lida Aronne-Amestoy, *Utopia, paraíso e historia: Inscripciones del mito en García Márquez, Rulfo y Cortázar* (Amsterdam: Benjamins, 1986).

64. See Augusto Roa Bastos, "Crónica paraguaya," *Sur,* March–April 1965, 102–12.

The following works also convey ideas of the novelist pertinent to this chapter: Augusto Roa Bastos and Saúl Sosnowski, *Augusto Roa Bastos y la producción cultural americana* (Buenos Aires: Ediciones de la Flor; Mexico City: Folios Ediciones, 1986); Augusto Roa Bastos, *Carta abierta a mi pueblo* (Buenos Aires: Frente Paraguayo en Argentina, 1986); and Augusto Roa Bastos, *Las culturas condenadas* (Mexico City: Siglo Veintiuno, 1978).

65. Augusto Roa Bastos, "Carta [a Roberto Fernández Retamar]," *Casa*

de las Américas (July–August 1967): 135–40. The letter was written in September 1966.

66. Augusto Roa Bastos, "Imagen y perspectiva de la literatura latinoamericana actual," *Humboldt*, January–April 1967, 47–52.

67. See Augusto Roa Bastos, "Aventuras y desventuras de un compilador," *Inti*, Spring 1979, 1–4.

68. Augusto Roa Bastos, "Augusto Roa Bastos sobre *Yo el supremo:* Entrevista [a] Alain Sicard," *Inti*, Spring 1979, 5–12.

69. Ibid., 11.

70. See Augusto Roa Bastos, "Escritura y liberación (la narrativa paraguaya en el contexto de la narrativa hispanoamericana," in *Perspectivas de comprensión y de explicación de la narrativa latinoamericana*, ed. José Manuel López y Abiada and Julio Peñate Rivero (Bellinzona, Switzerland: Edizioni Casagrande, 1982), 133–55.

71. Carlos Pacheco, "El escritor es un producto de mentiras: Diálogo con Augusto Roa Bastos," *Actualidades* 6 (1980–82): 35–45. The citation comes from p. 36.

72. Augusto Roa Bastos, "Paraguay: Anatomía de una 'democracia' totalitaria," *Plural*, July 1984, 5–11.

73. Roa Bastos, *Carta abierta*, esp. 11–16.

74. See Roa Bastos, "Ecritura y liberación," in López y Abiada and Peñate Rivero, *Perspectivas de comprensión;* Roa Bastos, *Carta abierta;* and Augusto Roa Bastos, "Una cultura oral," *Río de la Plata*, November 1987, 3–33, passim.

75. See Augusto Roa Bastos, "Entrevista con Augusto Roa Bastos," interview by Héctor Febles, *La Torre*, January–March 1988, 173–89.

76. See Augusto Roa Bastos, prologue to *Amérika, Amérikka, Amérikkka: Manifiestos de Vietnam*, by Fernando Alegría (Santiago: Editorial Universitaria, 1970), 9–22; Roa Bastos, "La agonía de un pueblo que canta sumuerte," *Humboldt* 55 (1974): 50–63; and Pacheco, "Diálogo con Augusto Roa Bastos."

77. See Roa Bastos, "Imagen y perspectiva de la literatura," 47–52, passim.

78. Roa Bastos, "Crónica paraguaya," 104–12, passim.

79. Roa Bastos, "Carta [a Roberto Fernández Retamar]," 137.

80. Augusto Roa Bastos, "Pensar es insalubre," *Crisis*, July 1973, 36–37.

81. Roa Bastos, "La agonía de un pueblo," 50–53, passim.

82. See Augusto Roa Bastos, prologue to *El dolor paraguayo*, by Rafael

Barrett, comp. and ed. Miguel A. Fernández (Caracas: Editorial Ayacucho, 1978), ix–xxxii.

83. See "Entrevista [a] Alain Sicard," 11. On this point see also Roa Bastos, "Ecritura y liberación," López y Abiada and Peñate Rivero, *Perspectivas de comprensión,* 137–55, passim.

84. Pacheco, "Diálogo con Augusto Roa Bastos," 45.

85. Roa Bastos, "Paraguay: Anatomía de una democracia," 5–11, passim.

86. See Augusto Roa Bastos, "Hacia el pluralismo en El Paraguay," *Cuadernos americanos,* July–August 1985, 7–17.

87. Roa Bastos, *Carta abierta,* 22.

88. Augusto Roa Bastos, prologue to *Manifiesto democrático: Una propuesta para el cambio,* by Euclides Acevedo and José Carlos Rodriguez (Asunción: Editorial Araverá, 1986), 17–29. The citation is from p. 17.

89. Augusto Roa Bastos, *El tiranosaurio del Paraguay da sus últimas boqueadas* (Buenos Aires: Frente Paraguayo en Argentina, 1986).

90. Augusto Roa Bastos, "El dilema de la integración iberoamericana," *Cuadernos hispanomamericanos,* January 1986, 21–41.

91. Augusto Roa Bastos, "El Quinto Centenario," *Nexos,* October 1991, 5–8.

92. Roa Bastos, "Tiranosaurio del Paraguay," 22.

93. See Roa Bastos, "Entrevista," 183.

The following sources also contain information on the thought of Roa Bastos: David William Foster, *Augusto Roa Bastos* (Boston: Twayne, 1978); Rubén Bareiro Saguier, *Augusto Roa Bastos: Semana de autor* (Madrid: Instituto de Cooperación Iberoamericana, Ediciones Cultura Hispánica, 1986); Ludwig Schrader, ed., *Augusto Roa Bastos: Actas del coloquio franco-alemán, Düsseldorf, 1–3 de junio de 1982* (Tübingen: Niemeyer Verlag, 1984); Adriana J. Bergero, *El debate político: Modernidad, poder y disidencia en Yo, el Supremo de Augusto Roa Bastos* (New York: P. Lang, 1994); Silvia Pappe, *Desconfianza e insolencia: Estudio sobre la obra de Augusto Roa Bastos* (Mexico City: Universidad Nacional Autónoma de México, 1987); Julio Calvino Iglesias, *Historia, ideología y mito en la narrativa hispanoamericana contemporánea* (Madrid: Ayuso, 1987); Liliana Befuma Boschi and Mónica Marione de Borras, *El hombre y su mundo en Hijo de hombre de Augusto Roa Bastos* (Concepción del Uruguay: Ediciones El Mirador, 1984); Juan Manuel Marcos, *Roa Bastos, precursor del post-boom* (Mexico City: Katún, 1983); and Gladys Vila Barnes, *Significado y coherencia del universo narrativo de Augusto Roa Bastos* (Madrid: Orígenes, 1984).

Chapter 5

1. Fidel Castro, *Palabras a los intelectuales* (Havana: Ediciones del Consejo Nacional de Cultura, 1961 [Año de la Educación]), 11.

2. Ibid., 8.

3. See David Viñas, et al, *Más allá del boom: Literatura y mercado* (Mexico City: Marcha Editores, 1981).

4. Tulio Halperín Donghi, "Nueva narrativa y ciencias sociales hispanoamericanas en la década del sesenta," in Viñas, *Más allá del boom*, 144–65. The passage cited appears on p. 156.

5. Alain Touraine, *Critique de la modernité* (Paris: Fayard, 1992), 395–98.

6. See Alain Touraine, *The Voice and the Eye: An Analysis of Social Movements* (Cambridge: Cambridge University Press; Paris: Éditions de la Maison des Sciences de l'Homme, 1981).

7. Jacques Derrida, *Acts of Literature*, ed. Derek Attridge (New York: Routledge, 1992), 37; Derrida's italics.

8. Raymond Williams, *Writing in Society* (London: Verso, 1983), 229–38. The citation is from p. 234.

9. Octavio Paz, *Los signos en rotación*, ed. and int. Carlos Fuentes (Barcelona: Círculo de Lectores, 1974), 265. See also Paz, *Frustraciones de un destino: La democracia en América Latina* (San José, Costa Rica: Libro Libre, 1990).

10. Octavio Paz, "A Literature of Convergences," in *Convergences: Essays on Art and Literature*, trans. Helen Lane (London: Bloomsbury Publishers, 1987), 217–26. The cited passage is from p. 219.

11. Julio Cortázar, "Carta," *Casa de las Américas*, November–December 1967, 5–12.

Following is a selected list of works conveying the ideas of the novelist pertinent to this chapter: Julio Cortázar and Saúl Yurkievich, *Argentina, años de alambrados culturales* (Buenos Aires: Muchnik Editores, 1984); Julio Cortázar, *Nicaragua tan violentamente dulce* (Managua: Editorial Nueva Nicaragua, 1983); Julio Cortázar, *Obra crítica*, ed. Saúl Yurkievich, Jaime Alazraki, and Saúl Sosnowski (Madrid: Santillana, 1994); and Julio Cortázar and Volodia Teitelboim, *Policrítica en la hora de los chacales/ Cortázar por Volodia Teitelboim* (Concepción: Ediciones LAR, 1987).

12. Julio Cortázar, "Literatura y revolución," *¡Ahora!* July 5, 1971, 64–69.

13. Julio Cortázar, "Mi ametralladora es la literatura," *Crisis*, June 1973, 10–15. Cortázar could also be less than positive about Latin America's great

NOTES TO PAGES 152-155

literary movement. In a 1978 interview he defined the boom as a "colonialist intromission into our vocabulary." See Orlando Castellanos, "Un cronopio llamado Cortázar," *Bohemia*, February 8, 1985, 14-18. This interview was published in the famed Cuban journal to commemorate the first anniversary of the Argentine's death.

14. Julio Cortázar, "América Latina: Exilio y literatura," *Arte Sociedad Ideología*, no. 5 (1978): 93-96.

15. See Eduardo González Bermejo, *Conversaciones con Cortázar* (Barcelona: Editora y Distribuidora Hispanoamericana, 1978), 15.

16. Julio Cortázar, "América Latina: Exilio y literatura," *Eco*, November 1978, 59-66.

17. Julio Cortázar, "Verlangen nach Brüderlichkeit," *Neue deutsche Literatur*, December 1979, 74-79.

18. Julio Cortázar, "Discurso en la constitución del jurado del Premio Literario Casa de las Américas 1980," *Casa de las Américas*, March-April 1980, 2-8.

19. Julio Cortázar, "Realidad y literatura en América Latina," *Revista de Occidente*, April-June 1981, 23-33.

20. Ibid., 26-27.

21. See comments to this effect in Cortázar, "Mi ametralladora."

22. See Julio Cortázar, *Vampiros multinacionales* (Mexico City: Libros de Excelsior, 1975).

23. See Julio Cortázar, "Literatura en la revolución y revolución en la literatura: Algunos malentendidos a liquidar," in *Literatura en la revolución y revolución en la literatura*, by Oscar Collazos, Julio Cortázar, and Mario Vargas Llosa (Mexico City: Siglo Veintiuno, 1976), 38-79.

24. See Julio Cortázar, "Entrevista Julio Cortázar," interview by Saúl Sosnowski, *Hispamérica* 313 (1976): 51-68.

25. See Julio Cortázar and Evelyn Picón Garfield, *Cortázar por Cortázar* (Mexico City: Centro de Investigaciones Lingüístico-Literarias, Universidad Veracruzana, 1978), 15-27.

26. In González Bermejo, *Conversaciones con Cortázar*, 86.

27. Gustavo Luis Carrera, *Nuevas viejas preguntas a Julio Cortázar* (Caracas: Ediciones de la Facultad de Humanidades y Educación, Universidad Central de Venezuela, 1978), 12-23 passim.

28. Cortázar, "Verlangen nach Brüderlichkeit," 77.

29. Julio Cortázar, "Ein Volk in der Schule der Freiheit," *UNESCO Kurier*, June 1980, 12-13.

30. See Julio Cortázar, "La literatura latinoamericana a la luz de la historia contemporánea," in "Julio Cortázar en Barnard," by Mirella Servodidio and Marcelo Coddou, *Inti,* Fall 1979–Spring 1980, 11–20; and Cortázar, "Discurso," 4–8, passim.

31. Cortázar, "Realidad y literatura," 24.

32. Julio Cortázar, "Entrevista a Julio Cortázar: Las palabras son como pequeñas carabelas que sirven para descubrir nuevos mundos," interview by Xavier Arguello [*sic*], *Nicaráuac,* June 1982, 137–41.

33. Karl Kohut, "Julio Cortázar," *Iberoamericana,* no. 1 (1984): 76–84.

34. Julio Cortázar, *Textos políticos* (Barcelona: Plaza y Janés, 1984), 125–30, 109–35, passim.

35. Ibid.; and see Julio Cortázar, "Entrevista con Julio Cortázar," interview by Walter Bruno Berg, *Iberoamericana,* nos. 2, 3 (1990): 126–41.

The following works contain further information on the thought of Cortázar: Alfred J. Mac Adam, *Modern Latin American Narratives: The Dreams of Reason* (Chicago: University of Chicago Press, 1977); Carlos J. Alonso, ed., *Julio Cortázar: New Readings* (New York: Cambridge University Press, 1998); Bernard McGuirk, *Latin American Literature: Symptoms, Risks, and Strategies of Post-Structuralist Criticism* (New York: Routledge, 1997); Ana Maria Simo, *Cinco miradas sobre Cortázar [por] Ana María Simo* (Buenos Aires: Editorial Tiempo Contemporáneo, 1968); Université de Poitiers, Centre de Recherches Latino-Americaines, *Coloquio Internacional Lo Lúdico y lo Fantástico en la obra de Cortázar* (Madrid: Editorial Fundamentos, 1986); Julio Rodríguez-Luis, *The Contemporary Praxis of the Fantastic: Borges and Cortázar* (New York: Garland, 1991); Estela Cedola, *Cortázar: El escritor y sus contextos* (Buenos Aires: Edicial, 1994); Rosario Ferré, *Cortázar: El romántico en su observatorio* (Silver Spring, Md.: Literal Books, 1991); Mercedes Rein, *Cortázar y Carpentier* (Buenos Aires: Ediciones de Crisis, 1974); Evelyn Picón Garfield, *¿Es Julio Cortázar un surrealista?* (Madrid: Gredos, 1975); Jorge Ruffinelli, *La escritura invisible: Arlt, Borges, García Márquez, Roa Bastos, Rulfo, Cortázar, Fuentes, Vargas Llosa* (Mexico City: Universidad Veracruzana, 1986); Jaime Alazraki, *The Final Island: The Fiction of Julio Cortázar* (Norman: University of Oklahoma Press, 1978); Helmy Fuad Giacoman, *Homenaje a Julio Cortázar: Variaciones interpretativas en torno a su obra* (Long Island City: Las Américas, 1972); Evelyn Picón Garfield, *Julio Cortázar* (New York: Ungar, 1975); Terry Peavler, *Julio Cortázar* (Boston: Twayne, 1990); Joaquín Roy, *Julio Cortázar ante su sociedad* (Barcelona: Ediciones Península, 1974); Saúl Yurkievich, *Julio Cortázar:*

Mundos y modos (Madrid: Anaya and Muchnik, 1994); Saúl Sosnowski, *Julio Cortázar: Una búsqueda mítica* (Buenos Aires: Ediciones Noe, 1973); Graciela Maturo, *Julio Cortázar y el hombre nuevo* (Buenos Aires: Editorial Sudamericana, 1968); Jean Casimir and Carlos Fazio, *El militarismo en América Latina: Entrevistas con Jean Casimir, Julio Cortázar, Ariel Dorfman, Theotónio Dos Santos, Gabriel García Márquez, Pablo González Casanova, Carlos Quijano y René Zavaleta* (Mexico City: Proceso, 1980); Malva E. Filer, *Los mundos de Julio Cortázar* (New York: Las Américas, 1970); Santiago Colas, *Postmodernity in Latin America: The Argentine Paradigm* (Durham: Duke University Press, 1994); and Zheyla Henricksen, *Tiempo sagrado y tiempo profano en Borges y Cortázar* (Madrid: Editorial Pliegos, 1992).

36. María Angélica Meza, ed., *La otra mitad de Chile* (Santiago: Centro de Estudios Sociales/Instituto para el Nuevo Chile, n.d.), 265.

37. Ibid., 277.

38. See Isabel Allende, "The World Is Full of Stories: An Interview with Isabel Allende," interview by Linda Levine and Jo Anne Englebert, *Review: Latin American Literature and the Arts,* January–June 1985, 18–20.

39. Isabel Allende, "Hablamos por un pueblo, por un continente: Entrevista de Víctor Baccheta," *Cuadernos del Tercer Mundo,* October 1986, 75–80. See note 50, this chapter, for additional works containing information on the thought of Allende.

40. Ibid.; and see Adriana Castilla de Berchenko, ed., *La narrativa de Isabel Allende: Claves de una marginalidad* (Perpignan, France: Centre de Recherches Ibériques et Latin-Américains, 1990).

41. Michael Moody, "Una conversación con Isabel Allende," *Chasqui,* November 1987, 51–60.

42. See Volodia Teitelboim, "Isabel Allende delínea su concepción de la novela," *Plural,* March 1989, 29–33.

43. See Isabel Allende, "An Interview with Isabel Allende," interview by Virginia Invernizzi and Melissa Pope, *Letras Femeninas,* Spring–Fall 1989, 119–26.

44. See Castillo de Berchenko, *Narrativa de Isabel Allende,* 141–42.

45. See Isabel Allende, "Somos una generación marcada por el exilio: Conversación con Fernando Alegría et al.," *Nuevo texto crítico,* 2d sem., 1991, 73–90. The cited material appears on pp. 75–76.

46. Meza, *Otra mitad,* 266.

47. See Allende, "World Is Full of Stories," 18.

48. In Moody, "Una conversación," 57.

49. Allende, interview with Invernizzi and Pope, 125.

50. Castillo de Berchenko, *Narrativa de Isabel Allende,* 141.

See the following sources for further information on the thought of Isabel Allende: Juan Andrés Pina, *Conversaciones con la narrativa chilena: Fernando Alegría, José Donoso, Guillermo Blanco, Jorge Edwards, Antonio Skármeta, Isabel Allende, Diamela Eltit* (Santiago: Editorial Los Andes, 1991); Sonia Riquelme Rojas and Edna Aguirre Rehbein, *Critical Approaches to Isabel Allende's Novels* (New York: Peter Lang, 1991); Marcelo Coddou and Isabel Allende, *Los libros tienen sus propios espíritus: Estudios sobre Isabel Allende* (Mexico City: Centro de Investigaciones Lingüístico-Literarias, Instituto de Investigaciones Humanísticas, Universidad Veracruzana, 1986); Patricia Hart, *Narrative Magic in the Fiction of Isabel Allende* (Rutherford, N.J.: Fairleigh Dickinson University Press, 1989); Margarita Serrano, *Personas de mundo: Entrevistas* (Santiago: Zig-Zag, 1990); and John Rodden, ed., *Conversations with Isabel Allende,* foreword by Isabel Allende, translations by Virginia Invernizzi (Austin: University of Texas Press, 1999).

51. Mario Vargas Llosa, "Fate and the Mission of the Writer in Latin America," *Haravec,* December 1967, 55-59.

Following is a selected list of works conveying the ideas of the novelist pertinent to this chapter: Mario Vargas Llosa, *Sobre la vida y la política* (Buenos Aires: Editorial InterMundo, 1989); Mario Vargas Llosa and Alberto Fujimori, *El debate* (Lima: Universidad del Pacífico, Centro de Investigación, 1990), (text of candidates' debate between Vargas Llosa and Alberto Fujimori, Lima, June 3, 1990); Mario Vargas Llosa, *A Fish in the Water: A Memoir* (New York: Farrar, Straus and Giroux, 1994); Oscar Collazos, Julio Cortázar, and Mario Vargas Llosa, *Literatura en la revolución y revolución en la literatura: Polémica* (Mexico City: Siglo Veintiuno, 1975); Mario Vargas Llosa, *La verdad de las mentiras: Ensayos sobre literatura* (Barcelona: Seix Barral, 1990); Mario Vargas Llosa and Myron Lichtblau, *A Writer's Reality* (Syracuse: Syracuse University Press, 1991); and Herbert Morote, *Vargas Llosa, tal cual* (San Sebastián: Fundación Kutxa, 1998).

52. Vargas Llosa, "Fate and Mission," 58.

53. See José Miguel Oviedo, *Mario Vargas Llosa: La invención de una realidad* (Barcelona: Seix Barral Editores/Biblioteca Breve, 1977), 69. This book contains one of the best bibliographies, for the time, of works on Vargas Llosa.

54. Mario Vargas Llosa, "El elefante y la cultura," *Estudios Públicos,* Summer 1984, 241-49.

NOTES TO PAGES 163–167

55. See Ricardo A. Setti, *Sobre la vida y la política: Diálogo con Vargas Llosa: Ensayos y conferencias* (Buenos Aires: InterMundo, 1989).

56. See Mario Vargas Llosa, "¿Epopeya del sertão, Torre de Babel o manual de satanismo?" *Amaru*, April 1967, 70–72; Oviedo, *Mario Vargas Llosa*, passim; and Mario Vargas Llosa, *Carta de batalla por Tirant lo Blanc* (Barcelona: Seix Barral/Biblioteca Breve, 1991). Joanot Martorell's late medieval "novel" *Tirant lo Blanc* (1490) is to Vargas Llosa the equivalent—as literary inspiration and "founding novel"—of Cervantes's works to Carlos Fuentes and the saga *Amadís de Gaula* to García Márquez.

57. On this point see Rosa Boldori, "*La ciudad y los perros:* Novela de determinismo," *Revista peruana de cultura*, December 1966, 92–113.

58. Vargas Llosa, "Fate and Mission," 57.

59. Mario Vargas Llosa, *La historia secreta de una novela* (Barcelona: Tusquets Editor, 1971), 23–24. This volume began as lectures delivered at Washington State University while Vargas Llosa taught there in 1968. Much of this work deals with the writing of *La casa verde.*

60. See Mario Vargas Llosa, "Génesis de *La ciudad y los perros,*" *Studi di letteratura ispano-americana*, no. 3 (1971): 77–85.

61. See Mario Vargas Llosa, "La novela," in *La novela y el problema de la expresión literaria en el Perú*, by Vargas Llosa and José María Arguedas (Buenos Aires: América Nueva, 1974), 7–50. The quoted passage appears on p. 39.

62. Oviedo, *Mario Vargas Llosa*, 69.

63. Mario Vargas Llosa, *La Utopia arcáica* (Cambridge: Centre of Latin American Studies Working Papers, no. 33, 1977), 4. This is the printed version of a lecture given in the fall of 1977.

64. Mario Vargas Llosa, *José María Arguedas, entre sapos y halcones* (Madrid: Ediciones Cultura Hispánica del Centro Iberoamericano de Cooperación, 1978), 27.

65. Vargas Llosa, *Arguedas*, 27.

66. Mario Vargas Llosa, *La cultura de la libertad, la libertad de la cultura* (Santiago: Fundación Eduardo Frei, Problemas Contemparáneos, 1985), 18.

67. See Setti, *Vida y política*, 68.

68. Ibid., 133–79, passim. Padilla's public recantation of his opinions, deemed "outside the revolution," caused many Latin American intellectuals to reconsider what they had said and written favorably about the Cuban Revolution. As shown in these pages, not all changed their minds.

69. See Setti, *Vida y política*, 178, 208–11.

70. As an example of whom Vargas Llosa meant, see his "Respuesta a

Günter Grass," in *Contra viento y marea (1964–1988)* (Lima: PEISA, 1990), 330–35.

71. Ibid., 329–30.

72. Mario Vargas Llosa, *La verdad de las mentiras: Ensayos sobre literatura* (Barcelona: Seix Barral, 1990), 10–15.

73. See Vargas Llosa and Fujimori, *Debate,* 19. Text of the candidates' debate between Vargas Llosa and Alberto Fujimori, June 3, 1990. See also the following sources for further information on the thought of Vargas Llosa: M. J. Fenwick, *Dependency Theory and Literary Analysis: Reflections on Vargas Llosa's* The Green House (Minneapolis: Institute for the Study of Ideologies and Literatures, 1981); Carlos Iván Degregori, *Elecciones 1990: Demonios y redentores en el nuevo Perú, una tragedia en dos vueltas* (Lima: IEP Ediciones, 1991); Francisco J. Romero Carranza, *Estudios críticos sobre J. M. Arguedas y Vargas Llosa* (Trujillo, Peru: Editorial Libertad, 1989); Helmy Fuad Giacoman, *Homenaje a Mario Vargas Llosa: Variaciones interpretativas en torno a su obra* (Long Island City: Las Américas, 1972); Charles Rossman and Alan Warren Friedman, eds., *Mario Vargas Llosa: A Collection of Critical Essays* (Austin: University of Texas Press, 1978); Dick Gerdes, *Mario Vargas Llosa* (Boston: Twayne, 1985); Roy Boland, *Mario Vargas Llosa: Oedipus and the "Papa" State: A Study of Individual and Social Psychology in Mario Vargas Llosa's Novels of Peruvian Reality: From* La ciudad y los perros *to* Historia de Mayta (Madrid: Editorial Voz, 1988); Raymond L. Williams, *Mario Vargas Llosa* (New York: Ungar, 1986); Rosa Boldori de Baldussi, *Mario Vargas Llosa y la literatura en El Perú de hoy* (Santa Fe, Argentina: Ediciones Colmegna, 1969); Rosemary Geisdorfer Feal, *Novel Lives: The Fictional Autobiographies of Guillermo Cabrera Infante and Mario Vargas Llosa* (Chapel Hill: University of North Carolina Press, 1986); Mario Vargas Llosa, *Sobre la vida y la política* (Buenos Aires: Editorial InterMundo, 1989); Sara Castro-Klarén, *Understanding Mario Vargas Llosa* (Columbia: University of South Carolina Press, 1990); Carlos Zuzunaga Florez, *Vargas Llosa: El arte de perder una elección* (Lima: Peisa, 1992); Rosa Boldori de Baldussi, *Vargas Llosa: Un narrador y sus demonios* (Buenos Aires: F. García Cambeiro, 1974); and Jeff Daeschner, *The War of the End of Democracy: Mario Vargas Llosa vs. Alberto Fujimori* (Lima: Peru Reporting, 1993).

74. Darcy Ribeiro, "Civilización y creatividad," *Revista de la Universidad de México,* February–March 1972, 47–64. See note 89, this chapter, for further reading suggestions on Ribeiro.

75. Darcy Ribeiro, "Tipologia política latino-americana," *Contexto,* March 1977, 15–35.

76. See Darcy Ribeiro, "Sobre o óbvio," *Encontros com a civilização brasileira*, July 1978, 7–22.

77. Darcy Ribeiro, "¿A América Latina existe?" *Cadernos trabalhistas*, 1979, 85–93.

78. Darcy Ribeiro, "Nosotros Latino-Americanos," *Encontros com a civilização brasileira* 29 (1982): 33–55. The citation is from p. 52.

79. See Darcy Ribeiro, *América Latina: A pátria grande* (Rio de Janeiro: Editora Guanabara Dois, 1986), 83; and Darcy Ribeiro, *Universidade para quê?* (Brasília: Editora Universidade de Brasília, 1986), wherein Ribeiro likens a university without a plan to an entire region without an identity.

80. See Darcy Ribeiro, *Testemunho* (São Paulo: Edições Siciliano, 1991), 208–10, passim.

81. See Darcy Ribeiro, " The Social Integration of Indigenous Populations in Brazil," *International Labour Review*, April–May 1962, 1–40.

82. Darcy Ribeiro, "Nuevos caminos de la revolución latinoamericana," *Estudios internacionales*, April–June 1972, 3–28. The citation comes from p. 3.

83. Darcy Ribeiro, "Configuraciones históricas de los pueblos latinoamericanos," *Pensamiento político*, May 1976, 99–118.

84. See, for example, Darcy Ribeiro, *Teoria do Brasil: Estudo de antropologia da civilização*, vol. 4, *Os brasileiros* (Rio de Janeiro: Civilização Brasileira, 1975).

85. See Ribeiro, "Configuraciones"; and *Os índios e a civilização: A integração das populações indígenas no Brasil moderno*, 2d ed. (Petrópolis: Editora Vozes, 1977); *Ensaios insólitos* (Porto Alegre: L and PM Editores, 1979); "Nosotros Latino-Americanos"; and *América Latina: A Pátria Grande*.

86. See Darcy Ribeiro, "Los protagonistas" and *O dilema da América Latina: Estruturas de poder e forças insurgentes* (Petrópolis: Editora Vozes, 1978).

87. See, as one example, Darcy Ribeiro, "Sou Trabalhista: Não quero um Partido de Sabios," *Cadernos trabalhistas*, 1979, 67–82.

88. Darcy Ribeiro, "Entrevista com Darcy Ribeiro," interview by Getúlio Alencar, *Pau Brasil*, January–February 1985, 43–50.

89. Ribeiro, *Testemunho*, 209–10.

See also the following sources for further information on the thought of Darcy Ribeiro: Darcy Ribeiro, *Carta: Informe de distribuição restrita do Senador Darcy Ribeiro* (Brasília: Gabinete do Senador Darcy Ribeiro, Senado Federal, 1991); José Wilson de Silva, *O Tenente Vermelho* (Porto Alegre: Tche! 1987); Darcy Ribeiro, *The Americas and Civilization* (New York: Dutton, 1971); Darcy Ribeiro, *Brasil como problema* (Rio de Janeiro:

Francisco Alves Editora, 1985); Darcy Ribeiro, *The Civilizational Process* (Washington, D.C.: Smithsonian Institution Press, 1968); Darcy Ribeiro, *Configurações histórico-culturais dos povos Americanos* (Rio de Janeiro: Civilização Brasileira, 1975); Darcy Ribeiro and Carlos de Araújo Moreira Neto, *A fundação do Brasil: Testemunhos, 1500–1700* (Petrópolis: Vozes, 1992); Darcy Ribeiro, *Os índios e a civilização: A integração das populações indígenas no Brasil moderno* (Rio de Janeiro: Civilização Brasileira, 1970); Darcy Ribeiro, *Propuestas acerca del subdesarrollo: Brasil como problema* (Montevideo[?]: Libros de la Pupila, 1969); Darcy Ribeiro, *Teoria do Brasil* (Rio de Janeiro: Paz e Terra, 1972); Darcy Ribeiro, *A universidade necessária* (Rio de Janeiro: Paz e Terra, 1975).

Chapter 6

1. Indicative of shifts in emphasis, selection of causal factors, major themes, and increased interdisciplinary application of theory to social and economic as well as political problems are the following selected works: Pablo González Casanova, *Las categorías del desarrollo económico y la investigación en ciencias sociales* (Mexico City: Instituto de Investigaciones Sociales, 1967); Pablo González Casanova, *Imperialismo y liberación en América Latina: Una introducción a la historia contemporánea* (Mexico City: Siglo Veintiuno, 1978); Pablo González Casanova, *El estado en América Latina: Teoría y práctica* (Mexico City: Siglo Veintiuno, 1990); Florestan Fernandes, *Mudanças sociais no Brasil: Aspectos do desenvolvimento da sociedade brasileira* (São Paulo: Difusão Européia do Livro, 1974; Florestan Fernandes, *Poder e contrapoder na América Latina* (Rio de Janeiro: Zahar Editores, 1981); Florestan Fernandes, *Democracia e desenvolvimento: A transformação da periferia e o capitalismo monopolista da era atual* (São Paulo: Editora HUCITEC, 1994); Fernando Henrique Cardoso, *Ideologías de la burguesía industrial en sociedades dependientes (Argentina y Brasil)* (Mexico City: Siglo Veintiuno, 1971); Arnaud Pascal, *Estado y capitalismo en América Latina: Casos de México y Argentina* (Mexico City: Siglo Veintiuno, 1981); Félix Jiménez, *Perú: Economía no-neoclásica, modelo de acumulación, crisis y alternativa de desarrollo no-monetarista* (Lima: Centro de Estudios para el Desarrollo y la Participación, 1986); and Hernando de Soto, *Estimación de la magnitud de la actividad económica informal en el Perú* (Lima: Instituto Libertad y Democracia, 1989).

The following works, more familiar to English-language readers, should also be consulted: Guillermo O'Donnell, *Modernization and Bureaucratic Authoritarianism: Studies in South American Politics* (Berkeley: Institute of International Studies, University of California, 1973); Fernando Henrique Cardoso and Enzo Faletto, *Dependency and Development in Latin America,* trans. Marjory Mattingly Urquidi (Berkeley: University of California Press, 1979); Joseph L. Love and Nils Jacobson, eds., *Guiding the Invisible Hand: Economic Liberalism and the State in Latin American History* (New York: Praeger, 1988); Robert Devlin, *Debt and Crisis in Latin America: The Supply Side of the Story* (Princeton: Princeton University Press, 1989); Robert A. Packenham, *The Dependency Movement: Scholarship and Politics in Development Studies* (Cambridge, Mass.: Harvard University Press, 1992); and Jorge G. Castañeda, *Utopia Unarmed: The Latin American Left after the Cold War* (New York: Alfred A. Knopf, 1993).

2. Wallerstein, *Unthinking Social Science: The Limits of Nineteenth-Century Paradigms* (Cambridge: Polity Press, 1991), 14. That an intellectual whirlwind blows still, with no signs of surcease, can be seen in Plinio Apuleyo Mendoza, Carlos Alberto Montaner, and Alvaro Vargas Llosa, *Guide to the Perfect Latin American Idiot,* trans. Michaela Lajda Ames (Lanham, Md.: Madison Books, 1996); and Miguel Angel Centeno and Fernando López-Alves, eds., *The Other Mirror: Grand Theory through the Lens of Latin America* (Princeton: Princeton University Press, 2001).

3. *Washington Post,* December 24, 1996, C ("Style") 1–2.

4. See Sol Serrano, "América Latina y el mundo moderno en algunos ensayistas latinoamericanos," *Opiniones (Ex Alternativas),* September 1984, 56–100.

5. On this, see Tulio Halperín Donghi, "Nueva narrativa y ciencias sociales hispanoamericanos en la década del sesenta," *Hispamérica,* December 1980, 3–19.

6. See Jeffrey M. Puryear, *Thinking Politics: Intellectuals and Democracy in Chile, 1973–1988* (Baltimore: Johns Hopkins University Press, 1994). A series of short pieces in the Social Science Research Council's *Items* (June–September 1998), treats the council's initiative to "develop intellectuals on a global scale." This issue also contains excerpts from a 1998 council symposium, "Social Sciences Around the World," that underscore the significance of the social sciences as discussed herein.

7. See José Medina Echevarría, "América Latina en los escenarios posibles de la distensión," *Revista de la CEPAL,* 2d sem., 1976, 9–87. Hereafter *CEPAL.*

8. See Paulo Roberto Haddad, "Políticas de estabilização econômica: A dimensão regional," *Pensamiento iberoamericano*, July–December 1986, 245–60. Hereafter *PI*.

9. Ominami, "Doce proposiciones acerca de América Latina en una era de profundo cambio tecnológico," *PI*, January–June 1988, 49–65.

10. Jaguaribe, "América Latina dentro del contexto internacional de la actualidad," *Revista mexicana de sociología*, July–September 1989, 5–73. Hereafter *RMS*.

11. Jaguaribe, "Desarrollo recíproco: Perspectivas de una justa asociación," *Síntesis*, January–April 1988, 83–94.

12. See, for example, Carlos Fortín, "Las perspectivas del Sur en los años noventa," *PI*, July–December 1990, 183–201.

13. See José Ocampo, "Perspectivas de la economía latinoamericana en la década de los noventa," *PI*, January–June 1991, 65–79.

14. Luciano Tomassini, "La cambiante inserción internacional de América Latina en la década de los ochenta," *PI*, January–June 1988, 13–29.

15. See Carlos Rico F., "La influencia de factores extrarregionales en el conflicto centroamericano: El socialismo europeo, la Alianza Atlántica y Centro América: ¿Una historia de expectativas frustradas?" *PI*, January–June, 1988, 113–34. The citation comes from p. 124.

16. See, for example, Aldo Ferrer, "El sistema centro-periferia y la política económica: Una ilustración sobre el caso argentino," *PI*, January–June 1987, 59–82; and, in the same issue, Jaguaribe, "Autonomia e hegemonia no sistema imperial americano," 95–119.

17. See Osvaldo Sunkel, "Las relaciones centro-periferia y la transnacionalización," *PI*, January 1987, 31–52; and, in the same issue, Norberto González, "Vigencia actual del concepto de centro-periferia," 17–29.

18. See Juan Rial, "Transición hacia la democracia y gobernabilidad en Uruguay," *PI*, July–August 1988, 247–60. The quoted passage is found on p. 259.

19. See Mara d'Alva Gil Kino, "Considerações sobre a transição democrática no Brasil," *PI*, July–August 1988, 241–46.

20. As an example see Luiz Carlos Bresser Pereira, "La crisis de América Latina: ¿Consenso de Washington o crisis fiscal?" *PI*, January–June 1991, 13–35.

21. See Edelberto Torres-Rivas, "Centroamérica: Democracia de baja intensidad," *PI*, July–December 1988, 221–30.

22. Héctor Aguilar Camín, "PRI: Descenso del milagro," *PI*, July–December 1988, 209–20.

23. On this see Carlos Huneeus, "La democracia en Chile: Un enfoque institucional," *PI,* July 1988, 93–108.

24. Amparo Menéndez-Carrión, "La democracia en Ecuador: Desafíos, dilemas, y perspectivas," *PI,* July–December 1988, 123–42.

25. See Carlos Iván Degregori, "Guzmán y Sendero: Después de la caída," *Nueva sociedad,* March–April 1993, 53–58 (hereafter *NS*); and Gert Rosenthal, "América Latina y el Caribe: Bases de una agenda de desarrollo para los años noventa," *PI,* January–June 1991, 55–79.

26. See Norbert Lechner, "El debate sobre estado y mercado," *NS,* September–October 1992, 80–89.

27. See Gert Rosenthal, "Democracia y economía," *CEPAL,* April 1991, 7–10.

28. Jorge G. Castañeda, "Latinoamérica y el final de la Guerra Fría," *Leviatán,* Winter 1991, 67–89. The citation comes from p. 75.

29. See Ricardo Ffrench-Davis, Patricio Leiva, and Roberto Madrid, "Liberalización comercial y crecimiento: La experiencia de Chile," *PI,* January–June 1992, 33–55.

30. Enrique Ottone, "Los nuevos escenarios internacionales," *CEPAL,* August 1991, 127–36. The quotation appears on p. 131.

31. Héctor Aguilar Camín, "La transición mexicana," *Síntesis,* September–December 1988, 91–103.

32. Fernando Calderón and Mario R. Dos Santos, "Hacia un nuevo orden estatal en América Latina: Veinte tesis socio-políticas y un corolario de cierre," *Revista paraguaya de sociología,* January–April 1990, 7–36. The quotation is from p. 36. Hereafter *RPS.*

33. See Meyer, "La debilidad histórica de la democracia mexicana," *Síntesis,* September–December 1988, 79–90. The cited passage is on p. 80.

34. Norbert Lechner, "De la revolución a la democracia: El debate intelectual en América del Sur," *Opciones,* May–August 1985, 57–73.

35. See Paz, *One Earth, Four or Five Worlds: Reflections on Contemporary History,* trans. Helen R. Lane (New York: Harcourt Brace Jovanovich, 1985), 142–43.

36. See Dieter Nohlen, "¿Más democracia en América Latina? Democratización y consolidación de la democracia en una perspectiva comparada," *Síntesis,* September–December 1988, 37–63.

37. See Guillermo Maldonado Lince, "Los desafíos de América Latina en el mundo de hoy," *CEPAL,* April 1988, 65–75; and Torres-Rivas, "Escenarios y lecciones de las elecciones centroamericanas, 1980–1991," *RMS,* July–September 1992, 45–67.

38. See Wilson Cano and Leonardo Guimarães Neto, "A questão regional no Brasil: Traços gerais de sua evolução histórica," *PI*, July–December 1986, 167–84.

39. Alain Touraine, "As possibilidades da democrácia na América Latina," *Revista brasileira de ciências sociais*, June 1986, 5–15. The citation is from p. 9. Hereafter *RBCS*.

40. See, for example, Rolando Ames Cobián, "Los estados latinoamericanos entre la democracia y la violencia: Equívocos mortales," *Síntesis*, September–December 1989, 15–29.

41. See Sonia Miriam Draibe, "La reforma del estado en América Latina: Observaciones sobre el caso," *Perfiles latinoamericanos*, December 1992, 55–83.

42. Atilio Borón, "Transición, vulnerabilidad externa, y autonomía nacional: El papel de las relaciones europeo-latinoamericanas," *Síntesis*, January–April 1988, 51–67.

43. See Luis Alberto Padilla, "Guatemala: ¿Transición a la democracia?" *Síntesis*, May–August 1989, 117–31.

44. Elisa Pereira Reis, "Política e políticas públicas na transição democrática," *RBCS*, February 1989, 15–23.

45. See Angel Flisfisch, "Gobernabilidad y consolidación democrática," *RMS*, September 1989; Luciano Tomassini, "Estado, gobernabilidad, y desarrollo," *Revista de ciencia política* (Chile) 1–2 (1992): 23–61. Hereafter *RCP*.

46. Readers would do well to consult Michel Foucault's "Governability" (a lecture given at the Collège de France in 1978, at about the same time governability was being mooted most vigorously in European and North American social science circles), translated and reprinted in *The Foucault Effect: Studies in Governability, with Two Lectures and an Interview with Michel Foucault*, ed. Graham Burchell, Colin Gordon, and Peter Miller (Chicago: University of Chicago Press, 1991), pp. 87–104. Foucault made the point that government—the *ability* to conduct it—may be considered to be more associated with "a complex of men and things" than with geographical space or territory. This is worth considering, given the perceived historical significance of the post-Cold War international paradigm and the impact of its economics on Latin America.

47. Rolando Franco, "Estado, consolidación democrática y gobernabilidad en América Latina," *RPS*, September–December 1990, 141–64.

48. See Carlos Barba Solano, José Luis Barros Horcasitas, and Javier Hurtado, eds., *Transiciones a la democracia en Europa y América Latina*

(Mexico City: FLACSO, Universidad de Guadalajara, Grupo Editorial Miguel Angel Porrúa, 1991).

49. See Pérez Fernández del Castillo, "Gobernabilidad y sistema político en México," *Revista latinoamericana de ciencias sociales* 1 (1991): 9–21. Hereafter *RLCS* . See also, in the same issue, Edelberto Torres-Rivas, "La recomposición del orden: Elecciones en Centroamérica," 2–28; and Daniel García Delgado, "La gobernabilidad en las condiciones débiles: El caso argentino," 40–50.

50. See Amparo Menéndez-Carrión, "Para repensar la cuestión de la gobernabilidad desde la ciudadanía: Dilemas, opciones y apuntes para un proyecto," *RLCS* 1 (1991): 79–98.

51. Ignacio Walker, "Transición y consolidación democrática en Chile," *RCP* 1–2 (1992): 89–104.

52. See Alfonso Arrau C., "Modernización y redemocratización en Chile," *Revista de sociología* 6–7 (1992): 7–19. See also Francisco Rojas Aravena, ed., *América Latina y la iniciativa para las Américas* (Santiago: FLACSO, 1993).

53. See Leal Buitrago, "Democracia, oligarquía, y rearticulación de la sociedad civil: El caso colombiano," *PI*, July–December 1988, 53–65.

54. For applications to the Southern Cone, see, on Chile, Rodrigo Baño's, "Tendencias políticas y resultados electorales después de veinte años," *RMS*, October–December 1990, 69–82; and in the same issue, on Argentina, Isidoro Cheresky, "Argentina: Un paso en la consolidación democrática: Elecciones presidenciales con alternancia política," 49–68.

55. See Carmen Fariña Vicuña, "El pensamiento corporativo en las revistas *Estanquero* (1946–55) y *Política y Espíritu* (1945–75)," *RCP* 1–2 (1990): 119–42.

56. See, for example, Rodolfo Stavenhagen, "Los conflictos étnicos y sus repercusiones en la sociedad internacional," *Revista internacional de ciencias sociales*, March 1991, 125–40. Hereafter *RICS*.

57. See Julio Labastida, "México: Transición democrática y reforma económica," *RMS*, April–June 1991, 127–39; and Francisco C. Weffort, "¿Qué es una nueva democracia?" *RICS*, June 1993, 279–91. The citation is from Weffort, p. 281.

58. Enzo Falleto, "Cultura política y conciencia democrática," *CEPAL*, August 1989, 77–81.

59. See Jorge G. Castañeda, "La decadencia del comunismo y la izquierda latinoamericana," *Revista occidental: Estudios latinoamericanos*, Winter 1993, 63–80. The citation is from p. 71. Hereafter *ROEL*. See also

H. C. F. Mansilla, "¿El fin de la historia, o el fin de la reflexión crítica?" *ROEL*, Spring 1992, 103–15.

60. See Manuel Antonio Garretón M., "La democracia entre dos épocas: América Latina 1990," *RPS*, January–April 1991, 23–37.

61. See, for example, Daniel García Delgado, "La gobernabilidad en las consolidaciones débiles: El caso argentino," *RLCS* 1 (1991): 40–50; and, in the same issue, Gustavo Cosse, "La gobernabilidad en Uruguay: Desafíos y perspectivas de la democracia," 51–79.

62. Walder de Góes, "Os Militares e a Democrácia," *Política e estratégia*, July–September 1985, 443–54. Hereafter *PE*. My emphasis.

63. General (ret.) Horacio Toro I., "Segurança Nacional: Uma Visão Chilena," *PE*, January–March 1989, 98–114.

64. See, for example, Enrique Bernales B. and Diego García Sayan, "Peru: Defesa, Segurança, e Paz," *PE*, July–September 1989, 338–65.

65. Paulo Kramer, "As relaçoes militares Brasil-Estados Unidos," *PE*, January–March 1986, 45–53.

66. Some recent thoughts on this subject appear in Frederick M. Nunn, "Can Some Things Change and Remain the Same? Post–Cold War Officer Corps Thought and Self-Perception in Argentina, Brazil, Chile, and Peru," paper presented at the meeting of the Latin American Studies Association, Miami, March 16–18, 2000.

67. See Thomaz Guedes da Costa, "La percepción de amenazas desde el punto de vista de los militares brasileros en las décadas del setenta y ochenta," in *Percepciones de amenaza y políticas de defensa en América Latina*, ed. Admiral Rigoberto Cruz Johnson and Augusto Varas Fernández (Santiago: FLACSO, CEEA, 1993), 193–210. The quotation comes from p. 209.

68. See the Chilean Admiral Jorge Martínez Busch's "La carta de París para una nueva Europa: Algunas cuestiones políticas estratégicas para las relaciones militares entre Iberoamérica y Europa," *Ciencia política*, May 1991, 35–52. The cited passage comes from pp. 36–37.

69. See Augusto Varas Fernández, "La post-guerra fría, la seguridad hemisférica y la defensa nacional," in Cruz Johnson and Varas Fernández, *Percepciones de amenaza*, 3–69.

70. As evidence of Mercado's role in the professional military version of the intraregional social science dialogue to which this study speaks, see his "As doutrinas de segurança e as forças armadas na América Latina," *PE*, July–September 1989, 325–37.

71. A recent model for this kind of inquiry is David Ralston, *Importing*

the European Army: The Introduction of Military Techniques and Institutions into the Extra-European World, 1600–1914 (Chicago: University of Chicago Press, 1990). Similar approaches to the study of civil-military relations guided my *Yesterday's Soldiers: European Military Professionalism in South America, 1890–1940* (Lincoln: University of Nebraska Press, 1983); and *The Time of the Generals: Latin American Professional Militarism in World Perspective* (Lincoln: University of Nebraska Press, 1992).

Timely social science literature from Latin America pertinent to this discussion includes works already cited in this study and the following (selected) titles: Andrés Serbín, "Percepciones y equipamiento en Venezuela," in Cruz Johnson and Varas, *Percepciones de amenaza*, 269–316; Alexandre Barros, "Problemas de transição democrática na frente militar: A definição do papel dos militares, a mudança de doutrina, e a modernização do país," *PE*, April–June 1988, 206–13; and, in the same issue, Ubiratan Borges de Macedo, "A escola superior de guerra: Sua ideología e tránsito para a democrácia": 215–22; Walder de Góes, "Os militares e a constituição: Uma estrategia para a democrácia," *PE*, July–September 1986, 342–54; Carlos Portales, "Las relaciones internacionales de las fuerzas armadas chilenas: De la guerra fría a los años ochenta," *Opciones*, January–April 1986, 199–233; and Carlos María Lezcano, "Constituição e crise do estado militar no Paraguai," *PE*, October–December 1987, 426–38.

72. See Raúl Barrios Morón, "Militares y democracia en Bolivia: Entre la reforma o la desestabilización," *ROEL*, Winter? 1993, 81–108.

73. Admiral Rigoberto Cruz Johnson, "El Pacífico Sur Oriental y la post guerra fría," in Cruz Johnson and Varas Fernández, *Percepciónes de amenaza*, 77–87. The citation is from p. 87.

74. See Edgardo Mercado Jarrín, "Los cambios internacionales y sus probables efectos en la situación estratégica y de seguridad de América Latina," in *Cambios globales y América Latina: Algunos temas de la transición estratégica*, ed. Augusto Varas Fernández and Isaac Calvo (Santiago: Centro Latinomericano de Defensa y Desarme [CLADE] and FLACSO, 1993), 17–36.

75. Francisco Rojas Aravena, "América Latina en la post guerra fría: Nuevas oportunidades para la concertación estratégica," in *La situación estratégica latinoamericana: Crisis y oportunidades*, ed. Agustín Toro Dávila and Augusto Varas Fernández (Santiago: FLACSO, Instituto de Estudios Internacionales, Universidad de Chile, 1992), 142–70. The quoted passage comes from p. 143.

76. Norbert Lechner, "Problemas de la democratización en una cultura postmoderna," *Mundo*, Winter 1987, 53–61. The citation is from p. 59.

77. Karl Mannheim. *Essays on the Sociology of Culture* (London: Routledge and Kegan Paul, 1992), 161.

78. See Enrique Krauze, "Old Paradigms and New Openings in Latin America," *Journal of Democracy*, January 1992, 15–24.

79. Joseph A. Schumpeter, *Capitalism, Socialism, and Democracy*, 6th ed. (London: Unwin Paperbacks, 1987). The remarks come from pp. 59, 167, and 236 respectively.

80. As recalled in Leopoldo Zea, "Liberación nacional y socialismo en América Latina," *RMS*, July–September 1989, 149–60.

81. Bernardo Subercaseaux, "La década de los ochenta: Un nuevo clima intelectual," *Mundo*, Winter 1987, 443–51. The quotation is from p. 445.

82. In an article on economic growth, *Manchester Guardian Weekly*, April 21, 1996.

83. John Le Carré, interview by David Streitfeld, *Manchester Guardian Weekly*, December 29, 1996. See also George Soros, "The Capitalist Threat," *Atlantic Monthly*, February 1997, 45–58.

Conclusions

1. See *New York Times*, April 25, 2000, A3.

2. Patricia Nelson Limerick, "Layer upon Layer of Memory in the American West," *Chronicle of Higher Education*, March 3, 2000, B4–B7.

Index

INDEX

Jaguaribe, Hélio, 185, 187
Jaimes, Roberto, 118
Jamaica Letter, 51
James, Henry, 73, 121
Jesuits (Society of Jesus), 58–59, 69
Jews, 17, 19, 69, 92
    in fictional history, 24–25, 29, 34–39
John Paul II, 208
Joyce, James, 11, 130, 163
Juana Ines de la Cruz, Sor, 44, 123
Judaism. *See* religion

Kafka, Franz, 130
Kundera, Milan, 114–16

Las Casas, Bartolomé de, 24
Lastarria, José Victorino, 11, 27, 99, 123
Latin American Social Sciences Faculty
    (FLACSO), 184, 193
latinomericanidad (Latin Americanness),
    4–5, 31, 179–223
    and El Boom, 5, 109–42, 143–76
Lazarillo de Tormes, 130
Leal Buitrago, Francisco, 197
Lechner, Norbert, 193
Leenhardt, Jacques, 146
Lezama Lima, José, 122, 136, 154, 163
López, Francisco Solano, 119
Lopéz Rega, José, 84
Lost Generation, The, 217
L'Ouverture, Toussaint, 119
Loyola, Ignatius, 24
Lukacs, Georg, 112, 116
Luther, Martin, 23

Machado, Gerardo, 119
Machado de Assis, Joaquim Maria, 163
Machiavelli, Niccolò, 24, 179
Maciel, Antônio, 78
Mannheim, Karl, 206
Mariátegui, José Carlos, 114, 118, 165, 170
Martí, José, 27, 109, 118–20, 123, 126, 142,
    170, 217
Martínez, Tomás Eloy, 84, 104, 114, 182
Martínez Estrada, Ezequiel, 114
Martínez Moreno, Carlos, 90, 104
Martorell, Joanot, 163
Marxism (and Marxists), 2, 93, 143–76,
    179–210. *See also* fiction; fictional his-
    tory; history
Mattos, Gregório de, 170
Melgarejo, Mariano, 119

Melville, Herman, 164
Menéndez-Carrión, Amparo, 190, 197
Mercado Jarrín, Edgardo, 204
metaphor, 74–79, 101, 157, 162, 213
Mexico, 28, 46, 120, 125, 137, 188, 192–93
Meyer, Lorenzo, 192
Mier, Fray Servando Teresa de, 57
military, 3–4, 76, 81, 144, 166, 199, 211–23
    and military-civilian relations, 158, 166,
    199–200
    and professionalism of, 81
    and professional militarism, 3–4, 144,
    153, 200–204
    and U.S., 93–95
militarization of history. *See* history
Miranda, Ana, 48, 69, 71, 173
    fictional history by, 69–71
miscegenation. *See* race relations
Moctezuma, 64
Montalvo, Juan, 140
Mora, José Joaquín, 123
More, Sir Thomas, 24
Morelos, José María, 45, 50
Morison, Samuel Eliot, 23
Moyano, Daniel, 122
Mutis, Alvaro, 129

nationalism (in history), 44–47, 58, 211–23
Neruda, Pablo, 158
New World Order, 9, 75, 112, 124, 161, 175,
    179–210, 211–23
Nicaragua, 85, 87, 90, 130, 157
Nostromo, 138
novelists. *See* El Boom; fiction; fictional his-
    tory; *and by author*

OAS (Organization of American States), 8
Odría, Manuel A., 96
Odyssey, The, 132
"Oedipus Rex," 130
O'Gorman, Edmundo, 27
O'Higgins, Bernardo, 50, 52, 220
Ominami, Carlos, 185
Oña, Pedro de, 20
Onetti, Juan Carlos, 122, 136
Orientalism, 63
Ortega y Gasset, José, 113–14
Orwell, George, 73–102
Ottone, Enrique, 191
Oviedo, José Miguel, 165

Padilla, Heberto, 128, 167

264